BY CHARLES PETERS

*We Do Our Part*

*Five Days in Philadelphia*

*Lyndon B. Johnson*

*How Washington Really Works*

*Tilting at Windmills*

# WE DO
# OUR PART

# WE DO OUR PART

*Toward a Fairer
and More Equal America*

★

## CHARLES PETERS

Foreword by Jon Meacham

RANDOM HOUSE

NEW YORK

Published in the United States by Random House, an imprint and division
of Penguin Random House LLC, New York.

RANDOM HOUSE and the HOUSE colophon are registered trademarks of
Penguin Random House LLC.

Grateful acknowledgment is made to the following for permission to reprint previously pub-
lished material:
*The Guardian:* Excerpt from "Get Carter" by Gaby Wood (*The Guardian,*
November 10, 2002), copyright Guardian News & Media Ltd. 2016.
Reprinted by permission of *The Guardian.*
**Perseus Books, an imprint of the Perseus Books Group:** Excerpt from *How to Lose Friends
and Alienate People* by Toby Young, copyright © 2002 by Toby Young. Reprinted by
permission of Perseus Books, a member of the Perseus Books Group.
**Errol Lincoln Uys:** Excerpt from *Riding the Rails: Teenagers on the Move During the Great
Depression* by Errol Lincoln Uys (Boston: T. E. Winter & Sons, 2014), copyright © 2014 by
Errol Lincoln Uys. Reprinted by permission of the author.

LIBRARY OF CONGRESS CATALOGING-IN-PUBLICATION DATA
Names: Peters, Charles, author.
Title: We do our part : toward a fairer and more equal America / Charles Peters.
Description: New York : Random House, [2017] | Includes index.
Identifiers: LCCN 2016043513| ISBN 9780812993523 | ISBN 9780679645665 (ebook)
Subjects: LCSH: Equality—United States. | United States—Politics and government.
Classification: LCC JC575 .P44 2017 | DDC 323.420973—dc23
LC record available at https://lccn.loc.gov/2016043513

Printed in the United States of America on acid-free paper

randomhousebooks.com

2 4 6 8 9 7 5 3 1

First Edition

Title-page image: copyright © iStock.com/© MicroStockHub

*Book design by Victoria Wong*

# FOREWORD

★

## Jon Meacham

B y any measure, his is a great American life. From the legislature of his native West Virginia to the founding of the Peace Corps; from the Columbia College of Lionel Trilling to the creation of bracing public-service journalism at *The Washington Monthly;* from a Depression-era youth to a spectacular series of books written late in life, Charles Peters occupies a unique place in American life and letters. At once wise and street-smart, idealistic yet hard-headed, he, at ninety, has much to say about who we were, who we are—and who we ought to be.

He is a Renaissance man, great in years but forever young in spirit and in energy. Born in Charleston, West Virginia, in 1926, Charlie attended public schools and enlisted in the U.S. Army in 1944. Injured in a training accident, he recovered and enrolled at Columbia in New York after World War II. Reading widely and deeply, a devotee of the theater—he worked in summer stock, learning the great truth that the show must always go on—Charlie found his way to the University of Virginia law school. Practicing in Charleston and serving in the legislature, he ran John F. Kennedy's campaign in West Virginia's largest county in 1960. Charlie joined the nascent Peace Corps in Washington, serving as the agency's director of evaluation. In 1969 he became an unlikely entrepreneur, founding *The Washington Monthly* to, as he put it, cover the capital in the way an anthropologist might cover a South Sea Island. Celebrated for discovering a remarkable array of talented editors and writers who would go on to distinguished careers at more prominent journals, Charlie has led one of the great journalistic careers of this or any era.

I first encountered Charlie in the pages of the *Monthly* and in *Tilting at Windmills*, his sage, sprightly 1990 memoir. Sensible, earnest, and wry, Charlie's voice resonated with me. His is a political worldview in the purest sense of *political*, meaning it encompasses all of life, not just the public sector: his cares and concerns include art, culture, faith, honor, and love. He often writes of the state, but his true focus is the soul.

Here is a generous-spirited Democrat with little to no time for liberal pretensions or hypocrisies, a believer in government who labors under no illusions about the limitations of the state. He takes on selfishness wherever he sees it, whether in the boardrooms or CEO suites of American corporations or in the smugness of public-employee unions. He worries about the quiet compromises and corruptions of the meritocratic class, fearing that lives better spent in pursuit of true happiness are instead being consumed by anxieties about money and taste. The Peters "gospel," as his *Monthly* editors referred to it, is both empirically based and big-hearted. In the early 1980s, defining his philosophy, Charlie wrote: "We . . . believe in liberty and justice and a fair chance for all, in mercy for the afflicted and help for the down and out. But we no longer automatically favor unions and big government or oppose the military and big business. Indeed, in our search for solutions that work, we have come to distrust all automatic responses, liberal or conservative."

A voice in the wilderness, crying out for compassion and common sense: Charlie penned that plea for a more rational politics more than three decades ago. (And when I say "penned," I mean "penned": much to the frustration of his editors over the years, he has never learned to type, preferring instead to scribble in green ink on yellow pages—or in the margins of old-fashioned newspaper clippings.) In the ensuing years, the nation has become ever more partisan and ever more polarized—a state of things that makes the message of the wonderful book you are holding all the more essential and urgent.

The 1930s may seem as remote as Agincourt or Appomattox, but the forces that shaped the decade are familiar in our own time. Demagoguery is on the rise, as is unease about the durability of the basic institutions of society. In the summer of 1932, Franklin Roosevelt remarked that the two most dangerous men in America were Huey Long and Douglas MacArthur—Long because he could lead a populist revolt from the left, MacArthur one from the right.

As Charlie movingly—and often wittily—argues, we emerged from the crisis of the '30s by heeding the better angels of our nature. This is not a sentimental point, for the salvation of democratic capitalism was, as Wellington remarked of Waterloo, a close-run thing. Which is why Charlie's searching, challenging, and indeed brilliant survey of the last eighty years is so important: Those who came before us managed to make the world better not because they were superhuman. They were like us—subject to appetite and ambition, jealousy and pride—and yet fought through the shadows of selfishness toward the light. And if they could do so, then we can, too.

For Charlie is always about hope—hope that our politics can be more fulfilling, hope that our lives can be varied and various, hope that the history we make can stand the test of time, illuminating a path forward to what Churchill, himself a voice in the wilderness in the 1930s, called the sunlit uplands of happiness and peace.

This book is Charlie's valedictory, his view from the mountaintop after decades in the arena. Like its author, it is knowing, funny, smart, and—to use an appropriate if antiquated term—*honorable*. "We have made dividing ourselves against ourselves into a virtue," Charlie has written. Such reflexive divisions are anything but virtuous. For those looking to survive and even thrive in an age when the shadows seem to be lengthening, begin here, with this good man's account of other, darker days—and how Americans found the light. It is the story Charlie Peters was born to tell, and we are blessed that he has chosen to share it with all of us.

*Jon Meacham*

# CONTENTS

# WE DO
# OUR PART

*Those dying generations—at their song*
William Butler Yeats, "Sailing to Byzantium"

———————— ★ ————————

# Why This Book

When I was a college student in the late 1940s, I rarely trusted authors who were much older than sixty. I was not interested in the songs of dying generations. Even the thought was vaguely depressing. Ironically, as I entered my forties in the late 1960s, I found myself dealing with young writers who did not trust anyone over thirty. Now that I am eighty-nine, I am painfully aware that there are many younger people who will doubt that I have anything useful to say.

But since you have started to read this book, you must be willing to consider the possibility that I may be worth listening to. I have written it precisely because of those eighty-nine years and what I have learned living them. I have seen this country become better in some ways and worse in others. Actually, in the case of income inequality, I have seen things go from bad to much better and back to bad again. I have seen times when the average white man was respected, not disdained, when more of us listened to those with whom we disagreed, when more of us viewed each other as human beings, not as some hated or feared "other," when there was more concern for public service and less for personal gain. I have seen my home state go from being politically liberal and among the nation's leaders in desegregating its schools to admiring Donald Trump and hating Barack Obama. But I have also seen women go from having their choice of work limited to nurse, teacher, secretary, or sales clerk to supplying the majority of our new physicians, running major corporations, occupying three seats on the Supreme Court, and winning the most popular votes for president. I have seen gays leave the closet, serve openly in the military, and marry the person they love. I have seen cellphones and body and squad car cameras make white people face the danger blacks endure every day. I have not only witnessed these changes but have participated in many of them, making it possible for me to tell you the story of what happened and to have some ideas on how we can keep the good we have attained while recapturing the good that we have lost.

I was born in Charleston, West Virginia, in December 1926, so my memories include the Depression and the New Deal. Charleston combined cultures of the South, the Midwest, and Appalachia. There were Babbitts and hillbillies as well as those who still thought of Robert E. Lee as very nearly divine. Indeed, I was one of the latter until I was six, when FDR replaced him. And I still speak with a southern Appalachian accent. I sound like a hillbilly because my father was a hillbilly. He came from a farm in the mountains of eastern West Virginia. He was fortunate enough to come of age just before World War I, when American farming was enjoying some of its most prosperous years, so my grandfather was able to send him to college and law school. By the time I was a boy in the early 1930s he was a successful lawyer in Charleston, but the Depression had brought hard times for his brothers on the farm. The fact that his own brothers were struggling was one reason my father identified with others in similar straits during the Depression. Coal miners were the most conspicuous sufferers in West Virginia. My father made sure I understood their plight.

When I was only six or seven he took me to a company town. This was before the New Deal legislation permitted the United Mine Workers to organize the majority of miners—back when the mine company owned all the houses in the town and the only store. Miners were paid partially in scrip, which they could use only at the company store. What made this a radicalizing experience for a six-year-old was that the store charged a dime for a pack of chewing gum that could be bought for a nickel at any other store.

My other radicalizing experience came when I was seventeen and, on Students Day in Charleston, served as student chief of police. The real chief took me around the station and, trying to treat me as a man of the world, said he wanted to show me how they dealt with niggers. He opened a door to a closet that was full of bloody garments.

On the other hand, as I attended the then-segregated public schools in Charleston, I heard the word "nigger" from the other kids but not very often. My parents never used it, nor did their friends. Blacks were called "colored" back then, not only by whites but by blacks themselves. Whites could be condescending in speaking of them but seldom expressed hatred and often spoke of blacks they knew with affection. So, though I knew from the police chief that ugly attitudes might lurk underneath, what I usually saw was a better and more benign side of whites.

When I was in the army toward the end of World War II, my back was broken during infantry training so I spent several months in the orthopedic ward of the hospital at Fort McClellan in Alabama. During one of those months, four of us were assigned to a partially partitioned-off section of the ward. Two were farmers: one was from Alabama, the other from Mississippi; one was white, the other black. (Even though the armed forces were segregated back then there was only one orthopedic ward at the hospital.) Both farmers had a sense of humor as did a third occupant, a navy pilot whose plane had crashed near Fort McClellan. Our laughter came so frequently and with enough volume that the nurses would tell us to quiet down. There was absolutely no racial tension. The ease of the relationship between the two farmers—Huck and Jim in real life—made you think of what could be.

The army did two other things that took me into different

worlds. Before the infantry it sent me to Ohio University, in Athens, Ohio, for six months. It would later become Roger Ailes's alma mater, and my affectionate memory of both the school and the town gives me some understanding of a man I do not admire. After Fort McClellan I was sent to Ashford General Hospital, where there were a large number of seriously wounded veterans of the war in Europe. There were some genuine heroes among them—they came from all over the country and from all kinds of backgrounds.

From Ashford I went to New York City, where I entered Columbia College in January 1946. Most of my first friends there were veterans. Indeed, the student body seemed largely composed of veterans and bright young Jews from the New York area. (They had to be very bright because Columbia had a quota system at the time.) At the beginning of my second term I encountered two people who had immense influence on me. One was a teacher, Lionel Trilling; the other was a student, Allen Ginsberg.

Trilling was brilliant, but he was also an intellectual snob and taught me to be one at the time. Allen was good at implying that he held the keys to the kingdom of hipness and, like many other nineteen-year-olds, I desperately wanted to be considered hip.

Allen was the first openly gay person I had ever known. Even in New York, that was not common. There were a lot who were closeted—as were all gays almost everywhere else—and some who were semi-closeted, meaning they were open in situations they thought sympathetic. One of my veteran friends who was gay took two years to tell me that he was.

Allen was also the first person I knew who smoked marijuana—he called it "tea"—and he and his friends remained the only users I knew until the 1960s.

A chance encounter with a New York actress from my hometown led to an opportunity to work in summer theater in 1946, an experience that temporarily changed my ambition from becoming a lawyer and politician to becoming a theater director. Ever since I was a boy watching circus trains being unloaded and tents being erected, the process of putting on a show had fascinated me. And it was undeniable that there was a light in young women's eyes when I said I was in the theater that was absent when I said I was a pre-law student. For the next eight years, when I was not a student I would be involved part- or full-time in working backstage at the theater. It was a world where people were more open about their sexuality and in which women could achieve more recognition for their talent and, indeed, power—I know because I was fired by two of them—than they attained in fields other than the arts until the 1960s.

In the '50s I entered two new worlds: One was advertising, where I worked at J. Walter Thompson. The company's appeal for me was that it had a television department that, in a holdover from the custom of radio days, produced several major drama and variety shows for the networks. The other new world was law school at the University of Virginia. In each of them I became immersed in the conformity that characterized the 1950s. Thompson was better than most agencies in that it refused to take cigarette advertising, and Virginia was better than many southern schools in that two of its law professors were able to take firm stands against those, like the editor of *The Richmond News Leader,* who urged massive resistance to the desegregation of the public schools. Otherwise, as exemplified by the dress code at both Thompson and UVA—suits and ties, preferably by J. Press or Brooks Brothers—the culture was primarily go along to get along.

By the time I entered law school my ambition had returned to law and politics. The first indication that my mind would change again came in 1949 when my father led a fight in the West Virginia legislature to pass a bill to control the pollution that fouled the air above many of the state's towns and cities. Giant chemical plants both east and west of Charleston belched noxious fumes into the air and into the lungs of residents twenty-four hours a day. Even though my father was far ahead of his time—this was twenty-one years before the Environmental Protection Agency came into being—he managed to get his bill passed in one house of the legislature only to see it defeated in the state senate by the combined lobbies of the coal, chemical, and steel industries. I could not help feeling that I should have been at his side fighting the same fight. That spring I handed out brochures for the campaign of Franklin D. Roosevelt, Jr., who was running for Congress on New York's west side. I lived around the corner from his headquarters at Ninety-first and Broadway. In 1951 and 1952 I volunteered in two other campaigns, including Adlai Stevenson's for president.

After graduating from law school I joined my father's firm, where my experiences varied from the tedium of searching real estate titles to the excitement of trying cases, and my first contact with journalism advising the editors and reporters of *The Charleston Gazette* on libel law. I also did a considerable amount of work as a court-appointed attorney for criminal defendants. Unfortunately, all of my clients were guilty, but in several instances I was able to persuade the prosecutor to drop the case or reduce the sentence.

I decided I would personally rehabilitate the first to be freed. I gave him a suit and bought him a bus ticket to Pittsburgh, where I arranged for a friend to give him a job. Chicago Red had other ideas. He cashed in the ticket, used the proceeds to buy a shotgun, and broke into the jail in an attempt to free his former fellow inmates. Though my own effort at rehabilitation flopped, I saw the six county probation officers do a remarkable job of keeping their clients out of trouble. (But it should be noted that their successes came with first offenders whose crimes had been nonviolent.)

By chance my criminal clients all happened to be white. From them I learned that police brutality is not confined to blacks. Rather, when police perceive people as powerless, they feel safe from repercussion for any brutality they may be guilty of. But there had to be something more than the powerlessness of the victims that led that Charleston chief of police to preserve those bloody garments.

Not all the police were brutal. Some were just ordinary guys doing a job. If there was a pervasive problem with law enforcement in my county it was inefficiency. If the police caught a criminal it was usually because the squad car happened to be passing by as one culprit was handing a TV set to another out the broken window of a store.

The contrast between the relative ineffectiveness of the police with the effectiveness of the probation officers was one of my first lessons in the danger of making generalizations about government—that it is all bad or all good.

Late in 1958 I got a call from a high school friend who was then the chairman of one of the two main committees of the West Virginia House of Delegates offering me a job as his clerk. I know that sounds less than exciting, but at that moment I was mired in the record room and would have welcomed any life preserver thrown my way. I also knew—because I had been a legislative page while in high school—that the clerk's job could be interesting and actually have considerable influence. If the clerk became known as a source of objective information about pending bills, the members who were either too busy or too lazy to inform themselves would rely on his advice on how to vote. In 1960, hoping to have an even greater voice, I ran to become a member myself. That year, as the primary election drew near, I was asked to run the campaign in my county for John F. Kennedy. Kennedy won, and so did I.

The 1960 West Virginia primary would be decisive in determining if John Kennedy would become the Democratic nominee for president. Kennedy had won the preceding primary in Wisconsin, but lost in the state's Protestant districts. Now the question was could a Catholic win in a state that was 95 percent Protestant. The candidate spent more than half his time in West Virginia during the five weeks leading up to the May ninth primary, as did his brother Robert. Most of their top aides were there the entire time. Thus I was able to get an inside look at the workings of a national campaign at a crucial stage. I saw a bad side of politics as the campaign paid influential county leaders for their support, but I also saw an operation that was brilliant and inspiring in its ability to bring out the voters' better angels and overcome their latent anti-Catholicism.

In January 1961 I began serving the sixty-day term of the legislature. I was able to get bills passed, establishing the state's first civil service and its first human rights commission. But I also, as my father had before me, learned of the power and devious tactics of the state's largest industries. In April I went to Washington, D.C., to join the staff of the Peace Corps, then just seven weeks into its new life.

The idealism of the Roosevelt era that had been dormant during the 1950s had been reawakened by the challenge in Kennedy's inaugural address to "ask what you can do for your country." I wanted to be part of the response to that challenge, but I also planned a political career in West Virginia so I intended to stay in Washington only a short time to help launch an agency that I very much believed in and, incidentally, to share in the excitement of the early days of the New Frontier. But I became so involved in my work at the Peace Corps that, after briefly returning to Charleston in 1962 to complete my service in the legislature, I ended up staying at the Peace Corps for the next six years. That excitement I had hoped to share lasted not only through the Kennedy administration but during the first two years of LBJ's Great Society. It was a time when, as hard as it may be to believe today, most of us felt proud to be working in the government and proud of the country we were serving.

I found that my work at the Peace Corps meant so much to me that I had nightmares about leaving—until I thought of starting *The Washington Monthly*. My job at the Peace Corps had been to evaluate our programs overseas to find out what we were doing right and wrong, and to figure out how we could do better. The idea for the magazine was to do the same thing for the entire government.

Even as I was planning to leave the Peace Corps it turned out to play a major role in the launch of the magazine. *The Washington Monthly*'s original staff had all worked with me in evaluating the Peace Corps, and our first prominent writers were recruited from those who had worked with me as part-time evaluators, including Richard Rovere and Calvin Trillin. Russell Baker and Murray Kempton knew about my work from mutual friends at the Peace Corps. The first investor was a former Peace Corps colleague, Jay Rockefeller. Another, Warren Buffett, was referred to me by a Peace Corps friend. Though Buffett had not yet become well-known—when he asked me to introduce him to Katharine Graham she said she had never heard of him—his two sides, the good citizen and the shrewd investor, were already evident. They were to come in conflict in the case of *The Washington Monthly*. The good citizen would tell him that it was something he should support, and his other side would tell him that its slim financial prospects made it unlikely to enhance his reputation as a shrewd investor.

The first year of the *Monthly* the staff and the writers were paid competitive rates. By the end of that year, however, it became clear that Warren's shrewd investor side was right and that the magazine was fiscally challenged, enough so that we could no longer afford those rates. I decided to apply the lesson I had learned from the Peace Corps that young people in their twenties were capable of remarkable achievements. The first to be hired was Taylor Branch, then a twenty-two-year-old graduate student. I found out about him when he was in Washington for an antiwar rally in the fall of 1969 and dropped by the *Monthly* office to offer us an article about his experience trying to register black voters in rural Georgia. When Taylor left in the summer of 1972 I spent a week worrying about how I could ever replace him, and then I was told there was a young man waiting to see me. He was James Fallows, another twenty-two-year-old. After interviewing him for fifteen minutes I knew I had found Taylor's replacement, and I also knew that the Peace Corps idea was going to work at the *Monthly*.

My original intent was to devote the *Monthly* entirely to covering government and making it work better, but the events of 1968 changed all that. The Tet offensive in late January made the Vietnam War look unwinnable. The April riots in the wake of Martin

Luther King, Jr.'s assassination dealt a severe blow to the hopes of racial harmony inspired by the 1963 march on Washington and the great civil rights bills that passed in 1964 and '65. The assassination of Robert Kennedy following as it did the murders of his brother a few years earlier and of King just two months before deprived the nation of yet another one of its most promising leaders. The chaos of the Democratic convention in August seemed to signal that we had serious class and generational differences to add to the racial ones, and Richard Nixon's victory in the November presidential election did not inspire hope that things would get better.

It was clear that the *Monthly*'s purpose should broaden from what was going wrong with government to understanding what was going wrong with the country as a whole. Examining why top officials had been deceived or deceived themselves about what was going on in Vietnam would lead us to a failure of bureaucratic culture: Bad news was filtered out as it traveled from the field to the White House. Some officials were afraid to pass it on and others did not want to hear it. But it would also lead us to Lyndon Johnson's conviction that the war was a test of his manhood and thus lead us to articles like "Violence and the Masculine Mystique" and "Gay Is Good for Us All."

So we were finding ourselves involved in advocating new causes at the same time we were trying to warn of the dangers of losing the good the country had attained in the Roosevelt era.

One of those causes was trying to make the country aware of the kind of snobbery that we had first seen in the disdain that many of the student antiwar demonstrators displayed toward the workers and cops who supported it. Snobbery was not unknown as I was growing up. Usually it involved members of the social elite looking down on the rest of us. In the 1970s, however, there was a new kind of snob, one who thought of his status as being achieved by merit, not conferred by birth, of being earned by scoring the best on tests, by gaining admission to the most selective universities, and by having the right taste in everything from art to beer.

School snobbery is an example of what troubled me about this trend. At its worst, it had students thinking they were doomed if they didn't make it into one of the Ivies. But I knew there were plenty of good institutions. After all, I had attended Ohio University and evaluated Peace Corps training programs at schools like Iowa State, Michigan, Penn State, and Texas Western (now UT at El Paso).

Along with the growth of snobbery, we saw the first signs of an increase in greed. (I should make clear that I think "greed" is a word that no one understands as applying to themselves. Perhaps the definition that communicates best is simply the desire to have more and more.) In any event, of my four hundred or so classmates from Charleston High School, I can recall only one who showed any signs of wanting to be wealthy. The same was true of my friends at Columbia and in the theater. I can't remember any of my friends talking about making a lot of money. Even at the ad agency and law school, the aspiration was more toward leading a comfortable life than toward accumulating great wealth. It was not until the 1970s or '80s that I began hearing about wealth as an end in itself. By 1988, I was concerned enough to write at the conclusion of a book, "Above all, do not betray your potential in life for the sake of money—Jesus Christ and Mahatma Gandhi are better spiritual guides than Ronald Reagan."

You could see the beginning of the wanting more by the late 1970s. It was truly amazing how quickly the baby boomers' idealism turned into materialism, how those who had marched against the Vietnam War and, as underpaid Nader's Raiders, attacked corporate bad guys decided they had to get MBAs and seek careers as corporate executives or on Wall Street. They also sought law degrees, not so they could join Nader but so they could land jobs at big-time law firms that promised lucrative careers.

Their need for more money was quite understandable. After all, boomers born in 1946, the year after World War II ended, were in 1976 thirty years old, probably married and beginning families.

Naturally they needed homes, and so increasingly their conversation turned to real estate prices. The Volkswagen Beetle that had been their vehicle of choice during the 1960s and '70s could not contain their expanding families, and Beetle sales plummeted as boomers purchased larger cars and station wagons. The more expensive Volvo became the preferred wagon—it's safer for children, you know. And they were right, the Volvo was safer, but the boomers were launched on a lifestyle that required more and more income, the need for which they could always see compelling justification.

Soon you began to hear them talk of how they had to have larger houses. They needed workout rooms. They needed home offices. They needed walk-in closets. And of course they had to have state-of-the-art kitchens and bathrooms.

If they did not go to work on Wall Street to make the money to buy all the things they wanted, they became investors. And as investors, they began to identify with management and with the CEOs who were maximizing profits that could increase the dividends paid to investors. In the process, they tended to forget the workers.

When a worker's job was downsized, his plant closed or his work shipped overseas, all in the name of maximizing profits for managers and stockholders, you could see and feel the workers' resentment rising. And when workers realized that the same people who were taking away their jobs were also looking down their noses and seeing them as tasteless boobs, they began to get angry. White workers also resented blacks who they felt were beneficiaries of government programs that injured workers—programs like busing and affirmative action. Black people, on the other hand, were angered by white resentment of measures that to blacks seemed only fair to make up for the years of degradation and slavery to which they had been subjected.

Right-wing media and political leaders fanned the flames of white anger, while self-righteous liberals encouraged that of blacks. In politics, the Gingrich revolution of 1994 intensified partisanship, deepening the divide between right and left. It only got worse when the Republicans decided to just say no to everything President Obama tried to do. The Internet has made things even worse by creating a means of instant reply or comment, meaning the message was more likely to be ill considered or anger provoking. I have heard the word "outrage" used more in the past twenty years than ever before. Indeed, "I am outraged" has become a cliché of modern discourse.

So much of the anger comes from a failure to understand the other side, and to realize that its members are human beings just like us. We have seen the problem illustrated at Trump rallies in ugly exchanges between protesters and Trump's followers, in the clashes between whites and blacks in Ferguson, Missouri, and between pro-life and pro-choice factions outside Planned Parenthood clinics.

It is hard to see how we can have a fairer and more equal society as long as we are divided into groups that see only their own side and not the other fellow's. Blacks and whites have to understand why they fear each other and acknowledge the fault on both sides. Occupy Wall Streeters have to understand that capitalism is the best way to generate wealth. On the other hand, Wall Streeters and corporate leaders have to understand that wealth should be created in a way that does no harm to the rest of us, and that it should be fairly distributed among all the people who helped create it. Each of us has a vital interest in listening to the other side. If we don't listen to them, why should they listen to us?

Listening should inform our politics, making our causes reflect the legitimate concerns of those on the other side. But—and this is crucial—we must make political choices. When we don't choose, when we don't participate, when we don't even bother to vote, bad things can happen. But when we make choices, participate, and get out and vote, in midterm as well as presidential elections, great good can result. Consider the New Deal reforms described in the next chapter. Those reforms could never have been made if Democrats had not chosen to participate in the 1930s, first winning majorities in the House and Senate in the 1930 midterms and then electing Franklin D. Roosevelt and giving him substantial Democratic majorities in the House and Senate in 1932, increasing those majorities in the 1934 midterms, and reelecting him in 1936 with even greater congressional majorities. The New Deal reforms enacted as a result of those elections led to four decades of the fairest sharing of the nation's income in our history. Democrats who are discouraged by Donald Trump's victory in the 2016 election can take heart from the fact that their comeback could also begin in a midterm election—the one coming in 2018.

# CHAPTER 1

# The Age of Roosevelt

"I want to get out of this Wall Street racket."

This sentence was part of a letter written by Jerome Frank in early 1933 seeking help in landing a job with Franklin D. Roosevelt's new administration in Washington. At age forty-three, Frank had already established himself as a successful lawyer in New York and as one of the nation's most original legal thinkers. He soon became the general counsel of the New Deal's Agricultural Adjustment Administration. Fifteen of the twenty-six lawyers who joined him to defend the AAA from conservative attacks in the courts were recent graduates of Harvard Law School. They and Frank were part of the flood of talented, mostly young people attracted to Washington by the New Deal.

This was, of course, the exact opposite of what has happened since the early 1980s. Steve Rattner, a graduate of Brown University who in the 1970s had emerged as an able young reporter covering Washington for *The New York Times,* decided to leave journalism to go to Wall Street in 1982. "It begins to get to you after a time that you are writing about people who have far more power than you, more influence and more money and are not any more capable," Rattner's wife explained. "Why in the world are you traipsing around the world and writing about them when you are smart enough to make the money and have the influence commensurate to theirs?"

By the end of 1984 Rattner's friend the journalist Walter Shapiro was writing an article, subtitled "Money Madness in Manhattan," announcing that Wall Street had become the destination of choice for the best and brightest. By 1985 there were more investment banks conducting job interviews at Harvard than any other profession. (In 2012, Harvard officials had become so disturbed by the trend that they formed a special task force to consider how to reconnect their graduates with public service.) And by 1987 Oliver Stone was making a movie called *Wall Street* with the intention of disclosing the evils of the financial world, some of which had already become obvious.

The effect of the movie, however, was not what Stone expected. Michael Douglas, the actor who portrayed the movie's villain, Gordon Gekko (whose motto was "Greed, for want of a better word, is good"), found himself hailed as a role model. Instead of being offended by Gordon Gekko's corner cutting, ambitious young people who watched the movie hungered for the money Gekko made and the lifestyle it conferred: limousines, luxurious apartments, beachfront houses, and beautiful women. Twenty-three years after the movie came out, Douglas said in an interview that he was still being stopped by Wall Streeters who would say, "Man, I want to tell you, you're the biggest single reason I got into this business. I watched *Wall Street* and found I wanted to be Gordon Gekko."

In the 1930s, however, the attitude of most people toward attaining wealth found perfect expression in the title of a play that became a big hit on Broadway in 1936 and was made into a popular movie in 1938: *You Can't Take It with You.* Carrie Lee Nelson, who became an army nurse during World War II, recalled, "We just didn't care that much about having a lot of money." Perhaps nothing better illustrates the difference in values between the 1930s and more recent times than the way the leading character was changed when the 1940 movie *The Shop Around the Corner* was redone as

*You've Got Mail* in 1998. In the 1940 version, the hero, played by James Stewart, is a clerk in a small retail store. By 1998, with Tom Hanks in the role, he had to be not only a store owner but the rich owner of a chain of big stores. The Hanks character was living in Manhattan, where, as Walter Shapiro had observed back in 1984, "something . . . makes it hard to think of anything other than how much money you don't have." The hunger for more and more money may have first become obvious in New York, but it soon spread throughout the country, fueled by the need for more and more things, like the new electronic devices that seemed to appear every other month, and for larger and larger homes with more and more rooms to house all those new things.

The change in attitude toward money was reflected in a change in political philosophy. This change could be seen in Ronald Reagan's personal journey from ardent supporter of FDR and the New Deal in the 1930s to champion of conservatism—as eloquent in its advocacy as Roosevelt had been in the cause of liberalism. These disparities in attitudes toward money and politics are just two of the differences between then and now to be explored in this book. It is a story about Washington, D.C., and the nation its leaders govern, beginning with the era of Franklin D. Roosevelt. FDR was president from 1933 to 1945, but the values of those days generally prevailed into the mid-1960s and, in a few respects, including those values governing the distribution of income, through the 1970s. It is also a story about how the city and the country changed, sometimes gradually and sometimes with eye-blinking rapidity as we made the transition to the era of Ronald Reagan, whose presidency in the 1980s was characterized by a set of values that—as with FDR's before him—have continued to rule much of our political and economic life long after his administration ended.

There are countless ways that life is much better today than it was back then. The most recent development is the treatment of gays, who are now accepted to an extent unimaginable in the Roosevelt era. But that era was better in one important way: People were considerably more willing then to share the burdens and benefits of society. For example, for two decades, the top income tax rate was 90 percent. For a bit more than two decades, men from all walks of life felt an obligation to serve in the military. The most dramatic difference, the one that people today are most aware of, is that incomes were much more equal, with workers, executives, and owners each receiving a much fairer share. Contrast this with the Reagan era, which from the beginning saw a decline in the workers' share and an increase in that of executives and owners.

In telling the story of what was good about the Roosevelt era, my aim is not to urge that we go back to that world and try to re-create it. It is, rather, to show that as a people we are capable of the kind of behavior that was so admirable then, and that there is no reason why we are not capable of the same kind of behavior today.

IF THE NEW Dealers didn't come to Washington to make money, why did they come? Of course they wanted to make a decent living, and a government salary was welcome in those days. But government salaries were not going to make them rich. Indeed, back then, public service was rarely looked upon as a way to cash in. It's revealing to recall that through the entire decade of the 1930s only eight retiring congressmen became lobbyists, whereas among retirees from the class of 2010 alone, forty-one became lobbyists.

Jack Abramoff offers some insight on this development. Abramoff was a successful lobbyist during the early George W. Bush years, with friends such as Karl Rove, Grover Norquist, and House majority leader Tom DeLay. His career was cut short when his corruption became a bit too blatant, and he ended up doing time in prison. Afterward, he explained to an interviewer how he would reel in members of Congress and their staffs. First he would show them the good life that a lobbyist could lead, traveling in private jets and dining in the fanciest restaurants. Then, "I would say or my staff would say to him or her at some point, 'You know, when you're done working on the Hill, we'd very much like for you to consider coming to work for us.' Now, the moment I said that to them or any of our staff said that to them, that was it. We owned them."

Jerome Frank said he had come to Washington because the struggle against the Depression seemed to be "the equivalent of war. I want to sign up for the duration." Certainly there was an excitement about being where the action was. For Charles Wyzanski, Jr., a lawyer at the Department of Labor, it was a "feeling that one really counted, that what we did was very important." For Francis Biddle it was "the satisfaction derived from sinking individual effort into the community itself, the common good and the common end." Their cause seemed far more important than any individual.

Adlai Stevenson, who, like Jerome Frank, came to Washington as a young New Deal attorney in 1933, observed that people were working twelve hours a day and sleeping on couches. And they were getting things done, sometimes with remarkable speed.

In the first months of 1933 there had been a rash of bank failures. Depositors in the remaining banks worried that theirs would fail, too, so they withdrew their money, causing more banks to fail. In his first week in office, after his inauguration on March 4, Franklin Roosevelt closed all the banks for four days, Congress passed the Emergency Banking Act providing federal aid for banks sound enough to survive, and Roosevelt gave a fireside chat explaining what the government had done and why. On March 13, the healthy banks started reopening, the panic withdrawals stopped, and the banking system did not face another crisis for more than half a century. The people had believed FDR when he told them in his fireside chat that it "is safer to keep your money in a reopened bank than under the mattress."

Walter Lippmann, an influential columnist and not always a friend of FDR, wrote, "In one week the nation which had lost confidence in everything and everybody had regained confidence in the government and in itself." That probably overstates what happened in one week but it does capture the spirit of how, in the early years of the New Deal, one action after another demonstrated that government was making life significantly better for most Americans.

The New Dealers persuaded Congress to enact a record amount of legislation in the first hundred days of the new administration, including the Agricultural Adjustment Act, the Federal Emergency Relief Act, the National Industrial Recovery Act, and the law authorizing the Civilian Conservation Corps. By July the CCC had put 275,000 young men to work clearing roadsides and planting trees in forests that had been severely depleted by a rapacious timber industry and by farmers hungry for more land to till. That fall and winter, Harry Hopkins, the head of the Federal Emergency Relief Administration, established the Civil Works Administration, which put four million people to work in two months, an incredible accomplishment.

How did the New Dealers do so much so fast? They thought they had no choice. They had to act. And they had to think big. They couldn't just sit there or take tiny tentative steps the way Herbert Hoover had done. They had to risk making mistakes, and they made some lulus.

In 1933, millions of Americans flocked to movie theaters to see "The Three Little Pigs," Walt Disney's longest cartoon to date, in which the pigs foil their foe and end up singing "Who's Afraid of the Big Bad Wolf?" The song became immensely popular, with the wolf widely understood to symbolize the Depression. Meanwhile, the Agricultural Adjustment Administration was pushing a program to slaughter small pigs to help put a floor under hog prices. Needless to say, this did not make a favorable impression on the nation's children or on many of their parents.

But the New Dealers did enough right to get the country going again. By restoring the people's confidence that the government could solve problems, even major ones, they inspired Americans to believe in themselves and the ability of the government they chose to do great things—which is exactly what it proceeded to do, from ending the Depression to winning World War II to providing a college education for millions of veterans to saving Western Europe with the Marshall Plan to building the interstate highway system and sending men to the moon.

Needless to say, making New Deal programs such as the CCC and the CWA work required able people to run them. But they weren't just drawn from the Harvard Law School. Harry Hopkins, who led the CWA, was an Iowan who had graduated from Grinnell College. The CWA in Missouri was run by Harry S. Truman, a graduate of Independence High School. FDR delegated the running of the CCC to the army. Among the officers it assigned to the task were Colonel George C. Marshall, a graduate of the Virginia Military Institute, and Major Dwight D. Eisenhower, a graduate of the U.S. Military Academy.

Democratic majorities in Congress were also an important factor in speedy action on the New Deal measures. In 1933 the Democratic margin in the Senate was 59 to 36, and in the House it was 311 to 117. By 1935 the Democrats' lead in the Senate had grown to 60 to 35 and in the House to 322 to 103. Indeed, from the Roosevelt administration through that of Lyndon Johnson, the Democrats controlled Congress and the White House twenty-eight of thirty-six years. But in the years since, from 1981 to 2016, they have controlled both houses of Congress and the White House for only four years.

Another important factor in the success of the New Deal was the fact that there were actually liberal Republicans in those days. In the Senate, a dozen or so of them voted at one time or another for New Deal measures, and in the House a couple of dozen. "The admirable trait in Roosevelt has been that he has the guts to try," observed one of the liberal Republicans in the Senate, Hiram Johnson of California. "He does it all with the rarest good nature. . . . We have exchanged for a frown [Hoover] in the White House a smile. . . . Where there was hesitation and vacillation, always weighing the political consequences, feebleness, timidity and duplicity, there are now courage and boldness and real action."

In addition to the liberal Republicans there were liberal southern Democrats. Although almost all of them were conservative on racial issues, a substantial number were liberal on other New Deal programs. In the Texas delegation alone, the liberals included Sam Rayburn, Wright Patman, and Maury Maverick.

Unlike today, the threat of a filibuster was rarely used in the Roosevelt era. Back then it took 64 votes to break a filibuster—two-thirds of the 96 senators from the 48 states. Among the New Deal bills that did not attain 64 votes—in other words, bills that could have been filibustered successfully—were the Tennessee Valley Authority legislation, the Fair Labor Standards Act, the National Labor Relations Act, and the Securities Exchange Act. All could have failed in the face of a filibuster.

The three main purposes of the New Deal were to put a floor under falling prices (both on the farm and for small businesses, particularly retail); to create jobs, putting people back to work rather than having them on relief; and to create fairness for both labor and investors. By the end of the 1930s, despite some New Deal legislation having been declared unconstitutional by a conservative Supreme Court, the fundamental aims of the New Deal had been accomplished. Prices for small retail stores had been stabilized; the principle of keeping a reasonable floor under prices and income of farmers, insuring them against the extremes of the market and of weather, had been established, as was the principle of fair labor practices. And the Securities and Exchange Commission helped to level the playing field for investors.

As for creating jobs, both the CCC and the Civil Works Administration achieved impressive results. The CCC continued until 1942, but Roosevelt, worried about Republican criticism of the government's directly hiring the unemployed, disbanded the CWA in the spring of 1934. On reflection, however, he decided he had made a mistake, and after the Democrats' great victory in the 1934 midterm elections, he established the Works Progress Administration (WPA), again under the leadership of Harry Hopkins. The

WPA would ultimately put eight million people to work. The CCC added three million more. This was perhaps the greatest accomplishment of the New Deal. By 1936 it had cut unemployment by more than half. (The reason most historians don't acknowledge this fact is that WPA and CCC workers were not included in the official employment statistics.)

But the job figures do not tell the whole story of the CCC and the WPA. Equally impressive is what the workers accomplished. The CCC reforested the country, planting three billion trees all over America. The WPA built 650,000 miles of roads, 78,000 bridges, 125,000 civilian and military buildings, 700 miles of airport runways, and built, improved, or enlarged 800 airports. It served almost 900 million school lunches, operated 1,500 nursing schools, presented 225,000 concerts, and produced almost 475,000 works of art and at least 276 full-length books.

A sister agency of the WPA called the Public Works Administration (PWA), run by Harold Ickes, was another major factor in not only creating jobs, but in changing the face of America. It is impossible to find an actual number of people who were employed by the PWA, because it worked by letting out contracts to private organizations to do the actual work. So its workers weren't direct hires like those of the CCC and the WPA, but the scale of the projects undertaken by the PWA suggests that it must have taken millions of workers to accomplish all that the agency did. Those projects included the Triborough Bridge and the Lincoln Tunnel in New York; the Overseas Highway connecting Key West with the mainland of Florida; the San Francisco–Oakland Bay Bridge in California; the Grand Coulee Dam in Washington State; the electrification of the railroad between Washington and New York; and the construction of the aircraft carriers *Yorktown* and *Enterprise,* from which planes took off to sink four Japanese carriers at Midway, the most decisive naval battle in American history.

My family would take motor trips within West Virginia and to the neighboring states of Virginia, Ohio, and Kentucky. It was amazing how in almost every town there would be at least one building being constructed by the PWA and the WPA. And as for their efforts on roads, I can testify to the misery of summer travel during the 1930s, when we would encounter one road construction project after another, and have to sit in long lines under the hot sun in un-air-conditioned vehicles waiting for the cars in the other lane to pass. (In those days all but a few highways consisted of just two lanes.) In my hometown of Charleston, the WPA or the PWA built the South Side Bridge, the municipal auditorium, the post office, and a riverfront parkway along the four-mile length of the city.

Perhaps the most significant impact of these New Deal agencies, however, was on the lives of the men to whom they gave work. Jim Mitchell of Kenosha, Wisconsin, described how he drifted around from one odd job to another, barely eking out an existence, until he joined the CCC in 1934:

> You had three square meals a day with good food and a good place to sleep. . . . To this day I can go and see parks that we built in the CCC. I can see trees that we planted. . . . The CCC shaped my life. . . . I stayed in . . . for two years, getting thirty dollars a month. At last I could bring some help to my family. Ma's first letter gave me a big boost.

> *Dear Son,*
>     *I want you to know how grateful we are to you, and proud too. The $25 we get each month goes a long way in holding us together. It's good to look Dmitri in the eye and plunk cash down for groceries and not be obliged to Merri-weather for the rent.*

For the first time in my life I felt good about myself.

Still, there was criticism of the CCC and WPA, especially the latter. Those liberal Republicans mentioned earlier were not a majority of the party in the Roosevelt era. Tea party–types existed then, too, complaining loudly about paying taxes to support a bunch of loafers. Conservative cartoons in the newspapers typically depicted a WPA worker as leaning on his shovel or asleep on the job. One conservative columnist named Jay N. ("Ding") Darling delighted in depicting the New Deal brain trusters as demented professors running around erecting Rube Goldberg–like bureaucratic structures. Sometimes the criticism was justified. One New Dealer at the Agriculture Department told a group of macaroni makers that "we need to involve the macaroni growers in this discussion."

As for the majority Republican attitude toward taxes, the comedian Will Rogers observed, "I really believe that if it came to a vote whether to go to war with England, France and Germany combined [the dominant military powers of the day] or raise taxes on incomes over a hundred thousand dollars, [the Republicans] would vote war."

The business community tended to go easy on Roosevelt in 1933, but by 1934 it had turned against him, sometimes viciously. Bernard Baruch, who later became an adviser to Roosevelt during the war, called one New Deal measure "mob rule" and "more drastic than the French Revolution." Lewis Douglas, Roosevelt's first budget director, said of another measure, "Well, this is the end of Western Civilization." The American Liberty League, a group of conservative businessmen, called old-age pensions "the end of democracy" and the Agricultural Adjustment Act part of "a trend toward fascist agriculture."

Nonetheless, the unity in the country in the Roosevelt era was remarkable. In his presidency, perhaps it was strongest on New Deal issues in his first term, 1933 to 1937. On foreign policy the unity was strongest from 1940 to 1945, of course. Republican presidential nominee in 1940, Wendell Willkie, actually joined Roosevelt in backing the peacetime draft and Lend-Lease, both of which almost certainly would not have passed without his support.

The words "We Do Our Part," the slogan of the New Deal's National Recovery Administration (NRA), captured the prevailing

attitude of the American people in the fight against the Depression
and in winning the war. That attitude led millions to march during
the winter of 1933–34 in support of the NRA, and millions more to
collect scrap metal, buy war bonds, and share the burden of military
service during World War II, long after the agency itself had been
dissolved.

Historians tend to underestimate the importance of the NRA to
the people of America in the depths of the Depression. It created
codes of conduct for almost every occupation, including barbers, in
which they pledged fair treatment to other occupations in return for
fair treatment of themselves. Most of all, it represented a compact
among Americans to help one another, for businessmen to help
workers get fair treatment, and for workers to help business by
agreeing to pay fair prices. One reason it may be discounted by historians is that deflation, which was a terrible problem back then,
has not been a problem for America since, so putting a floor under
prices seems anti-competitive now, or anti-consumer. But then it
was essential to the survival of the small retailer in particular. And
even though the U.S. Supreme Court declared the NRA unconstitutional in 1935 it's important to understand that its principles were
continued under other legislation. The labor provisions of the NRA
continued under the Wagner Act, the National Labor Relations Act
that was passed in 1935. And federal and state fair-trade laws kept
a floor under retail prices for several decades to come.

As for the NRA's meaning to unions, the United Mine Workers,
within eight months of the passage of the NRA, increased its membership from 100,000 to 400,000, and in less than a year the garment workers doubled their membership. That the NRA involved
people from all walks of life was demonstrated by the march in
New York. For ten hours, 250,000 bankers, brokers, stock exchange workers, barbers, jewelers, garment workers, pawnbrokers,
butchers, firemen, policemen, librarians, druggists, book publishers,
bartenders, and more marched. I watched the parade in downtown
Charleston for about half an hour in the morning as it started, but

I was bored by the lack of uniforms, and there were not nearly enough bands. (I should note that I was seven years old at the time.) That night my father, mother, and I were listening to *Amos 'n' Andy*, which came on at seven P.M., and a man knocked at the door. He said, "They're still marching." The same story was repeated all over America. In Hollywood, Busby Berkeley, the great musical comedy director, was working on a film called *Footlight Parade*. He got so excited about the march that he rewrote the finale so that his stars and extras would form an American flag in the profile of FDR and the NRA's blue eagle.

Behind the "We Do Our Part" spirit was a dominant quality Americans displayed during that period: generosity. The most commonly cited memory by many who lived through that time is of mothers feeding hungry people who came to the kitchen door. My boyhood Charleston friend Cabell Davis recalls how his mother never failed to feed the hungry even though their clothes were tattered and they sometimes didn't smell too good. My mother did the same. Manuel Chavez of Las Cruces, New Mexico, recalled that when he was ten years old "my mother . . . never turned down anyone. She would prepare delicious chili from Mesilla Valley, a big pot of pinto beans, and hot tortillas. She'd put a table under the shade of a mulberry tree where the hobos could enjoy their meals with a little dignity. I would hear them say 'Thank you' and then leave with a smile on their faces." Ollie Gossard of Omaha recalled how "a man would knock on the back door seeking something to eat. My mother always fixed a sandwich and a glass of milk. These men were always appreciative."

The spirit of generosity was accompanied by a sense of neighborliness. Gossard recalled a typical evening:

My father would sit in front of our big radio to hear Lowell Thomas and then laugh at the antics of *Amos 'n' Andy*. He would then go out on the front porch to read the afternoon paper. Soon he would be talking with Mr. Keller next door, and then each of them would haul a chair off his front porch and place them near each other on the two concrete driveway paths between the houses. And then another neighbor would join them and another. Then their wives would have finished cleaning up the kitchen and joined their husbands and neighbors in the expanding circle. We kids would play kick the can or some other kid game, but eventually we would slip into the circle and lean against the back of a parent's chair.

Those who had little helped those who had even less. One young hobo told a story in the book *Riding the Rails* of how he stopped at a shack by a cotton field in Mississippi:

A wrinkled old man with white hair sat in front of a tiny cabin with clapboard windows and no glass. His rickety chair appeared to be ready to fall apart and he looked the same. I told him I hadn't eaten in three days and asked if I could buy some food. The old man pulled himself out of his chair and walked over to the cabin door.

"Mandy, this white boy says he is hungry." . . .

A gray-haired lady stepped out of the cabin. She looked even older than her husband and had trouble carrying a blackened kettle. The bottom held the congealed remains of a butter-bean stew. It didn't look appetizing but it smelled delicious.

The old couple smiled and watched as I scraped the pot clean. In the cabin's dim light I could see how poverty-stricken they were.

Another young man told the story of how he and a companion

ran across a log cabin deep in the blackjack oaks. It had a well in the backyard with a rope and a pulley. A man who must have been close to ninety years old came out of the cabin. We asked if we could have a bucket of water.

"When did you boys last eat?" he asked.

When we told him, he asked his wife to bring us food.

She set out a gallon crock that was half full of milk, a pone of cornbread, and a bucket of sorghum molasses.

One reason people didn't look down on those who were down and out was that 80 percent of those born before 1920—in other words, 80 percent of those above age fourteen when Roosevelt came to office—came from rural America. The Great Depression had hit those rural areas first; there was an agricultural decline even before Wall Street fell apart. Almost everyone had friends whom they knew to be good people who were out of work. They were not inclined to look down on people who were like themselves. Will Rogers called himself an old country boy. My father, who was a successful lawyer, referred to himself as a common man. The journalist Ernie Pyle called Harry Hopkins, the head of the WPA, a common man, and made clear he meant it as a term of praise. Interestingly enough, Pyle went on to exalt the common man as enlisted soldier during World War II, as did Bill Mauldin in his cartoons portraying the GIs Willie and Joe.

Behind the greater political unity of the 1930s was an even greater cultural unity. People got their information from newspapers, which, in turn, relied largely on just three news services, the Associated Press, United Press, and the International News Service, to supply that information. There were three radio broadcast networks—Mutual, Columbia, and the National Broadcasting Company, which split its offerings into a "blue" and a "red" network, the blue later becoming the American Broadcasting Company. People listened to the same shows. The next day it would seem that everyone was talking about what Charlie McCarthy said to Edgar Bergen or what Rochester said to Jack Benny.

Public schools were another significant factor in that unity. A far larger part of the population attended public schools in those days, and there was a far greater diversity of students from different economic classes than exist today in much of American education. Schools were better back then because limited employment opportunities for women meant a much higher percentage of the brainiest went into teaching.

Parents put less pressure on children to get As and much less emphasis on getting them into the "right" schools (an endeavor that now begins, for many parents, at kindergarten or even nursery school). As a result, after-school activities were left pretty much to the imagination of the kids. The typical parent would send them out to play, with the only injunction being to come home in time for dinner.

The military draft played an important role in promoting cultural unity, bringing together men from all classes from 1940 through the mid-1960s. And it may well be that the restrictive immigration laws enacted after World War I, though otherwise odious, gave the nation breathing space to assimilate the waves of immigrants from Ireland, Italy, and eastern Europe that came into this country in the early part of the century.

Two other factors in that unity of the 1930s were the image of America projected in movies made by the mostly Jewish film industry in Hollywood, and the kind of Christianity preached by Franklin D. Roosevelt. The hero of a '30s movie was usually an average man, played by Spencer Tracy, Gary Cooper, Henry Fonda, Clark Gable, or James Stewart. Stewart's role in *Mr. Smith Goes to Washington* was typical. Comedies of the 1930s ridiculed pretension and snobbery. In *It Happened One Night,* the hero, a reporter played by Clark Gable—in those days, reporters thought of themselves as blue-collar employees—wakes up a spoiled rich girl played by Claudette Colbert to the pretensions of the wealthy. Another common theme of 1930s movies was an idealized portrait of the middle-class family, most notably as presented in the Andy Hardy movies, which starred Mickey Rooney.

In *Andy Hardy Meets Debutante,* a typical film in the series,

Andy goes to New York and pretends that he is rich in an attempt to impress an attractive socialite. His wise father, Judge Hardy, played by Lewis Stone, gently and with a good-humored understanding of the travails of adolescence, helps Andy see the folly of pretension and the falseness of values that make being rich or being a socialite seem important.

Respect for the authority figure, for the father, was another common feature of the culture of the Roosevelt era, and it extended through the 1950s in, for example, the television series *Father Knows Best*. It may have been a factor in Roosevelt's losing his fight to expand the Supreme Court, which could have been regarded as an attack on the authority of the judiciary. But it also may have been a factor in Roosevelt's success because of the automatic respect accorded the president.

As for Roosevelt's Christianity, it is hard to say whether it was his faith that influenced other Americans or that his faith merely exemplified the Christianity that was prevalent at the time. The key to understanding that Christianity is the failure of Prohibition. Prohibition had been adopted just after World War I as part of a moral crusade led by evangelists such as Billy Sunday and Aimee Semple McPherson and by organizations such as the Woman's Christian Temperance Union. Because Prohibition clearly had not worked—the moral absolutism behind it having failed to persuade much of the country—people were, as one theologian put it, "trying to find a new moral framework for improving America without so much pride and arrogance and self-assurance as the Prohibitionists had." Roosevelt's Christianity made little reference to hell and damnation and the sterner aspects of the Old Testament and the book of Revelation. Instead it emphasized the Sermon on the Mount.

"Probably no American politician," wrote FDR biographer James MacGregor Burns, gave "so many speeches that were essentially sermons rather than statements of policy." In 1932, when he was accepting his party's nomination for president, Roosevelt spoke of having come through "an era of selfishness among individual men and women. Many among us have made obeisance to Mammon" and "succumbed to the lure of the profits of speculation."

"Practical Christianity generally applied," he told a group of Methodist bishops, would help "solve the great economic problems confronting us, brought about in large part by greed and selfishness." In a speech in 1933 he charged that "the practices of unscrupulous moneychangers"—by which he meant dishonest financiers, shady stock traders, and corrupt bankers—had caused the Great Depression. At the Democratic National Convention three years later, he declared that "in the place of the palace of privilege we seek to build a temple out of faith, hope, and charity." Later in that 1936 campaign, he told an audience that after four years of the New Deal "your government is still on the side of the road with the Good Samaritan and not with those who pass on the other side."

Roosevelt saw the New Deal as applied Christianity, but he did not condemn or exclude other religions. As for the different sects of Christianity, while Roosevelt was an Episcopalian, his son James reported that he particularly enjoyed "hearing and singing rousing Methodist and Baptist hymns." FDR and Winston Churchill, when they met in 1941 to proclaim the Atlantic Charter on the British battleship *Prince of Wales,* joined the crew in singing "Onward, Christian Soldiers" and "Eternal Father Strong to Save."

In his annual Christmas Eve speech in 1939, Roosevelt was anticipating that benefits under the Social Security law, passed in 1936, would begin to be paid on January 1, 1940. He quoted the Sermon on the Mount and asked his audience to "pray that we be given the strength to live for others." Then he tied the story of Scrooge— Roosevelt was famous for reading "A Christmas Carol" to his grandchildren on Christmas Eve—to the Social Security program:

Old Scrooge found that Christmas wasn't humbug. He took to himself the spirit of neighborliness. But today neighborliness can no longer be confined to one's own little neighborhood. Life has become too complex for that. In our country neighborliness has gradually spread to boundaries—from town to country to state, and now at last to the whole nation.

For instance, who . . . would have thought that a week from tomorrow, January 1, 1940, tens of thousands of elderly men and women in every state and every county and every city in this nation would begin to receive checks every month for old age retirement insurance?

The next leader of the Roosevelt era to use Christianity to advance a great cause was Martin Luther King, Jr. Recall that King's organization was named the Southern Christian Leadership Conference. King challenged whites to do unto others as they would have others do unto them, and when they did just the opposite, he asked blacks to turn the other cheek. The result was a contrast that seared the conscience of anyone who considered himself a Christian: the dignity of blacks, even as they lay beaten and bleeding, contrasted with the ugliness of white anger and hatred.

After King, liberals began to lose faith in Christianity, and only one Democratic president emphasized his religion: Jimmy Carter, who was born-again and thus part of the evangelical movement that increasingly dominated Christianity. The evangelicals emphasized their salvation, the idea that Jesus could save them. Carter, in his own life, practiced FDR's "What can I do for Jesus?" kind of Christianity, but unfortunately most of his fellow evangelicals were more concerned with what Jesus could do for them, and the great majority of them were—and remain—conservative in their politics.

If Franklin Roosevelt's relationship to the Christianity of his day and the nature of that Christianity proved essential to his success, an equally significant factor was his relationship to the media, which mostly meant newspapers at that time, and the nature of journalism in that era.

Roosevelt liked reporters. He enjoyed the give-and-take of press conferences. Indeed, he held two a week throughout his presidency,

many more than any other president. Only John F. Kennedy re-
sembled him in terms of seeming to actually take pleasure in meeting the press. When Roosevelt came to office, reporters were
required to submit their questions in writing in advance. In other
words, reporters had to let the White House know what their questions would be so that the president could have canned answers
ready for them.

But at Harvard, Roosevelt had run *The Crimson,* the college
newspaper, so he understood what reporters needed. He abolished
the requirement that questions be put in writing and submitted in
advance; reporters were free to ask whatever they wanted, without
informing the White House. The columnist Heywood Broun called
Roosevelt "the best newspaperman who has ever been president of
the United States." Roosevelt's sense of the news, moreover, would
not only help reporters do their job; it also helped him in anticipating what questions would be asked and what would help him get his
message across to reporters. As Graham J. White wrote in *FDR and
the Press,* "Far from being a burdensome chore, press conferences
were stimulating and enjoyable interludes to which Roosevelt
looked forward, in the later estimation of one newsman, with the
same enthusiasm with which Dwight Eisenhower contemplated a
game of golf."

Arthur Sears Henning, a Washington newsman for twenty-three
years and chief of the *Chicago Tribune*'s Washington bureau for
nineteen of those years, said the relationship between president and
press had never been as satisfactory as it was under Roosevelt, at
least from the newspaperman's point of view. This from a correspondent for a newspaper that was implacably hostile to Roosevelt.
Raymond Tucker wrote in *Collier's* magazine that "the reportorial
affection and admiration" for the president was "unprecedented. . . .
He has definitely captivated an unusually cynical battalion of correspondents."

All this did not mean that a reporter would tilt his story in
favor of Roosevelt. The fact that most reporters' bosses—their

publishers—were against Roosevelt guaranteed that that would not happen. Another guarantee was the respect for objectivity in reporting. This kept stories from being tilted against FDR, but it also meant Roosevelt's message would be reported. Objectivity had become the aim of reporters for the better newspapers as a reaction to the excesses of partisanship in the past. It remained the standard throughout the Roosevelt administration. Even in the most heated period of election campaigns—the two months preceding the fall election—coverage was mostly straightforward and unbiased. A study of forty-seven stories reporting on Roosevelt's speeches during that period in the 1936 and 1940 campaigns found that the number of those that were sharply tilted either for or against the president was in the single digits. Most of the reports were deemed "fair and accurate."

Roosevelt's first "fireside chat" was given on March 12, 1933, just eight days after his inauguration. The radio audience for the fireside chats reached a top figure of sixty million, almost half the population of the United States at the time. In the mid-1930s, *Billboard* magazine published a list of the most-listened-to radio shows, and fifteen of the top thirty were speeches by Roosevelt. Barack Obama, by contrast had an audience of thirty-seven million for his 2012 State of the Union speech, approximately one-ninth of the population. One problem a president faces today, of course, is the vast array of competing entertainments. The major networks might broadcast a presidential speech, as do the three main cable news networks, but hundreds of other cable channels are available to distract the viewer, as are a vast array of other possibilities opened up by the Internet and video games.

The coverage by Fox News, the nation's most popular cable news channel, has been constantly slanted against Obama and the Clintons. The most influential radio voice is that of Rush Limbaugh, who is joined by a chorus of lesser conservative voices that together dominate the airwaves. The coverage of presidential speeches and White House press conferences is so full of reporters' opinion and interpretation as to obscure whatever it is the president is trying to convey.

For instance, Obama is often criticized in the media for not making it clear that his healthcare reform plan did not pose a threat to Medicare. In fact, he began a press conference in July 2009 by doing exactly that, but his words all but disappeared in subsequent accounts of that press conference, which dwelt almost exclusively on Obama's answer to the last question in the session, concerning the treatment by Cambridge, Massachusetts, police of the black scholar Henry Louis Gates, Jr. As for coverage of Obama's speeches, a thirty-two-paragraph article in *The New York Times* by Jackie Calmes on an Obama speech in Cleveland not only began on an inside page—Roosevelt usually got front-page coverage not only for his speeches but for his press conferences—it also contained exactly two paragraphs of quotes from the speech, and these were near the end of the piece. The emphasis on the reporter's take on a speech rather than on what the speaker actually said is demonstrated by the first sentence of her story: "Seeking to rally his struggling party for the final weeks of the midterm election President Obama made the most partisan speech of the campaign."

Most editorial pages were anti-Roosevelt—probably more than have been anti-Obama today—and most of the columnists were similarly opposed to FDR, including David Lawrence, Frank Kent, Mark Sullivan, Westbrook Pegler, and Arthur Krock. William Randolph Hearst turned sharply against the New Deal in 1935, when the president called on Americans to "foreswear that conception of the acquisition of wealth which through excessive profits creates undue power over private affairs and . . . public affairs." Hearst was outraged and wrote to his editors, "It's essentially communism." A message went out from Hearst executives to Hearst editors that "the chief instructs that the phrase 'Soak the Successful' be used in all references to the administration's tax program. . . . He also wants the words 'Raw Deal' used instead of New Deal."

But such voices could not compete with that of the most popular columnist and commentator of the day: Will Rogers, who was a strong supporter of the president until his untimely death in a plane crash in August 1935. Rogers had a column that appeared in *The New York Times* and approximately one hundred other papers, but his greatest influence was through his radio show, which had an audience of 30 million. (This out of a population of between 120 million and 130 million. Rush Limbaugh has an audience of about 20 million in a population of 310 million.) When Rogers's show came on the air on Sunday evenings, churches noted that their attendance dropped by about half. His commonsense, country-boy arguments against Prohibition were devastating to its self-righteous proponents. Rogers was a capital-d Democrat. He not only supported FDR in the 1932 election campaign but became an advocate of almost all the New Deal programs. He was even called "an unofficial spokesman for the new president." When one critic wrote, "Here people are wondering if the president is writing your speeches or if you're writing the president's speeches," Rogers denied the suggestion, but said that he was proud that he and Roosevelt were "of the same mind." Rogers's biographer Richard D. White, Jr., said in his book *Will Rogers: A Political Life* that he "probably did more than any other American to convince the public to accept the New Deal."

Roosevelt was well aware of Rogers's importance, wooing him with invitations to Hyde Park, Warm Springs, and the White House, and complimenting him on his performances. It is hard to imagine Roosevelt, with his elite accent and background, gaining the tremendous popular acceptance he achieved so quickly without the support of the "old country boy."

When Rogers died, his place as influential Roosevelt supporter was taken by two men, neither of whom was as powerful as Rogers had been but who, taken together, had the most popular appeal of any commentators then in the press or radio. Drew Pearson wrote a column called "The Washington Merry-Go-Round." It was carried by more than six hundred newspapers with a total circulation of over twenty million. One critic commented that the column was regarded as a kind of "White House pet." The gossip columnist Walter Winchell had a crush on Roosevelt, and interspersed his items about Hollywood and Broadway stars with praise for the president and support for his programs.

Winchell's influence was not always for the best—if celebrityism is one of the curses of modern American culture, he was its original Typhoid Mary—but his support for FDR was ardent. His newspaper column had ten million readers, and there were probably twice that number of listeners to his radio program, a fifteen-minute Sunday night news show called *The Jergens Journal,* which ranked as high as fifth among all radio shows. As with Rogers, Roosevelt appreciated the influence of Pearson and Winchell, and leaked items to them through his conduits, Tommy Corcoran for Pearson and Ernest Cuneo for Winchell.

There were, of course, a great many things wrong with the 1930s. For one thing, there was little air-conditioning (which may, in fact, have been valuable in helping FDR get a record amount of legislation passed in the first hundred days of the New Deal, since members of Congress were desperate to escape Washington before the heat of summer turned it into an oven). Boredom was more a fact of life in those days. There simply weren't as many diversions as we have now. Television didn't become widely available until the late 1940s, and, of course, there was no cable or Internet. I can remember long summer afternoons when I was a kid and my friends were away at camp. I would sit through a movie twice, sometimes a double feature twice, just to while away the hours.

More seriously, cigarette smoke fouled the air of homes and offices throughout the country. It seemed like practically every adult and a goodly number of adolescents were puffing away unaware of the harm they were doing to themselves and others. They included Franklin Roosevelt, whose smoking contributed to his death before age sixty-four.

There wasn't much in the way of consumer protection in the

'30s either. Part of the reason for this was that society's respect for authority figures, such as, say, physicians, meant that if a doctor in an advertisement said that Camel or Lucky Strike cigarettes were not only safe but healthful, people believed the doctor. That's why the scene in the movie *Kings Row,* in which a sadistic physician amputates the legs of a character played by Ronald Reagan, was so shocking.

And immigration restrictions, which may have helped in the assimilation of earlier immigrants, had a cruel exclusionary effect, the most memorable of which was the 1939 incident of the steamship *St. Louis,* which, crowded with Jewish refugees from Nazi oppression, was refused entrance to the United States by a State Department official named Samuel Miller Breckinridge Long, one of the more shameful episodes in American history. Jews in America in the 1930s were the victims of hatred by homegrown Nazis, but more often anti-Semitism wasn't hatred so much as unfair characterizations of them as being guilty of sharp practices in business, having too much concern with making money, of being vulgar, pushy, and not the kind one would want in his club. They were, in fact, excluded from most clubs and from many of the best hotels. The word "Restricted" meant, simply, "No Jews." For gays, the situation was pretty much summed up in the title of a Senate report published in 1950: "Employment of Homosexuals and Other Sex Perverts in the Government." Needless to say, except in a few large cities, gays had to remain in the closet.

For Catholics, there was less outright hostility than for Jews and gays, but there was certainly denial of employment in sought-after positions such as those in elite law firms in Boston, New York, Philadelphia, and Washington. And Catholics were, of course, the targets of undisguised hatred from the Ku Klux Klan.

As for women, their preferred occupation, at least so far as men were concerned, was housewife. If women had to work, they were expected to choose employment as teachers, nurses, secretaries, or sales clerks. Unwed motherhood could bring shame and a back-alley abortion, often at the hands of incompetents. Interestingly enough, women were still given a considerable measure of respect, reflected in the movies of the 1930s, in which the leading women characters were often shown as having lots of spunk, character, intelligence, and a great sense of humor. Actresses who played such roles included Claudette Colbert, Jean Arthur, Myrna Loy, Rosalind Russell, and Carole Lombard. Indeed, they were almost always as smart as the leading men in their movies—maybe smarter. And on occasion they were portrayed in jobs generally reserved for men. Rosalind Russell, for example, played a newspaper reporter in *His Girl Friday* who wanted to get married but also wanted to remain a reporter, which was quite unusual but not unheard of at the time.

One job that women had never held was as a member of the president's cabinet. Franklin Roosevelt changed that in 1933 when he named Frances Perkins secretary of labor. Her appointment was a triumph for her sex, but when she arrived at the department in 1933, she encountered a small but revealing sign that it was still a man's world: a brass spittoon stood in the corner of her office. Public expectoration, often involving a juice produced by chewing tobacco, was still widespread among American males, and spittoons could be found in most offices, as well as in building lobbies and next to the elevators. Since the male marksmanship did not always match male vanity, the spittoon and its surrounding area constantly reminded women that in the workplace, their needs and preferences ranked second.

Another fact of life in the '30s became clear on Frances Perkins's first day in office. She opened her desk drawer to find it inhabited by a large cockroach. She soon learned that many desks at the Labor Department were infested with the insects. Although the roaches were an irritation, what was more troubling was the reason for their presence: Black employees in the department had to bring their own lunches to work because they were refused service by restaurants. Even the department's own cafeteria was segregated by race, a situation that Perkins soon remedied, though she could do nothing about the restaurants. Harold Ickes, the secretary of the interior, also removed racial restrictions in his cafeteria, but in many other departments the lunchrooms remained segregated, as they did in Congress. In 1934, a North Carolina congressman, defending segregation in the House cafeteria, said that he was as free of racial and religious intolerance "as any man in this House," but that attempts to change the policy were the tactics of "toughs and hoodlums from Howard University."

Even in the 1940 movie *His Girl Friday,* which was the most progressive of the era in terms of women's rights, a reporter casually referred to a black child as a "pickaninny."

Well into the 1950s, black people in Washington could not sleep in downtown hotels, could not be served in downtown restaurants (not even those in department stores), and were excluded from major movie theaters and the National Theatre, where road companies of Broadway plays performed. Schools were segregated, as were public swimming pools and the local amusement park at Glen Echo in Maryland. The good news was that blacks were able to get government jobs. By the end of the New Deal, they held a percentage of federal jobs pretty much equal to their share of the country's population—indeed, an even higher percentage at the post office. But they were concentrated in jobs that tended to be at the lower end of the ladder. Lester Perry, who had a degree from Howard University and was hired by the Department of Commerce in 1937, described his duties: "I came in the morning and dusted off the desk for the chief of my division. I usually went down and got the mail, and I opened that and put it on the desk of the secretary to the chief of my division, and for the rest of the time I ran such errands as were assigned."

But Perry had it easy compared with many of his brothers in this country. In 1933, a total of thirty-four blacks were lynched in America. One lynching occurred as close to Washington as Princess Anne, Maryland, where on October 19 a mob smashed in a jail door with a battering ram, seized a twenty-three-year-old man, and "dragged him by the neck through the streets," according to an account of the event published by *The New York Times.* "While the prisoner pleaded desperately for his life and members of the mob shouted, 'Lynch him,' a rope was put around his neck. The other end was swung over the limb of a tree. . . . To accompanying shouts of 'Let him swing,' the struggling Negro was hoisted into the air. Five minutes later he was dead."

In 1937, after two black men were shot to death in Mississippi following their torture by blowtorch, the House of Representatives finally passed an anti-lynching bill. In the Senate, however, a filibuster by southern members such as Allen Ellender of Louisiana, who declared, "I believe in white supremacy, and as long as I am in this Senate, I expect to fight for white supremacy"—killed the legislation. During debate, Senator Josiah Bailey of North Carolina said of the anti-lynching legislation, "I fear it, I dread it, I fight it. . . . Reconstruction all over again . . . will destroy the South."

The blocking of anti-lynching legislation was probably the worst thing southern congressmen did during this time, but it was not the only evil offense. One was blocking measures to bring voting rights to blacks. Another was restricting the kinds of jobs black people could get in the government, which they did, not by making laws, but by intimidating federal officials. For example, when Arthur J. Altmeyer, the head of the Federal Security Agency, was questioned in 1941 by Representative Malcolm C. Tarver of Georgia, here's how the dialogue went:

MR. TARVER: "What about mixing of black and white and colored all in the same workroom?"

MR. ALTMEYER: "As far as I'm concerned, I will give you the assurance I gave before that we will certainly work that out in accordance with the space limitations so that there will be no greater offense to social sensibility than exists at the present time."

MR. TARVER: "What about the business of having colored stenographers called in to attend to the stenographic needs of white employees and conversely white stenographers called in to attend to the needs of colored employees?"

MR. ALTMEYER: "We will not have that done. Now, you were asking two questions. I do not think there has ever been any question raised of colored people serving the needs of white persons or furnishing stenographic assistance. I think you mean particularly the other situation."

MR. TARVER: "I think both are objectionable."

MR. ALTMEYER: "If there is objection, we will eliminate both."

There is no question, however, that the Roosevelt era brought about a softening of attitude toward segregation. Lynchings, which had numbered in the triple digits early in the century and in the double digits into the early '30s, declined to eight in 1937 and stayed in single digits until the figure reached zero in the '50s, which was the number for most years thereafter. Still, Emmett Till, a fourteen-year-old black boy from Chicago who was visiting his family in Mississippi in 1955, was murdered by white men after he was said to have whistled admiringly at a white woman. And one has to suspect that there were other murders of blacks by white people that went unreported.

Hollywood and radio played a major role in changing racial attitudes. Sometimes their attempts to do so challenged credulity, as in 1934's *Judge Priest,* in which blacks and whites are shown marching together and celebrating the acquittal of a former Confederate general by singing "Dixie." But portrayals of black figures such as Jack Benny's valet, Rochester (played by Eddie Anderson), and Scarlett O'Hara's Mammy (played by Hattie McDaniel) as wiser and smarter than their employers helped to humanize and encourage respect for black Americans, as did the very popular radio show *Amos 'n' Andy.*

Many people look back on that show as being condescending, and perhaps it was. But it depicted blacks and whites as essentially the same people—black society as much the same as the white one.

The Mystic Knights of the Sea in *Amos 'n' Andy* was not that much different from the lodges that millions of white people joined. The Kingfish was the same sort of inept confidence man played by W. C. Fields and Groucho Marx in the movies. None of his schemes or theirs ever worked. Major Hoople, a widely popular white comic strip character in the 1930s and '40s, was practically identical to the Kingfish. Amos in the show was depicted as the average American good guy, a black version of the character often played by James Stewart in the movies.

*Amos 'n' Andy* was so popular among black Americans on radio and then in its television incarnation, which continued into the fifties, that when it was discontinued there was widespread distress. Henry Louis Gates, Jr., director of Harvard's Hutchins Center for African and African American Research, writes in his book *Colored People: A Memoir:* "*Everybody* loved *Amos and Andy*. I don't care what people say today. For the colored people, the day they took *Amos and Andy* off the air was one of the saddest days in Piedmont," his West Virginia hometown. In other words, *Amos 'n' Andy* was an expression of black and white reconciliation, people finding that beneath different exteriors beats the same heart.

Progress in race relations accelerated during the war. In 1941, Franklin Roosevelt, under pressure from black leaders, established the Fair Employment Practices Committee. It was far from totally effective, but did succeed in opening many jobs in war industries to blacks. Southern Democrats and conservative Republicans killed the FEPC in 1946, but in 1948, Harry S. Truman desegregated the army, which was a tremendous step forward. The 1940s also brought leading roles for blacks in movies, albeit in all-black casts, with Lena Horne and Bill Robinson in *Stormy Weather* and Ethel Waters in *Cabin in the Sky*. In 1949, a biracial woman was depicted in a movie, *Pinky*, with a largely white cast, but even so had to be portrayed by a white actress (Jeanne Crain). In the 1950s, however, black actors such as Harry Belafonte and Sidney Poitier had leading roles in mixed-race movies.

In 1954, the Supreme Court in *Brown v. Board of Education* decided that separate schools for black and white students provided in southern states and some border states were not equal. In 1957, Dwight Eisenhower sent federal troops to enforce the desegregation of Little Rock Central High School. This was the scene of the first photographs of young African American students being subjected to ugly white anger, which the nation would see repeated again and again, as young black students sat in at lunch counters in the South and as schools were desegregated, including the one in New Orleans that prompted Norman Rockwell, the artist who probably had the greatest impact on the American people, to do a cover illustration for the *Saturday Evening Post* showing one black child enduring the anger of the white mob. When this was followed by the 1963 bombing of the Birmingham church that resulted in the deaths of four young black children and the 1965 beating of ministers and marchers at the Edmund Pettus Bridge in Selma, Americans who had been indifferent to the cause of equal rights for blacks saw on their television screens exactly why they should care. And enough of them did care that the representatives they elected to Congress proceeded to pass two major bills that led to the end of the WHITES ONLY signs and gave black people the most important right of all: the right to vote.

The period 1941 through 1965 saw the elimination of legal obstacles to equal rights for blacks. It also saw a dramatic reduction in other prejudices.

Openly anti-Semitic statements decreased markedly in the 1940s. World War II movies were a major factor, often showing Jews fighting alongside wealthy WASPs from Manhattan, Italian Americans, Irish Americans, and farmers from the South or Midwest.

After the war Americans saw photographs and newsreels of stacked bodies and skeletal prisoners in Nazi concentration camps and then learned of the Nazis' attempt at extermination of the Jews at Auschwitz and other camps. Then came a movie, *Gentleman's Agreement,* that had enormous influence. Gregory Peck played a reporter posing as a Jew and encountering all the prejudices, subtle and not so subtle, to which American Jews were subjected every day. Gentiles were impressed by the dignity and courage of the Jewish struggle for a homeland as personified by the character played by Paul Newman in the movie *Exodus*. By the 1960s all those Restricted signs had disappeared.

As for Catholics, meaning Irish Americans and Italian Americans, they too benefited from those World War II movies. The prejudice against them softened through the 1950s and practically disappeared in the next decade in the wake of the immense popularity of John Kennedy and of John XXIII, the Pope Francis of his day.

In sum, the Roosevelt era from 1933 to 1965, despite its many faults, saw progress toward equality of income and social and legal status unparalleled in American history. Its roots were as varied as the humanizing of blacks by *Amos 'n' Andy;* the respect for the common man displayed by Will Rogers, Ernie Pyle, and Bill Mauldin; those World War II movies that showed Irish, Italian, and Jewish Americans fighting and dying for all of us; and finally those smart, spunky, and funny heroines of 1930s and 1940s movies who demonstrated beyond a shadow of a doubt that women were the equal of men, paving the way for the great women's movement that emerged in the 1960s.

The rest of this book is devoted to describing the advances and retreats from that progress, exploring why they happened and what we can do to become more equal.

Even as the progress of the Roosevelt era was still being made it was possible to see early warnings of the retreat that was to come. They are the subject of the next two chapters.

# CHAPTER 2

# From Doing Good to Doing Well: The Pioneers

If it was unusual for congressmen to become lobbyists in the 1930s, it was practically unheard of for New Deal officials to do so. Indeed, none did until Tommy Corcoran in 1941, and there wasn't another until 1946, when, after the death of FDR the year before, a couple of dozen left government, including Abe Fortas, a future Supreme Court justice. The first prominent Truman official to become a lobbyist was Clark Clifford in 1950. Clifford joined Fortas and Corcoran as the leading purveyors of influence in Washington for a decade to come.

They were the forerunners of the modern mass movement of public officials from doing good to doing well, a movement that grew into the hundreds in the 1970s and into the thousands thereafter. Their careers ended with their reputations tarnished, and their stories should have stood as a warning to those who followed. As with Gordon Gekko, however, the only lesson learned by their emulators was that they should make sure whatever they did was legal, if still morally dubious. To me, the three men also stand as illustrations of a major truth: that the contest between our better and lesser angels is usually a close call.

Corcoran had joined the government at age thirty-three—like Jerome Frank he was a little older than most of the lawyers attracted to the New Deal. And like Frank, he had enjoyed success practicing law in New York. He had moved to the city after serving as a clerk to Justice Oliver Wendell Holmes, Jr., and having been recommended by Felix Frankfurter, one of his law professors at Harvard and a future Supreme Court justice. He said his goal, one widely shared in the Roaring '20s, was to make a million dollars, and as of October 1929 he had been sufficiently successful to have accumulated a fourth of his goal: $250,000. But much of that was lost in the October Wall Street crash and the Great Depression that followed. His firm lost clients and cut his salary, and he began to consider employment opportunities elsewhere. Frankfurter recommended public service. Frankfurter had taught Corcoran about the economic theories of Harold Laski and John Maynard Keynes, who believed in government action to jump-start depressed economies. One government agency, recently established by Herbert Hoover, had the potential to do just that. It was the Reconstruction Finance Corporation, created to make loans to businesses in order to promote economic activity. When Corcoran was offered a job as the RFC's assistant general counsel, he accepted and moved to Washington in 1932.

The columnist Walter Lippmann called the RFC "the first New Deal agency" even though it was started under Hoover. Lippmann's description proved more hopeful than realistic. Conservatives on the RFC staff, definitely not among the admirers of Laski and Keynes, tended to drag their feet on any remotely imaginative project designed to promote economic activity. But things changed when Franklin D. Roosevelt became president in March 1933, and the RFC's and Corcoran's fortunes underwent dramatic improvement. His mentor, Frankfurter, turned out to be a man whose advice Roosevelt frequently sought and, especially on personnel matters, relied upon. So when Roosevelt decided to reform Wall Street, he asked Frankfurter to recommend a lawyer to write the necessary legislation. Frankfurter suggested Tommy Corcoran and another brilliant young lawyer, Ben Cohen. This team would, in the words of a contemporary reporter, "have more influence at the White House . . . and more throughout the government than any pair of statesmen in Washington" in the 1930s.

The only word that rings wrong in that quotation is "statesmen." It could apply to Ben Cohen, but Tommy Corcoran and most of the people who knew him would laugh at the gravity of demeanor it suggests. Tommy had a hint of rogue about him, a twinkle in his eye, a devilish grin, and a delight in making a deal.

FDR met Corcoran at a luncheon at the home of Oliver Wendell Holmes on the occasion of the justice's ninety-second birthday in March 1933. Frankfurter was also there. There is no record of FDR's reaction to Corcoran at the time, but it was clear that Frankfurter was responsible for Corcoran's involvement with the SEC legislation. When Roosevelt asked Frankfurter to take over the drafting of the bill, Frankfurter chose Cohen and Corcoran to work with him. Cohen, unlike Corcoran, was "shy and professorial," but the two men immediately established an intellectual rapport that would continue for the rest of their lives. Cohen, like Corcoran, had a job with a relatively innocuous title, associate general counsel of the Public Works Administration.

When Frankfurter left for London during the drafting of the bill, the two young lawyers sought the counsel of Justice Louis Brandeis, considered one of the most brilliant, and liberal, members of the largely conservative court. In Congress they formed a friendship with Representative Sam Rayburn, the liberal Texan who then chaired the House Banking Committee. "Taken together," Rayburn said of Cohen and Corcoran, "those two make the most brilliant man I ever saw." Rayburn would prove to be their most valuable friend on the Hill, fending off objections from Wall Streeters such as J. P. Morgan and John Foster Dulles, the future secretary of state under Eisenhower who was then a lead partner in the New York law firm of Sullivan and Cromwell.

As a matter of strict court propriety, Corcoran's use of Justice Brandeis, and the justice's participation in giving advice to administration lawyers, may have been questionable, but on this issue it was defensible as being in the public's interest. Later in life, Corcoran's habit of consulting justices outside normal court channels would be reinforced by his relationship with Frankfurter, when Frankfurter became a member of the court. Ultimately the habit was to lead him into the far more dubious practice of privately consulting with justices on behalf of corporate clients.

In 1933, once he had the president's support, Corcoran knew he faced two obstacles: Congress and the Supreme Court. Could he and Cohen draft a bill that would pass Congress and then pass the constitutional test of the Supreme Court, which was conservative enough to be proven hostile to New Deal regulation of business?

By getting Brandeis's guidance on how to draft a courtproof bill and having Sam Rayburn on their side in Congress, Corcoran and Cohen dotted one of Washington's i's and crossed a t. And to advance Corcoran's cause in the third center of Washington power, the White House, Frankfurter wrote a letter to Marguerite ("Missy") LeHand, Roosevelt's secretary and closest confidant, introducing "Tommy" and describing him as "an indefatigable worker for the success of the administration, a very close friend of mine," and "a person of entire dependability. He may come to you from time to time about matters and I commend him to you warmly."

As LeHand got to know Corcoran, she found herself charmed by the handsome Irishman. She put his name on a guest list for a small dinner party given for the president. Tommy played the piano, sang Irish songs, and soon had the president under his spell. By this time Corcoran's boss in the general counsel's office at the RFC was Stanley Reed, who would later become another justice of the Supreme Court.

Corcoran spread his influence by placing young lawyers, often recommended by Frankfurter, who was still on the Harvard law faculty, in jobs throughout the administration. They became known as the "Corcoran gallery of lawyers," a play on the name of Washington's Corcoran Gallery of Art.

By the end of 1933, Roosevelt knew that the SEC bill had not done enough to control Wall Street's excesses. He asked Corcoran and Cohen to come up with new and tougher legislation. Richard Whitney, the head of the New York Stock Exchange, a prominent Wall Streeter at the time though he later fell into disgrace and went to prison, came to Washington to lead the lobbying effort against the bills. Whitney had powerful allies, not only in the financial community but in the government itself and in the business press. The head of the National Recovery Administration, Hugh Johnson, opposed tougher regulation because he felt it would act as a brake on economic recovery. *Business Week* magazine called it "ruthless," and the publisher of *The Washington Post,* Eugene Meyer, said that it would put the nation on the path to socialism. But some Wall Streeters, including Robert Lovett and James Forrestal, were more farsighted in realizing that their business had to be regulated for its own sake. They testified in favor of the bill before Congress, as did Tommy Corcoran, who appeared alone before a House committee. His knowledgeable answers impressed the committee so much that Roosevelt called him, declaring, "By God, you're the first man I've had who could handle himself on the Hill."

Corcoran's next major challenge came when Roosevelt decided to go after the holding companies that dominated the electric utility business and were used to hold enough of a utility's profits to enable the company to plead poverty and obtain rate increases from state regulators. "A holding company," Will Rogers explained, "is something where you hand an accomplice the goods while the policeman searches you."

The lobby for the holding companies had tentacles reaching into just about every corner of the country, with its network of local utility companies, lawyers, and bankers to pressure their members of Congress. In the Senate, on the crucial vote on an amendment that could have emasculated the bill, the one-vote margin of victory was secured by Tommy Corcoran's promise to a Colorado senator to locate an SEC office in Denver.

A House Republican from Maine, Ralph Owen Brewster, accused Corcoran of trying to get his vote by threatening to stop construction of the Passamaquoddy Dam in his home state. Corcoran
denied the accusation, but some members immediately suspected
that the accusation was true because it sounded just like Tommy.
Others, however, suspected that Brewster's vote had been bought by
the utility lobby, a suspicion that tended to be confirmed by his later
reputation as the "senator from Pan Am," a reputation won by his
tireless service to the interests of Pan American Airways, which
helped it dominate international air travel from the United States
for forty years. Whatever its truth, however, the accusation served
to buttress Corcoran's notoriety as a slightly shady political ma-
nipulator who specialized in behind-the-scenes intrigue. And it was
this reputation that ultimately deprived Corcoran of the public offices he most sought—first to be solicitor general (the lawyer who
argues for the U.S. government before the Supreme Court), and, to
cap his career, an appointment to the court itself. Nonetheless, for
the time being, Corcoran had won himself a place as Roosevelt's
most influential adviser, a role he was to play until 1939, when
Harry Hopkins began to supplant him as FDR's closest confidant.

Until 1935 Louis Howe had filled that role, but by the summer
of that year, Harold Ickes, the secretary of the interior and PWA
head, noted in his diary, "Recently Louis Howe has been put out of
business by his illness and Corcoran has been called in to help in the
White House office and the liberals are certainly hoping that he will
become a permanent fixture because not only is he a liberal, he is a
very able lawyer with good all around ability and, I believe, a keen
political sense."

For the next four years Tommy would fulfill liberal hopes. He
continued to be Roosevelt's leading advocate on Capitol Hill.
Corcoran would often draft the president's speeches. Perhaps his
most memorable contribution came in Roosevelt's speech accepting
the nomination for a second term at the Democratic National Convention in Philadelphia, in which Roosevelt declared: "There is a

mysterious cycle in human events. To some generations much is given. Of other generations much is expected. This generation of Americans has a rendezvous with destiny."

The prophetic nature of these words would become clearer as that generation went on to overcome the Depression and win World War II, but even then the crowd sensed their importance and gave the words "sustained applause."

Playing the accordion and telling jokes to entertain the president at small White House dinner parties, and using his friendship with Missy LeHand to find out the best times to seek a private moment with FDR, Corcoran was able to maintain his influence without actually having an office in the White House. He became known in Congress as the best way to reach the president, and played an important role in passing Social Security and getting Sam Rayburn elected Speaker of the House.

The American people proved their support of the New Deal in the 1936 presidential election, and did it so enthusiastically that Roosevelt swamped his Republican opponent, Governor Alfred Landon of Kansas, by a count of 523 electoral votes to 8. (The Republicans were able to carry only Maine and Vermont.) But then Roosevelt made three crucial mistakes that threatened to take the steam out of the New Deal. First, because the economy was looking so rosy by the end of 1936, he decided to cut back on programs that had been stimulating growth. The result was a brief but nonetheless widely felt recession. And, angered by the Supreme Court's rejection of his programs—it had declared both the Agricultural Adjustment Act and the National Recovery Act unconstitutional—he decided to propose a reform of the court that would enable him to appoint enough liberal justices to create a majority sympathetic to the New Deal.

Critics called it his "court-packing scheme." The label stuck, and the public, which accorded high esteem to the nation's Judge Hardys, instinctively opposed it. Then, in 1938, his court proposal having failed, Roosevelt attempted to eliminate some of the conservative Democratic senators who had opposed him on the court issue and on other New Deal measures. The critics dubbed this effort a "purge." Again, the label stuck, and it resulted in Roosevelt's losing all but two of the races that he'd attempted to influence. It did not help Tommy's standing with the boss that he had been the closest to the throne at the time of these failures. None of them had been Corcoran's idea, but such is human nature that bosses sometimes blame the person nearest to them.

Still, Corcoran remained, until 1939, the most powerful of Roosevelt's advisers. He helped engineer the appointment and confirmation of Supreme Court justices William O. Douglas, Stanley Reed, Felix Frankfurter, and Hugo Black, who would turn that body into a bastion of liberalism, and gain for Roosevelt exactly what he had sought from his court-packing scheme, only it was done by using his power of appointment to replace retiring justices rather than by adding to their number. Corcoran's sage advice also played a crucial role in saving Black, whose appointment to the court had only just been confirmed, from impeachment when his past association with the Ku Klux Klan was revealed. In each of these cases Corcoran had done a good deed by helping men who turned out to be good members of the court, but it was also true that he was earning the gratitude of men who would be in a position to rule on cases in which he was involved.

With Europe in a state of crisis as Hitler took over Austria and Czechoslovakia, then invaded Poland in 1939, bringing France and Britain into what became World War II, Roosevelt's attention turned increasingly to that part of the world. As it did, Corcoran's position declined. Roosevelt was an Anglophile; the Irishman Corcoran was not. In addition, Roosevelt was not fond of hearing from Corcoran's rivals and from the press that Corcoran had manipulated him. Gradually Roosevelt turned to Harry Hopkins, who had made a huge impression on FDR with his running of the WPA. In late 1938, Roosevelt moved Hopkins into his cabinet as secretary of commerce, and Corcoran actually helped get him confirmed. But at about the same time, Roosevelt refused Corcoran's request to be appointed solicitor general, the job he wanted as a stepping-stone to his ultimate ambition, a seat on the Supreme Court.

When Hopkins was invited to move into the White House residence in April 1940, the writing was on the wall for Corcoran. At the same time, the fall of Denmark, Norway, Holland, Belgium, and, by June 22, France, focused Roosevelt's attention almost exclusively on what was happening in the war, on keeping Britain out of Hitler's hands, and on preparing America for its entry into the conflict. When, that spring, Roosevelt decided to run for a third term, he chose Hopkins, not Corcoran, to represent him at the Democratic National Convention in July.

Corcoran's decline was probably hastened by the people close to the president who didn't like him, including Roosevelt's wife, Eleanor, and press secretary Stephen Early. He also had angered at least a third of the Senate with his tactics during the 1938 purge.

When he didn't get the solicitor general job, Corcoran turned elsewhere. Resurrecting an ambition from his days on Wall Street, he told Samuel Rosenman, Roosevelt's principal speechwriter, "I want to make a million dollars in one year." His government salary at the time was $9,000. In March 1940 he married his secretary, Peggy Dowd (who would become much like an aunt to her cousin, the future *New York Times* columnist Maureen Dowd). His new wife soon became pregnant and did not want to move to New York, the place where Tommy had gone earlier when he wanted to make money in the 1920s.

So how could Corcoran make that million while remaining in Washington? He could use all the inside knowledge of government that he had acquired at the RFC, and as a top adviser to a president and a close friend of Speaker Sam Rayburn and many other members of Congress. And if one-third of the senators didn't like him, many of the remaining two-thirds not only liked him but had received favors from him. In addition, Corcoran had cultivated powerful members of the press, notably Drew Pearson, the most influential of all the journalists then covering Washington.

So in early 1941 Corcoran let Roosevelt know that he had decided to go into private law practice in Washington. Roosevelt signed a letter eloquently imploring him to remain in government, but Corcoran knew the letter had been drafted by Ben Cohen and a White House assistant and Corcoran admirer, Jim Rowe. The truth probably was that Roosevelt wanted to maintain Corcoran's good will and make occasional use of his skills, but keep him at arm's length. So Tommy decided to return to private practice.

At the same time, Roosevelt was trying to come up with a way to get aid to China to enable it to continue to fight the Japanese, who had invaded China in 1937 and now controlled a substantial part of the country, including all the main ports. He decided to have Corcoran set up a private corporation to handle it. That corporation became Corcoran's first client, and through it, he helped form the Flying Tigers, a group of fighter squadrons led by former Army Air Corps captain Claire Chennault, whose mission was to protect the Burma Road, over which China received vital war matériel.

Corcoran's reputation as a New Deal insider would attract many other clients. As the defense industry grew exponentially during the early 1940s, businessmen seeking contracts to make military equipment felt the need for a Washington insider to open the right doors for them. So, for example, into Tommy Corcoran's office walked Henry Kaiser, who was to become one of the biggest shipbuilders and aluminum producers during the war. Corcoran introduced Kaiser to Lauchlin Currie, a White House assistant, and William Knudsen, the former head of General Motors who was now in charge of defense procurement for the War Department. *The Washington Times-Herald* published an article that fortified Corcoran's reputation as the lawyer to consult in Washington: It described what Corcoran had done for Kaiser and ran a photograph showing Kaiser and Knudsen, leading one reporter to say, "This is the sort of entrée Tommy Corcoran has in high-level government: Hire him and you too can walk right into Knudsen's office and ask for the big defense contracts."

Tommy Corcoran was not only the first of the prominent New Dealers who came to Washington to do good but ended up doing well, he was also perhaps the frankest of all of them about what he was doing. The reputation for dubious tactics in doing good for FDR and the New Deal followed him into his new practice. He became known as a "fixer."

An illustration of that label came when Thurman Arnold, FDR's assistant attorney general for antitrust, tried to prosecute one of Corcoran's first clients, Sterling Drug, for creating an aspirin cartel with the German firm I.G. Farben. Corcoran went to his pal the acting attorney general Francis Biddle and arranged a plea deal that resulted in Sterling's getting off the hook by paying a fine of only $5,000.

When Missy LeHand had a stroke in 1941, Tommy lost his closest ally and most influential connection in the White House. He would from then on concentrate on his private practice and never again seek a major government job.

Corcoran kept one hand in politics, however, helping Representative Lyndon Johnson, who was running for the Senate in a 1941 special election, to gain approval for a Rural Electrification Administration project in his district in Texas. Corcoran reportedly called an REA official and said, "This is Tommy Corcoran at the White House. Congressman Johnson wants this today, and the White House wants him to have it today."

The call worked, although Tommy was no longer at the White House or anywhere else in government. Johnson lost that Senate race, but he continued to be an influential member of the House. He and Corcoran helped each other. LBJ introduced Corcoran to future client Brown and Root, the construction firm that was to be a major military contractor during the Vietnam and Iraq wars. Corcoran, in turn, helped Johnson gain Federal Communications Commission approval for Johnson's purchase, in his wife Lady Bird's name, of the Texas radio station that became television station KTBC and made Johnson a wealthy man.

Henry Wallace, FDR's vice president from 1941 to 1945, and Harry Truman agreed on few matters, but Tommy Corcoran was one of them. When, in 1944, FDR asked Wallace to put Corcoran on the Economic Defense Board, which Wallace chaired, Wallace refused, explaining (according to the columnist Thomas Stokes) that he "disapproved of the way Mr. Corcoran has capitalized on his government associations to promote his lucrative law practice." In November 1941, just ten months after he opened his law practice, Corcoran was called before a committee headed by then-senator Truman to defend the fees he was charging defense contractors.

The classic example of Corcoran's brazenness in attempting to use his connections to influence legal outcomes came in October 1969 on behalf of his client El Paso Natural Gas. Corcoran visited both Justice Hugo Black and Justice William Brennan in their chambers seeking to influence their votes on a petition by the gas company. Corcoran barely escaped public scandal at the time, but later, in 1979, Bob Woodward and Scott Armstrong told the story in their book *The Brethren*. One of Corcoran's enemies wrote a letter to the Board on Professional Responsibility of the District of Columbia Bar complaining about the incident, resulting in a headline on the front page of *The Washington Post* that read: "Attorney Corcoran Faces Ethics Probe."

Corcoran turned to Robert Bennett, who was taking Edward Bennett Williams's place as Washington's leading defense attorney. Here again Corcoran found that the favors he had done others continued to stand him in good stead. Bennett said, "It was just my way of paying back, even though it was just a drop in the bucket for everything he had done for me." Since Black had died in 1971, Brennan was the only witness to Corcoran's misdeed, and his friendship with Tommy led him to say he had "no independent recollection" of the episode. The case against Corcoran collapsed. Once again he had dodged a bullet that seemed to be aimed directly at his heart.

Corcoran's seventieth birthday was celebrated at a dinner arranged by his friends at the Federal City Club. It was attended by many of his former New Deal colleagues, including Ben Cohen and William O. Douglas. When Tommy rose to speak, one of the first things he said was that he represented one of the largest oil companies in the country. Some of his old friends thought this was not something to boast about. Ben Cohen then told the other half of the truth about Tommy Corcoran: "I think we may count the New Deal years among the best years of your life."

In those years, Corcoran had used his incredible assortment of skills to serve the public interest. He had played an essential role in making the New Deal happen. Few men have done more.

ABE FORTAS WAS another brilliant New Deal lawyer who, like Corcoran, would have stayed in government if he had been offered the right job. In 1946 he hoped Harry Truman would make him secretary of the interior, but when it became clear that Truman did not intend to nominate him, he decided to go into private practice. Again, like Corcoran, if he couldn't get the government job he wanted, he would compensate by making money. His wife, Carolyn Agger, also a lawyer, would push him to higher and higher earnings during his life, and his personal tastes reflected them. Before long he would drive a Rolls-Royce, and the couple had an impressive residence in Georgetown as well as a summer home in Westport, Connecticut.

Fortas came from modest origins in Memphis, Tennessee, where his father was a cabinetmaker. He attended Southwestern College (now Rhodes College) and went on to Yale Law School, where he edited the law journal and gained a reputation as one of the most brilliant—if not the most brilliant—of its graduates. He attracted the attention of Professor William O. Douglas, who helped him land an assistant professorship. After Douglas went to Washington to become chairman of the Securities and Exchange Commission, he frequently brought Fortas to Washington as a consultant. While there, Fortas impressed interior secretary Harold Ickes, who made him general counsel of the Public Works Administration. Fortas continued to impress Ickes, enough that he was made undersecretary of the interior. But Truman later declined to elevate him to head of the department.

In private practice, Fortas was joined in 1946 by Thurman Arnold, the former head of the antitrust division of the Department of Justice, and in 1947 by Paul Porter, the former chairman of the Federal Communications Commission. The combined experience of these three men allowed them to offer an almost unparalleled ability to navigate the maze of regulatory offices in Washington that had been created under the New Deal. For example, Porter's experience at the FCC would have obvious appeal to the American Broadcasting Company, which did indeed become a client.

More than any other firm, Arnold, Fortas and Porter (now Arnold and Porter) came to epitomize the transition of New Dealers from wanting to do good to wanting to do well—to make money out of the understanding of government they had gained through drafting and enforcing the reforms championed by Franklin Roosevelt. Advocates of reform now became defenders of those whom they had sought to reform. When Cabell Phillips of *The New York Times* in 1946 took note of this development, Jerome Frank challenged him: Surely this couldn't amount to a significant trend. Phillips was able to come up with the names of twenty lawyers who had left the New Deal for private practice, but this was out of the hundreds of thousands of employees who left the government soon after World War II as the bureaucracy shrank by almost a third. But some of Phillips's readers got the queasy feeling that this might someday turn into a significant trend, as indeed it did beginning in the 1970s.

Fortas provides a vivid example of how one's point of view shifted after moving from government to private practice. When he had worked at the Interior Department, he was asked by Rexford Tugwell, then the governor of Puerto Rico, whether the island should be represented by a private attorney. Fortas replied, "Governments and government agencies should be represented by lawyers who are public officials." But when Fortas left the government for private practice, he took as his first client the government of Puerto Rico.

A couple of facts made the postwar movement of New Deal lawyers into private practice understandable. One that cannot be overestimated was the death of Franklin Roosevelt, and the replacement of their inspiring leader by the pedestrian Harry Truman, who definitely did not inspire them. (Truman looks far better in the eyes of today's historians than he did in the eyes of his contemporaries in 1946.) The other fact was that the rising cost of living was making government salaries—Arnold earned only $8,600 a year at Justice—more of a problem, with a brief but scary burst of double-digit inflation hitting the economy in 1946–47 as wartime price controls were removed and pent-up demand for things such as automobiles, not available to the public since January 1942, simply exploded.

Arnold, Fortas and Porter was not only the first firm formed by New Dealers who had enjoyed prominent positions in the administration but also a beneficiary of the fact that all three partners were Democrats, so that they had connections in the Truman administration to help cement their reputations as insiders. Fortas and his wife, Carolyn, were also examples of how some postwar Americans displayed class through their good taste as represented by their purchases, often costly, of Chinese and other works of art, owning the Rolls, and having classical musicians such as the Budapest String Quartet give concerts of chamber music in their home, joined by Fortas, a skilled violinist. Carolyn Agger's lifestyle was enhanced by three French poodles and 150 pairs of shoes.

Fortas played two roles in the firm. One, he was the most proficient of the appellate brief writers, an important skill in law firms. He was also the firm's manager, the one who supervised the firm's

young associates. Such associates in almost all law firms were and
are overworked, but Fortas was especially well-known for being a
son of a bitch to his subordinates. When he was at Interior he had
once tried to get an elevator operator disciplined because he'd failed
to stop at Fortas's floor. Arnold's role was, of course, to supply expertise in antitrust law, but he also—because he had briefly served
on the Circuit Court of Appeals—was entitled to lifetime use of the
title "judge," which lent some gravitas to the firm. Porter was the
best at schmoozing clients. His charm was enhanced by a keen sense
of humor. Once, a congressional critic accosted him with "I understand your firm represents only Communists and homosexuals."

"That's right, Senator," Porter replied. "What can we do for
you?"

The purpose of his law firm, Fortas wrote, was "to provide the
means for the three partners to make a living." He continued, "The
criterion to determine the lawyer's decision as to whether he would
represent a client, with few exceptions, was entirely pragmatic: Was
the prospective client's problem such that the firm could advise and
represent the client with a reasonable prospect that the firm could
contribute something of value for which payment *could* and *would*
be received." (Emphasis mine.)

Of course, the payment could be more in influence than in actual
cash. Fortas's representation of Lyndon Johnson was an example.
Johnson's 1948 victory, by an eighty-seven-vote margin, in the
Texas primary for a seat in the U.S. Senate, was contested by his
opponent, Coke Stevenson, who was suspicious of the fact that in
Jim Wells County, Johnson won by a margin several hundred votes
in excess of the number of registered voters. Stevenson appealed to
the State Democratic Executive Committee, which ruled in Johnson's favor.

A federal district court judge decided in Stevenson's favor. Fortas
found himself confronted not only with a ruling against his client
but with incredible time pressure—only seven weeks remained for
the ballots to be printed and distributed in time for the November

general election. By a feat of legal legerdemain, Fortas managed not in weeks but in days to land the case in the in-box of Justice Hugo Black, who was able to dispose of it in a way that let stand the State Democratic Committee's decision in Johnson's favor.

The favorable outcome of the case left Lyndon Johnson in awe of Fortas's skill, an awe that only continued to grow during the rest of their relationship. Although he could be very unpleasant with his subordinates, Fortas was almost unique in his ability to win the confidence of people he regarded as his equals or as potential clients. "He's the wisest man I have ever known," Johnson told members of his staff. Fortas had a particularly good bedside manner. James Jones, a White House aide, put it this way: "For someone like Johnson, who was very strong yet in many cases very insecure, Fortas was a great source of comfort." Part of the reason was that Fortas, having been a brilliant student and then a professor at Yale Law, could be Johnson's own Ivy Leaguer to compete with the others left on his staff from the Kennedy administration, many of whom sometimes seemed to Johnson to be more loyal to JFK than to his successor.

Fortas's skills were such that he could often benefit two clients at the same time. One example is how he exploited the fact that, in order to encourage domestic oil production, oil companies were given quotas for how much foreign oil they could import. Ordinarily, oil imported from Venezuela would count against the quota, but Fortas got an exception for Venezuelan oil that was refined in Puerto Rico. Thus his client, Puerto Rico, got new business and Phillips Petroleum got a break on its import quota.

In 1964, after the surgeon general warned of the dangers of smoking, the Federal Trade Commission proposed rules to require cigarette makers to put warnings on their packages and in their advertising. Fortas advised his client Philip Morris to get action on the rules transferred from the FTC to Congress, where the cigarette companies would have more influence. This he accomplished by drafting a letter for Representative Oren Harris, chairman of the relevant House committee, to send to the chairman of the FTC, telling him not to take any action until Congress could consider the matter. Fortas then advised the cigarette companies to accept a weak, watered-down health warning, which they did. The strategy had worked.

In one sense, at least, the idealism of the New Deal continued at Arnold, Fortas and Porter. The law firm performed an unusual amount of pro bono and reduced-fee work on behalf of people unjustly accused of being disloyal to the United States during the McCarthy era. It also—Fortas himself deserves most of the credit here—was a pioneer in the expansion of the rights of defendants in criminal cases, including those who were pleading insanity and juveniles accused of any crime. And in perhaps his most famous case, *Gideon v. Wainwright,* the Supreme Court ruled that a criminal defendant's right to counsel is a constitutional guarantee. In the juvenile case *In re Gault,* a fifteen-year-old had received six years in prison for making an obscene phone call. If he had been an adult, the punishment would have been a fifty-dollar fine or two months in jail. This was the nature of juvenile justice at the time. Fortas won a Supreme Court opinion extending the Fourteenth Amendment rights to juvenile defendants. In *Gideon,* he was appointed by the Supreme Court to represent an indigent defendant who had been denied the right to counsel because he couldn't afford one. On March 18, 1963, Fortas won a unanimous decision from the Supreme Court extending the right to counsel to defendants regardless of their ability to pay.

Ultimately Fortas's desire for money—though modest compared to the greed of today—would bring him down. In 1965, President Johnson appointed him to the Supreme Court, and in 1968 to be its chief justice. But by that time, Johnson had become widely unpopular because of the Vietnam War, and his enemies turned on Fortas when they found out that he had accepted a $20,000 annual lifetime payment (which was also to be paid to his widow for her lifetime) from a foundation controlled by Louis Wolfson, a former

Fortas client accused of securities violations in a case that was ultimately destined for the Supreme Court. It was suspected at the time that the payment was meant to help secure a favorable decision from Fortas—and there is evidence to support this accusation—and to induce Fortas to ask Lyndon Johnson to pardon Wolfson. Fortas not only lost his chance to be chief justice but in 1969 was forced to resign from the court. When he had joined the court, the firm had changed its name to Arnold and Porter, and so it remained. His former partners refused to take back the man who had done so much to help the firm attain its prominence. Arnold and Porter continued to prosper, however, expanding from one town house to a row of town houses to an eight-floor building of its own and then to the thirteen-floor office building that it now occupies.

FOR MOST OF the time between his departure from government and his ascendancy to the Supreme Court, Fortas was one of the three most influential lawyers in Washington, one of the new breed combining legal skills with entrée to the executive and legislative branches of government, and sometimes even the judiciary. Another of the three was, of course, Tommy Corcoran. The third, who had not been part of the New Deal but had served in the Truman White House from 1945 to 1950, was Clark Clifford. From the moment Clifford arrived at the White House he cultivated the press, gaining a reputation as one of the good guys of the Truman administration. This meant he gave sound, moderately liberal advice reflecting the positions of most reporters.

On one occasion, he leaked information that was not entirely truthful. In 1948 he took credit for authoring the strategy that won the election for Truman, which had astonished the world. But the real author of the memo laying out that strategy had been Jim Rowe, a Roosevelt holdover on the White House staff. Since Clifford had more access to Truman, a fellow Missourian, Rowe sent the memo to him. Clifford changed the name of the author and sent it on to the president. Rowe did not object at the time, because Clifford had more power than he did. When Rowe ultimately revealed that he was the author, twenty years later, he felt that he had to apologize to Clifford: "Really, I am terribly embarrassed that I embarrassed you." The apology may have been partially motivated by Clifford's power and standing in Washington, which had only grown, but there is no question it was also motivated by genuine respect for Clifford, who was about to embark on one of the most important episodes in his career, serving as the secretary of defense who helped persuade Johnson to stop the escalation in Vietnam and seek peace.

The standing of the three lawyers—Corcoran, Fortas, and Clifford—was demonstrated in 1964 as the presidential election neared. Lyndon Johnson, having succeeded the slain John F. Kennedy, was opposed by Senator Barry Goldwater. In October, one month before the election, a Washington policeman spying on a public restroom at the YMCA—an unfortunate custom of Washington law enforcement in those days—saw LBJ's closest aide, Walter Jenkins, performing a sex act with another man. Corcoran was assigned the job of persuading Jenkins to depart quietly and not write any tell-all book about Johnson. Fortas and Clifford took on the even more delicate task of keeping the story out of the Washington papers. Incredibly, they almost succeeded. Their standing was such in the Washington community that they were able to persuade the editors of *The Washington Daily News,* the *Evening Star,* and *The Washington Post* not to publish the news. It was only when an Associated Press reporter found the details of another Jenkins arrest for similar conduct that the story broke.

Clifford had an innate gift for hypocrisy. From the time he entered private practice in 1950 he was especially concerned about avoiding the appearance of selling influence. In part this was to distinguish himself from the so-called five percenters, mostly minor officials who, by charging a fee for the exercise of their influence, had sullied the reputation of the Truman administration. In part it was inspired by Clifford's extreme concern for presenting the right appearance. Here's how he handled the matter when Howard

Hughes called to ask him to represent his companies Hughes Tool, TWA, and RKO: "Mr. Hughes, I look forward to our association. But before we proceed, there's one point I must make clear. I cannot consider that this firm has any influence in Washington. We cannot represent any client before the president or his staff. If you want influence you should consider going elsewhere. What we can offer you is an extensive knowledge of how to deal with government. . . . We will be able to give you advice on how to present your problem to the appropriate department and agencies of government."

Wink, wink, nod, nod. Hughes and Clifford both knew that the officials Clifford dealt with would be well aware of Clifford's influence at the White House. And by the time Truman departed in 1953, Clifford had expanded his connections, especially among the media, members of Congress, and business leaders. He participated in Truman's famous poker games with George Allen, who just happened to be a member of a number of corporate boards. When Clifford decided to go into private practice, Allen was able to refer clients such as RCA and Republic Steel to his new firm. Another friend was Robert Kerr, whom Clifford had met in 1948 during the Truman presidential campaign, when Kerr was running for a Senate seat from Oklahoma. Kerr introduced him to the president of Phillips Petroleum, who then hired Clifford to represent the giant oil company. Kerr himself quickly became a player in the Senate, raising campaign funds for other senators and providing numerous favors. Kerr also befriended Bobby Baker, the Senate secretary, whose knowledge of each senator's vulnerabilities was legendary, as was his skill at exploiting them. A friend once observed of Baker, "There are some people who like to look crooked even when they aren't, and Bobby was one of those characters. He could always do the slightest thing in such a way as to make it look like a deep, dark plot hatched in a back room with thousands of dollars on the table." Sometimes there really was cash on the table, and then it was likely that Kerr would be involved, but as corruptor rather than corruptee.

So Clifford had friends and clients who were not exactly squeaky clean. Another example of this fact came in the late 1960s and early '70s, when he served on the board of the National Bank of Washington, which was then owned by the United Mine Workers, headed by the thoroughly corrupt Tony Boyle. Boyle was later convicted of ordering the murder of a reform candidate for UMW president, but while Clifford was on the union's board, Boyle was its leader. Boyle deposited the union's pension fund in a National Bank account that, instead of producing income in the pension fund, created generous dividends for the union leaders to use for their own purposes in hiring killers.

When *The Washington Monthly* revealed the scheme in an article, Clifford called me and said, "Mr. Peters, I want you to know that I read your magazine cover to cover every issue. I want you to know how deeply concerned I am about the matters you raise. You can be sure I will examine them most carefully." The flattery was typical of Clifford, who employed it generously among those whose favor he sought. The grave tone was also typical of Clifford. When you were with him in person, he would often emphasize his seriousness by steepling his fingers. Despite his pledge, he did not go public with the concern he expressed to me about the bank. He resigned from the bank board without a peep a year later.

Clifford got away with it then. The Washington press was so in awe of him that it couldn't believe our story. A decade later, when Clifford embarked on an equally if not more questionable relationship with a bank, he did not get away with it. But before we get to that story, it is important to emphasize that there was a basis in reality for the media's high regard for Clifford. The advice he gave was usually sound. When Lyndon Johnson named him secretary of defense in 1968, Clifford helped the president understand the futility of further escalation in Vietnam. And even in the case of Jim Rowe's memo, Clifford had been astute enough to realize that the advice it contained would win Harry Truman a victory in 1948. If Clifford, like Fortas and Corcoran, had wanted to get rich, he had not—again like Fortas and Corcoran—been concerned with getting filthy rich. This was generally true of the country as a whole through the 1960s, only beginning to change in the '70s as part of a transformation that came to full flower in the greed of the '80s and thereafter. Clifford became part of that change as he became involved with a second bank.

In 1978–79, Clifford began to represent BCCI, formally known as the Bank of Credit and Commerce International, but called by Robert Gates, when he was deputy director of the CIA years later, "the Bank of Crooks and Criminals." The bank's founder and head, a Pakistani named Agha Hasan Abedi, was introduced to Clifford by Bert Lance, a former Carter administration budget director whom Clifford had successfully defended during a Senate investigation. (Lance had to resign anyway as it became clear that he had been involved in some dubious financial ventures and had run up substantial debts.)

Abedi had arranged for a rich Saudi Arabian to bail out Lance financially and then hired Lance to find an American bank that BCCI could acquire. Lance induced a Naval Academy classmate of Jimmy Carter's to help him acquire a substantial interest in Financial General Bankshares, an American company that owned banks in New York and Washington. The bank's other investors sued Lance and the Arab investors of BCCI, accusing them of violating U.S. securities law by failing to disclose that they were operating as a group to acquire American banks. The investors succeeded in bringing about an SEC inquiry. Clifford, representing BCCI, managed to get the defendants off with a slap on the wrist, and BCCI was able to use front men to acquire Financial General.

Although Clifford continued to represent BCCI, he claimed that he did not know it controlled Financial General Bankshares, even when Abedi changed its name to First American, made Clifford the president, and was consulted by Clifford on all major decisions that Clifford would make there. Over the next few years, according to a federal indictment, Clifford and his partner received more than $40 million in "fees, sham loans and rigged stock deals." For almost a decade Clifford was able to use his reputation for probity to maintain his claim that Financial General was not controlled by BCCI, but the truth ultimately came out. Clifford's distinguished and long-cultivated reputation as a man whose word was his bond was lost. *The Washington Post,* which had done so much to burnish Clifford's stature over the years, revealed a rigged stock deal that made a profit of $9.8 million for Clifford and Altman. Even Clifford's law partners deserted him. His firm was dissolved, and he had to resign the presidency of First American. The public learned that BCCI had laundered money for drug dealers, that it had helped the Panamanian dictator Manuel Noriega siphon money out of his country, and that it was the bank for the infamous terrorist Abu Nidal.

Clifford was spared further torment by federal prosecutors and Senate investigators because of their concern about his increasingly frail health at age eighty-five. As testimony to what his reputation had been before its destruction in 1991, *The New Yorker* magazine continued serializing his memoirs, written with the assistance of Richard Holbrooke, even after news of the BCCI scandal broke in the newspapers.

Clifford's decline was in part due to a change in the culture of Washington journalism. Until the mid-1960s, Washington had tended to be automatically respectful of public men, but Johnson's lies about Vietnam, and Nixon's about Watergate, brought about a dramatic change. In the 1970s and thereafter, journalists were prone to look for the weaknesses of great men, and made their reputations on exposés.

Another factor in Clifford's involvement with BCCI and First American could have been a desire to remain relevant. Because he had helped make lobbying respectable, he now had scores of competitors. By the late '70s, when he began his connection with BCCI, he was competing with many lawyers who were younger and more well connected to those in power than he was. The political and corporate leaders Clifford knew had been largely replaced by a new generation, and he could no longer count on his Rolodex to yield the right person to call.

In the end, the search for more money blinded the three preeminent lawyers of the post–World War II era—Tommy Corcoran, Abe Fortas, and Clark Clifford—to the ethical constraints and idealism that had motivated them as New and Fair Dealers. These men demonstrated three trends in postwar America. First was the shift to materialistic goals from the idealistic ones of the New Deal era. Second, and related, was a regard for professional skills in themselves, as opposed to the goals for which those skills were used. Finally, there was a new emphasis on taste as a demonstration of class. Corcoran's offer to send his wife Peggy's cousin Maureen Dowd to Smith College instead of Washington's Catholic University. Maureen stuck with Catholic University, but Corcoran's offer illustrated how an institution's selectiveness now was coming to be seen as a measure of the value of one's education.

In another respect, Abe Fortas pioneered a trend of the time: the adoption by liberals of causes that, although admirable, had the effect of alienating one element after another of the old New Deal coalition that had supported FDR and enabled him to follow his politics of generosity. The worthy causes that Fortas and his firm were notable for serving—defending people accused of Communist connections and expanding the rights of defendants accused of crimes—unfortunately tended to alienate former supporters of liberal causes. Roman Catholics, who had been a major element of the big-city Roosevelt vote, were especially offended by the defense of Communists or suspected Communists, whom they saw as having demonstrated hostility to the church. Less costly politically but still another chip in the New Deal coalition was the sense that Democrats were soft on crime. Indeed, the mantra of soft on Communism and crime became a standard part of the Republican case against the Democrats.

The great success not only of Clifford but of Corcoran and the firm of Arnold, Fortas and Porter inspired an increasing number of Washington lawyers to go into lobbying. But through the 1960s only a relatively small minority actually followed their example. Most New Dealers remained in public service. Jerome Frank, for example, whose desire to go to Washington began this book, was appointed to the Federal Court of Appeals by Franklin Roosevelt in 1939 and continued in public service on that court for the rest of his life.

Perhaps the most unfortunate influence that Clifford, Corcoran, and Fortas had was on the motivation for public service. In the New Deal, almost no one entered public service with the idea of cashing in on that service when they left. By the 1970s, however, a substantial number of people entering public service were doing so with the knowledge that the experience they gained could be turned to profit when they departed.

And the numbers of those who, whatever their motivation for entering government, left it to make more money continued to grow, soaring from the twenty whom Cabell Phillips was able to name in 1946 to thousands during the administration of George W. Bush. They would become lobbyists or work inside corporations or law firms to formulate strategies for dealing with Congress and executive branch agencies. Or they would work as contractors as the practice of contracting out functions of government expanded. This, too, reached a peak in the administration of George W. Bush, during which the Republican desire to privatize the functions of government coincided with a need to expand government, particularly in the national security area. This produced a record number of contract employees performing government functions. Perhaps the most maddening example of this phenomenon was the group of former CIA agents who retired and took their pensions, then became contractors, charging three, four, or five times the salaries they were paid in the government.

Financial regulators from the SEC and other agencies have come to look forward to using their expertise to land lucrative positions on Wall Street and with large corporations. And cashing in has practically become a tradition among high-ranking military officers. They have come to regard a cushy job with a government contractor as almost as much of an entitlement in their retirement as their pensions and health benefits. The fact that this might have led them to initially favor the contractor in their official decisions is even less acknowledged by them than it is known to the public.

———————★———————

# CHAPTER 3

# The Snob Factor

The stories of Tommy Corcoran, Abe Fortas, and Clark Clifford are part of the change that was beginning to happen in America after World War II. But few individuals reflected that change as clearly as John F. Kennedy.

During his first campaign for Congress in 1946, Kennedy made a speech in Charlestown, Massachusetts, ending with thoughts about how his fellow veterans felt about coming back to peacetime America, and he suggested there were some things they actually missed about the service:

> They miss the close comradeship, the feeling of interdependence, that sense of working together for a common cause. In civilian life they feel they have only themselves to depend on. They miss their wartime friends, and the understanding of their wartime friendships. One veteran told me that when he brought one of his Army friends to his home, his wife said, "What can you possibly see in O'Brien?" The veteran remembered O'Brien in Italy, walking with him from Sicily to the Po Valley, every bloody mile of the way. He knew what he could see in O'Brien.

Though the average man had already become a cultural hero by the end of the 1930s, people as wealthy as John Kennedy had had little experience with the O'Briens of America until the war. But it was clear that Kennedy's relationship with the men in his PT boat crew was warm. Indeed, his heroism in saving them after a Japanese destroyer knifed through their PT boat showed how much he cared, towing a burned crew member more than a mile with the strap of the man's life jacket gripped in Kennedy's teeth.

Nonetheless, seven years after he made that speech about O'Brien, in 1953, John Kennedy married a woman who, though she helped him rise in status among the social elite, seemed unlikely to understand what he saw in O'Brien. Jacqueline Bouvier Kennedy stood as a bridge between the old-money Social Register ethos, of which her family (but not the Kennedys) was part, and the coming education and taste elite that she helped create. She attended Vassar when it was one of the most selective of the Seven Sisters, and demonstrated her good taste by hiring the first French chef at the White House and through her sense of fashion, for which she became famous. She was dressed by the best designers, led the effort to restore the White House interior with the best antiques, saved the architectural character of Lafayette Square, and supported efforts to preserve the monuments of Abu Simbel in Egypt. Later she would help save Grand Central Station in New York and become a book editor, one of the status positions for the "meritocrats"—the name bestowed on the education and taste elite.

John Kennedy did remember his PT boat crew and reunited with them several times in his later life. And his campaign staff was largely composed of regular guys. His White House staff reflected the mixture in his character. There was Ken O'Donnell and Larry O'Brien and David Power, regular guys like his PT boat crew, and then there were the members of the new, meritocratic elite, represented by speechwriters Ted Sorensen and Richard Goodwin. McGeorge Bundy and Kennedy's friend Ben Bradlee were, like Jackie, a bridge between the old social elite and the new. Kennedy's other friends, however—such pals as Lem Billings and Chuck Spalding—tended to be part of the old social elite or of another, new elite composed of celebrities like his friend Frank Sinatra.

The impact of the Kennedys on American society cannot be separated from the fact that in the minds of many of his countrymen, John Kennedy was becoming a great president when his life was cut short by an assassin's bullet on November 22, 1963. The impression he had made during his life, and that Jackie Kennedy had made in the White House, was only heightened by the nation's grief at his death and with her behavior in the aftermath of the assassination. Men wanted to be like Kennedy; they even stopped wearing hats because he did not wear one. More important, they wanted to imitate his manner—the cool good humor he displayed at White House press conferences and the grace with which he carried himself. Women saw that by showing good taste they could be like Jackie. The Kennedys were not indifferent to the old social aristocracy. Jack shared his father's Irish Catholic resentment of being looked down upon by the WASP elite and his simultaneous desire to be accepted by them. But even more he respected the new meritocrats such as Ted Sorensen who could help him do his job well and the celebrities who could bring excitement, sex, and glamour to his life.

The celebrities and the meritocrats had some things in common, among them a high regard for skill. Both groups played a part in bringing about an increasing emphasis on making money in society as a whole. But it was the meritocrats who were most responsible for the gradual growth of the snobbery that was probably the most unattractive aspect of the postwar world. Two otherwise highly desirable developments in postwar America contributed to the gradual growth of snobbery: a great increase in access to higher education and to travel abroad.

The GI Bill played a historic democratizing role by making college available to all veterans who were high school graduates. It brought higher education to families that had never considered college as a possibility. My first roommate at Columbia, a veteran of the Battle of the Bulge who had been an electrical worker before the war, told me that he would never have dreamed of going to college had it not been for the GI Bill. The number of male college graduates tripled from the 1939–40 academic year to the 1949–50 year. Soon the veterans' younger brothers and sisters, who hadn't been in the service, began to think that they, too, were entitled to a college education. The proportion of women in this group was especially impressive. The number of female graduates tripled between 1949–50 and 1969–70, and by 1984–85 exceeded the number of male graduates.

As bachelor's degrees became more common, the GI Bill elevated the importance of graduate degrees and the reputation of one's college in enhancing one's résumé. This made the ability to score well on tests such as the SAT important as a means of admission to an elite school, thereby creating a whole new profession of counselors and counseling organizations that coached students on how to do well on the tests.

And as people began to perceive that getting into the right college was facilitated by the right secondary school, then primary school, then kindergarten, and finally even the right nursery school, the counselors and coaches necessary to gain those admissions became more common. Meanwhile, the selectivity and all that went with it extended upward as well, including getting into the right law or business school. It was understandable that those who had scaled these heights would have some feeling of superiority to those who had not, and thus was born school snobbery. My wife, who worked on the staff of a private school, once told me of an application to the school that listed the Ivy League colleges attended by the applicant's parents.

ANOTHER SIGNIFICANT FACTOR in the gradual increase in snobbery was the postwar expansion of travel, especially to Europe. It began in the late 1940s and expanded in the '50s, with a record number of transatlantic voyages by ship, and then soared with the introduction of jet travel in 1959. The '50s saw the rapid growth of a new profession: travel agents. By the end of the decade they could be found in almost every city and town in America. They were paid commissions of 5 to 10 percent by hotels and airlines, which enabled a great many of them to make a comfortable living. On a trip to Europe in 1956 I encountered a travel agent from as small a town as Franklin, Tennessee, leading a tour of college and high school girls.

The yearning to travel was fueled by movies such as *An American in Paris* (1951), *Roman Holiday* (1953), *Three Coins in the Fountain* (1954), *Summertime* (1955) with its memorable portrait of Venice by the great director David Lean, and *Around the World in 80 Days* (1956), which became the most popular movie of the decade. *Funny Face* (1957) provided an enticing portrait of Paris while endowing the worlds of fashion and fashion photography with the status of high art, as in a scene showing Fred Astaire playing a character modeled on photographer Richard Avedon, who was working for a character modeled on fashion editor Diana Vreeland, taking pictures of a model played by Audrey Hepburn, clad in a striking red dress by Givenchy, walking down a staircase of the Louvre with the *Winged Victory* statue in the background.

The typical European tour would include stops in London, Paris, Rome, Florence, and Venice, often adding a Rhine cruise and a stop in either Switzerland or Austria. As people visited these places, they gained knowledge of art, food, and wine. When they came home, they wanted to know more, and newspapers and magazines responded by devoting an increasing amount of attention to these topics. Craig Claiborne, who had served an apprenticeship in a French restaurant, began his restaurant reviews in *The New York Times* in 1956. In 1961 Julia Child published *Mastering the Art of French Cooking* and soon thereafter her cooking show began appearing on Boston's WGBH and other public television stations.

By the late 1950s, Spain, Scandinavia, and Greece were offered on many tours. By the '70s it had become necessary to find ever more obscure towns and villages in Tuscany and Provence, or a Greek island that your friends hadn't heard of. In the '70s and '80s, the list of popular destinations expanded to Japan, India, and finally China. Just as Americans had learned that Italians didn't confine their diet to spaghetti, they learned that Chinese cuisine wasn't all chow mein and egg rolls and that the food in India was definitely not the kind of yellow lamb or chicken curry known back home. Much of the travel was democratic in the sense that it was affordable to a wide swath of Americans. One of the most popular guides, published in 1957, was Arthur Frommer's *Europe on Five Dollars a Day*, and backpackers staying in inexpensive hostels became a part of the tourist scene. But the best hotels and restaurants and the best wines tended to cost money—more and more of it as the years went by.

So did the works of art that people had begun to take an interest in during their travels. In fact, the growth in enthusiasm for art was dramatic. The lines at the Uffizi Gallery and the Louvre seemed to grow longer each year. In the 1950s *The New York Times* devoted one page to art. Now the *Times* publishes art news every day, with a whole section on Friday devoted to art and ads for museums, and galleries offering sculptures and paintings at prices approaching stratospheric heights.

It was good that Americans were learning to have better taste in food, wine, and art. There was, however, a downside. Not only would they find that demonstrating their good taste seemed to cost more each year but that it also carried with it the danger of feeling superior to those who were less discriminating. In this sense travel was like the influence of the Kennedys. Those who wanted to acquire Jackie's taste in clothes, furnishings, and architecture were prey to the peril of requiring higher incomes to satisfy those tastes and of feeling superior to people who did not share them.

But the postwar tendency to use taste as an indication of class had been noticed by at least one observer even before school snobbery developed, and those trips to Europe became common, and the

Kennedys became prominent. It was clear enough to Russell Lynes back in 1949 that he wrote an article in *Harper's* about how people were beginning to separate themselves into highbrow, middlebrow, and lowbrow, with distinctions being made in everything from food to periodicals. Highbrows mixed their salad in unwashed wooden bowls and read a magazine called the *Partisan Review.* By 1958 the need to make distinctions based on matters of taste had become so widely felt that *Life,* the mass-circulation picture magazine, felt the need to devote two pages to a chart identifying highbrow, upper middlebrow, lower middlebrow, and lowbrow classes by their taste in matters ranging, again, from salads to magazines, with those unwashed salad bowls and the *Partisan Review* still making the highbrow list.

I was a participant, sometimes as a pioneer, sometimes as a laggard, in many of the postwar trends. The silliest example of snobbery was my carrying around the Columbia campus copies of the *Partisan Review* and *The New Yorker* so that people, especially young women, would be aware of my sophisticated tastes. Or maybe it would be a copy of Baudelaire's or Rimbaud's poetry that I learned about from my friend Allen Ginsberg, who was for me what he proved to be for future generations, a guide to how to be hip—who, in fact, informed me that "the word is 'hip,' not 'hep.'" He also introduced me to marijuana, but I couldn't smoke it without making him and others laugh, so it didn't become a habit. Another friend I would rely on in my attempts to become sophisticated was James Lee. I met him when we were both working at a summer theater in Massachusetts in 1946. Jimmy would tell me about the latest theatrical gossip, as would the director of that theater, Don Richardson, and share with me the hip opinions about actors, writers, and directors, so that I could sound as though I were knowledgeable about the theater. Sometimes in trying to show my hipness I would reveal certain gaps in my sophistication, as when I referred to both the painter Miró and the poet Rilke as "she."

I had a preview of the sexual revolution that was to come along in the 1960s and '70s by hearing stories about Allen and his friends Jack Kerouac, Neal Cassady, and Bill Burroughs, and by my experience in the theater, where I worked several summers in the late 1940s and early '50s and where both women and men enjoyed a considerable amount of sexual freedom. I had two bosses during that time who were very strong women, Sarah Stamm, the producer of the Newport Casino Theatre in Rhode Island, and Audrey Wood, a literary agent who represented Tennessee Williams, among other writers. Thus sexual freedom and women's rights to do "men's" jobs were familiar to me, as was the concept of gay rights.

Some of the signals of the time were perplexing. While Allen and several of his friends were obviously gay, Jimmy Lee and Don Richardson would refer to gays as "faggots," even though many of the actors they respected were gay. And women, though respected as talents, would still be routinely treated as sex objects. This confused me for a while, but fortunately not for long. The bad influence that lingered longer was the beginning of the idea that expressions of elevated taste would make me rise in other people's esteem, and the snobbery that idea fostered.

That influence was heightened by the impact of a brilliant professor, Lionel Trilling. Trilling taught me to respect rigorous thought and the ability to make careful distinctions—for example, the ability to see what was wrong about McCarthyism without denying the guilt of Alger Hiss or Julius Rosenberg, or excusing the horrors of Stalinism. He also taught me that knowing what to teach was just as important as knowing how to teach, a distinction that, unfortunately, the Columbia Teachers College seemed to have difficulty making. But in describing the errors of the conventional left and of Teachers College, he could speak with a disdain that was not admirable and that I unfortunately imitated during my worst period. I think that in a way Trilling had a problem like my own. I was a boy from West Virginia who landed among all the sophisticates in New York (or who seemed like sophisticates to me). He was a Jew from the Bronx who landed on the Columbia faculty and had to deal with real prejudice. In 1946–47, the year I had classes with him, he was still an associate professor, even though he was one of the five or six most distinguished members of the entire faculty. The WASPs were reluctant to recognize his talent, and I think the insecurity that brought about may have led to his developing his own version of snobbery.

When my snob phase was at its worst in early 1948 and my grades were plummeting, I was called into the dean's office. The result was a visit to a psychiatrist, who turned out to be a salutary influence on my life. Under his treatment, I realized that my own snobbery was largely a result of trying to prove that I was smart without risking failure in class by actually trying. When I arrived at Columbia, a graduate of Charleston High School in West Virginia, I encountered a lot of people who knew a great deal more than I did, and I think I was afraid of failure if I made an all-out effort to compete with them.

Unfortunately, being able to say I had consulted a psychiatrist gave me entrée to another form of snobbism that came along at about that time: People were beginning to boast about being in treatment. The 1945 movie *Spellbound* with Gregory Peck and Ingrid Bergman contributed to the popularity of the ideas of Sigmund Freud. In the minds of many, Freud's ideas about sex were confirmed by the Kinsey report in 1948, which only added to the cachet of citing him in conversation. Even more impressive was disclosing that you were in analysis—the ultimate status symbol for decades to come. Fewer people undergo analysis these days, but the self-absorption it signified has, alas, become nearly universal. In 1948, however, I should hasten to add, while going to the psychiatrist was something one talked about in New York, it was still *not* something one talked about in Charleston, West Virginia.

In my experiences with travel I would continue to fall victim to the old snobbery from time to time. I remember on my first trip to Europe in 1952, rushing to the Basilica of San Francesco in Arezzo to see the Piero della Francesca frescoes, and to the Brancacci

Chapel in Florence to see the Masaccio frescoes—motivated in part, I'm sure, by the knowledge that neither of these attractions was on the usual tours at that time and that being able to refer to them would demonstrate my discriminating taste in art.

What had happened to me at Columbia was an experience common to many late adolescents—wanting to be hip didn't differ all that much from the desire to be "in" or "cool." Indeed, I was nineteen when I first encountered Allen Ginsberg, Lionel Trilling, Don Richardson, and Jimmy Lee. But the snobbery that showed in my 1950s travel was something that I shared with a growing number of Americans.

It is important to emphasize that the trend toward making class distinctions based on taste was still not dominant in the country as a whole. America in the 1950s, indeed until about 1965, continued to be recognizably the country it was in the days of Andy Hardy. In fact, many of the attitudes of the Andy Hardy movies were repeated in television series such as *Father Knows Best* and *Leave It to Beaver*. And all classes continued to feel an obligation to serve in the military, with celebrities such as Elvis Presley going into the army, as well as people as privileged as Ted Kennedy. The baseball great Ted Williams served as a marine pilot in Korea after having also served in World War II. At the end of the 1951 season, during which another future baseball Hall of Famer, Willie Mays, had proved himself as a rising star, no one even considered arguing that Mays should be exempted from the military draft. He served two years in the army, just as other draftees were doing. Few of today's sports stars have done the same. The average citizen of the 1950s not only continued to serve in the military but continued to believe in what government can do, supporting ambitious programs like the Marshall Plan to aid Western Europe and the construction of the interstate highway system. To finance them, he continued to pay taxes at World War II levels.

The key to understanding America from the end of World War II to the end of the 1950s can be found in the attitude of the returning veterans. They'd had enough risk and disruption. They wanted life to be regular again. They wanted to raise a family, to be good parents, and to have a house and a yard for the kids to play in, which led many of them to move to the suburbs. They wanted a job that offered both an adequate income and, perhaps most of all, stability, meaning many were attracted to careers in large corporations. Their needs were modest. The average size of their houses was eleven hundred square feet, far less than today's average. *Fortune* magazine found that even the typical corporate executive required a home of only seven rooms.

Politically they were moderates who resisted boat rockers from the left or the right. In 1946 they elected a Republican Congress because they did not want any more New Deal reforms, but when the Republicans started tampering with the existing New Deal reforms, most notably by passing the anti-union Taft-Hartley Acts, the voters responded by electing a Democratic Congress and giving the moderate liberal Harry Truman a full four-year term as president. To succeed him, they elected the moderate conservative Dwight Eisenhower in 1952 and reelected him in 1956.

They were disturbed by revelations in the late 1940s that there had been traitors in the government, but when Joe McCarthy and his allies went too far in trying to purge suspected left wingers, the public rejected them.

The veterans' distaste for boat rocking helped to explain why the 1950s was the decade of conformity. They were organization men because they wanted to be, but, in return, their bosses, who in many cases were veterans themselves and in other cases were mindful of the power given unions by the New Deal reforms, treated them fairly, sharing corporate income with them to a degree unheard of before the New Deal and since the 1970s.

Allen Ginsberg's "Howl," published in 1956, gave voice to an undercurrent of rebellion against '50s conformity, but it was a revolt that did not flower until the counterculture of the late '60s. But even Ginsberg had been tempted by conformity. When I saw him in

New York two years before the publication of "Howl" he was wearing a suit and tie and working as a market researcher. He still spoke admiringly, as he had for the entire time I had known him, of Wallace Stevens, T. S. Eliot, and William Carlos Williams, each of whom had managed to combine poetry and regular jobs: Stevens as an insurance executive, Eliot as a banker, and Williams as a public school administrator.

Just as America of the 1950s remained much the same country as it had been in the 1930s and 1940s, I remained in many ways the same person I had been growing up in West Virginia. I still loved politics and baseball. I attended Giants games at the Polo Grounds, Yankees games at Yankee Stadium, and Dodgers games at Ebbets Field. Ebbets Field was my favorite; I saw Jackie Robinson play there and got to know fans whose savvy about the game reminded me of the foolishness of my snobbery. FDR was still my hero. I followed the 1948 election closely, starting out as a supporter of Henry Wallace but switching to Harry Truman as I came to admire his campaign and his desegregation of the armed forces. On election night I stayed up until it became clear in the early morning hours that Truman had won. And in 1952 I served as a volunteer in Adlai Stevenson's presidential campaign.

By 1954 my desire for a life in politics and government became strong enough that I took the first step by entering law school at the University of Virginia that fall. During the 1956 presidential campaign I distributed brochures for the Adlai Stevenson campaign outside the polling place at the Albemarle County Courthouse in Charlottesville. After graduating the next year I was making political speeches in Charleston by 1958, and by 1959 I was working as a Democratic staff member in the state legislature, to which I was elected in 1960.

In 1960 I agreed to run Kennedy's campaign in my county, even though I was launching my own campaign for the legislature at the time. I did not think my Kennedy duties would be too distracting, since the West Virginia primary had never played an important role in national politics. That, however, did not prove to be the case in 1960. West Virginia's population was 95 percent Protestant. After Kennedy's Catholicism became widely publicized, a poll of the state's Democrats showed them favoring his opponent, Hubert Humphrey. Then the results of the Wisconsin primary showed Kennedy carrying the Catholic but not the Protestant districts. The big question confronting Kennedy's campaign was, could he carry a state as Protestant as West Virginia? Not only was the poll result depressing, but the first time I escorted Kennedy through downtown Charleston I was shocked to find he was shunned by several voters to whom I attempted to introduce him. Clearly things did not look hopeful. An emergency meeting was held at Robert Kennedy's home, Hickory Hill, outside Washington to which several of us from West Virginia were summoned and asked for our ideas on how the situation could be saved.

Our first recommendation, which illustrated how much this was still the FDR era, was that Franklin D. Roosevelt, Jr., campaign for Kennedy. We said FDR was practically a god in West Virginia and that a blessing from his son would help West Virginians overcome their suspicion that Catholics were agents of the pope. We then urged that a magazine article describing Kennedy's heroism during World War II be widely distributed among the state's voters, since West Virginia had among the highest percentage of veterans in any state—even nonveteran voters would be impressed at how a Catholic had risked his life for his country and theirs.

On a more practical political level, our state chairman had already urged generous contributions to the more influential of the county party leaders and their organizations. I know this sounds improper—and indeed it was—but it was so customary in West Virginia politics at the time that many campaign workers would have been insulted if they weren't compensated. Another improper suggestion made by some of us was that donations be made to the prominent radio preachers, whose influence was comparable to today's televangelists, to help them resist the temptation to inflame anti-Catholic sentiment among their listeners. I feared that if those preachers got really wound up before we'd had a chance to make the good case for Kennedy the momentum of their anti-papist message might be impossible to overcome.

It may have been that all this was unnecessary. John Kennedy's personality proved magnetic as the campaign went on. One county leader said that he would have supported Kennedy regardless of the contribution he had received from the campaign because his wife and daughter would have disowned him otherwise.

On May 10, 1960, Kennedy won West Virginia 60–40, reversing the result of a pre-election poll that had shown him losing by the same margin. There is no question that some of Kennedy's votes were bought by Kennedy money, but even in West Virginia, you can't buy a landslide. The better angels of the state's voters had won out, engraving on me the lesson that prejudice can be overcome. But I also knew that the result could have been different if we had not managed to appeal to the voter's good side with messages about FDR Jr.'s endorsement and Kennedy's wartime heroism, messages that they understood, that did not strike them as condescending political correctness—and that reached them before the opposition could exploit their potential for bigotry.

The campaign led to my joining the Kennedy administration in Washington as a member of the staff that launched the Peace Corps. It was a hopeful and inspiring time when there was still a belief that government could do great things. Thousands of young people responded to Kennedy's "Ask what you can do for your country" by volunteering for the Peace Corps. My job was to give my boss Sargent Shriver an independent report of the problems they were encountering in their training and as they served overseas. Many of those problems were daunting, and I was amazed by the courage and imagination with which the volunteers met them.

Indeed, the spirit that problems could be overcome seemed to grip the country. There was no better example than the 1963 march on Washington. I stood at the side of Constitution Avenue watching the marchers, black and white together, as they approached the Lincoln Memorial. They marched with great dignity, united in peaceful protest. There was no sign of violent opposition by any whites along the way. You could not escape the feeling that change was not only possible, but that it was happening before your eyes.

It was a feeling that continued through the early years of the Johnson administration, when most of the Great Society legislation was enacted, including the creation of Medicare, measures to carry out the War on Poverty, the Civil Rights Act of 1964, and the Voting Rights Act of 1965. The rejection of old prejudices embodied in the latter two laws culminated in the Immigration and Nationality Act of 1965 that removed the restrictions on Asians; on eastern Europeans, which had been largely aimed at Jews; and on southern Europeans, where the main target was Italians.

All of these changes made many of us feel that a good country was getting better. But in July 1965, Lyndon Johnson decided on a major escalation of the American commitment to Vietnam. Opposition to the war, though still coming from only a little over 10 percent of the population, would grow and become more vocal as the months went by. At first it was largely composed of young people, and we soon began to feel it at the Peace Corps. Looking back, we realized that our recruiting had peaked in 1964. If young people were less eager to join the Peace Corps, they were even less likely to want to serve in Vietnam. This was the first blow to what had seemed like a growing unity in the country. Now there was a generational conflict of youth against their elders and, more ominously, there was the beginning of class conflict between the college students at the heart of the antiwar movement and the less educated but patriotic working class.

An ancient American division that had seemed to be healing with the march on Washington and the civil rights laws quickly enacted in its wake now reappeared. The occasion was the assassination of Martin Luther King, Jr., in April 1968. Blacks in Washington, D.C., and other major cities rioted, reigniting white fear of black violence.

The year had begun with the Tet offensive in Vietnam, launched by the Vietcong and the North Vietnamese. It took American and South Vietnamese forces by surprise, with the Vietcong actually breaching the walls of the U.S. Embassy compound in Saigon and practically destroying Hue, the ancient capital of Vietnam. The effect on the American public was dramatic. The Johnson administration and the American commander, General William Westmoreland, had been promising that there was light at the end of the tunnel. After Tet, it was a light most Americans no longer saw.

Gloom descended over Washington, briefly lifted by antiwar candidate Eugene McCarthy's impressive showing in the March New Hampshire presidential primary, followed by Lyndon Johnson's decision to withdraw his candidacy for reelection. For a few days there was such good feeling in the country that when Johnson appeared at a ceremony at St. Patrick's Cathedral in New York he was cheered by the congregation, some of whom had doubtless been chanting, "How many kids did you kill today?" just shortly before.

But then came the King assassination and the riots that ensued. One of the participants in the Washington riots was Stokely Carmichael, a young black leader who had split with King. Carmichael favored the more assertive approach that had been advocated by Black Muslim leader Malcolm X, which involved an implicit or overt threat of violence as a tactic to gain black power. Carmichael was guilty only of throwing a brick through a store window, but the Black Panthers, a group formed out of justifiable anger at the beatings and other injustices to which blacks had been subjected by the Oakland, California, police department, not only carried weapons but actually waved them around (thereby scaring the pants off) white people.

The bad news of 1968 did not end with the riots. On June 6,

Robert Kennedy was assassinated. He was the one Democratic leader who appealed to blacks, working-class whites, and antiwar youth, as was movingly demonstrated by the crowds lining the railroad tracks as his funeral train passed by.

Kennedy had been running for the Democratic nomination for president, to succeed Lyndon Johnson. He had just won the crucial California primary, and seemed to have a good chance of winning at the Democratic convention in August. But without his presence, that convention turned into a nightmare as antiwar demonstrators voiced their frustration and anger that the convention would now nominate Hubert Humphrey, the candidate favored by Lyndon Johnson and party regulars. Demonstrators on the street provoked police by calling them pigs, and the police responded by beating and gassing them. There was even violence in the convention hall. In one memorable moment CBS anchor Walter Cronkite expressed anger at "a bunch of thugs" who roughed up the network's floor reporter Dan Rather. As the convention came to an end, the orchestra played a wonderfully jaunty tune from a Broadway play featuring the words "Let a Winner Lead the Way." The irony was heartbreaking, because you felt that Hubert Humphrey, who was, after all, a good man, was doomed to lose the election to Richard Nixon, who was not.

The demonstrators in the Chicago streets consisted largely of college students. Part of their motivation was an idealistic concern with stopping the war, but it was coupled with something less admirable, a desire to evade the draft and let someone else do the fighting and dying. The someone else, of course, consisted of the less educated. The response of the hard hats and the police fed a growing division between student and worker that was part of a growing class separation in a country that had liked to think of itself as classless.

In the early 1960s, the critic Dwight Macdonald wrote a book called *Masscult and Midcult* and a review in *The New Yorker* of Michael Harrington's book *The Other America*. Taken together they help explain the coming alienation of the liberal, educated elite from the middle class. In the book, Macdonald expressed contempt for the taste of both lower and upper middlebrows. In the review, the eloquence of the concern he expressed for the poor helped inspire John Kennedy to form the pilot agency that would lead to Lyndon Johnson's War on Poverty. As these two attitudes of Macdonald's spread, the "average" man began to feel that not only were his tastes being looked down upon but that his concerns, such as those about the impact of busing on his children, were being ignored, while those of the poor were being taken care of.

The mid-1960s saw the founding of two magazines that would satisfy this growing desire to display class through taste, *The New York Review of Books* and *New York* magazine. The *New York Review* was founded to replace *The New York Times Book Review* during a newspaper strike, but it quickly became the magazine for highbrows or those who wanted to be considered highbrows, replacing the *Partisan Review*. *New York* magazine catered to the meritocratic and celebrity classes, offering information on topics such as the best places to eat, the best art galleries, the latest in fashion, and other consumer advice on what was in while at the same time appealing to readers' intellects with well-written articles by a group that became known for the "New Journalism."

Using taste as a demonstration of class had become so common by 1975 that *The Washington Monthly* published an article entitled "Taste, Class and Mary Tyler Moore," in which the author, Suzannah Lessard, made the point that being in "is a condition which must be constantly and feverishly maintained." The Style section of *The Washington Post* and many of the city magazines that were subsequently established in imitation of *New York* began to publish lists of what was in and out each year, contributing to the nervousness. Woody Allen captured this feverishness in his 1979 movie *Manhattan,* in which the characters are shown one-upping each other in displaying their taste badges. Interestingly enough, Allen, after making fun of the other characters for their displays of refined taste, showed his own in a scene where he demonstrates his "original" taste by joining Mozart's "Jupiter" symphony and Woody Herman's "Woodchopper's Ball" in his list of favorite works of art.

This would become a trend among the cognoscenti: endeavoring to mix an occasional bit of lowbrow into their highbrow favorites. The best example of this tendency was the status of beer. In the 1958 *Life* magazine chart, beer was the beverage of the lowbrows. But as the years went by, one imported beer after another would become chic, and then there would be a return to a mass favorite such as Budweiser, followed by the microbrew trend, and then, perhaps, the traditional Pabst Blue Ribbon, and now by craft beer.

By the mid-1970s, there was at least one clear sign of the growing importance of displaying one's discriminating taste. In the 1940s and 1950s the *Partisan Review*'s circulation hovered around 10,000. By the mid-1970s the circulation of the *New York Review* exceeded 100,000 copies, many of which were displayed on coffee tables with an intent not dissimilar to Charlie Peters's as he carried the *Partisan Review* around the Columbia campus.

———————★———————

# CHAPTER 4

# The Rise of the Right

## A. Me, Money, and the Powell Memorandum

The movement for group rights, first for blacks and then for women, began in the 1960s under the influence of the counterculture to include the personal right to sexual freedom as well as the freedom to inhale or ingest illicit substances. In the 1970s, the assertion of these personal rights came to be the dominant concern of far too many, leading to the self-absorption and self-indulgence that Tom Wolfe called "the Me Decade" and Christopher Lasch called "the culture of narcissism." The bestselling book published in 1971 was entitled *How to Be Your Own Best Friend*. By the end of the decade, the concern for personal rights began to include the right to make more and more money. From the 1930s well into the 1960s, most educated people did not talk in social conversation about making a lot of money, but by the 1970s, a lot of those educated people were watching a public broadcasting show called *Wall Street Week* that gave advice on what stocks to buy. By the 1980s, it was the most popular show on public television. Money had become a major and open interest of the meritocratic class. And as money took over as a primary concern, of course, the cause of lower taxes and of conservatism in general flourished, as shown by the election of Ronald Reagan in 1980.

Liberalism had dominated campuses in the 1930s and '40s, but conservatism began to make inroads in the 1950s with William F. Buckley, Jr.'s *God and Man at Yale* and the publication of Russell Kirk's *The Conservative Mind*. The first conservative student movement occurred in the early '60s, forming around the candidacy of Barry Goldwater and the publication of his book *The Conscience of a Conservative*. But the real explosion of conservatism in Washington and on campuses throughout the country came in the 1970s.

Corporate leaders were shocked to see the Roosevelt era seem to continue into the 1970s. After all, a Republican, Richard Nixon, had been president since January 1969, yet here they were confronted by three new regulatory agencies: the Occupational Safety and Health Administration, the Consumer Product Safety Commission, and the Environmental Protection Agency. Movements led by Ralph Nader and by environmentalists, originally inspired by the publication of Rachel Carson's *Silent Spring* in 1962, had already succeeded in establishing new agencies and seemed to be gaining in strength. There was a growing sense in the business community that the situation had gotten out of hand.

In 1971 a prominent corporate attorney, Lewis Powell, Jr., later to become a Supreme Court justice, wrote a memo to the U.S. Chamber of Commerce that might have been called "The Corporate Manifesto." It urged corporate leaders to seize the kind of influence over the nation's political and intellectual life that, he lamented, liberals had too long enjoyed.

Looking back, it is not clear whether it was the Powell memo itself that was effective or simply that it captured the emerging conviction among corporate leaders that they'd had enough of the New Deal, Fair Deal, New Frontier, and Great Society. The move of the National Association of Manufacturers to Washington soon thereafter, in 1972, proved symbolic. In the next decade more than two thousand companies established Washington offices. Corporate funds poured into new conservative think tanks such as the Heritage Foundation and existing ones such as the American Enterprise Institute, as well as to the libertarian Cato Institute, staunchly allied with the conservatives in its resolute anti-tax, anti-regulation, and anti-government policies.

These efforts paid off, with corporate lobbyists dominating Washington and conservative thought dominating the Republican Party by the end of the decade. And in the opinion of many Americans, Jimmy Carter's Democratic administration from 1977 to 1981 confirmed that the conservatives were right in being anti-regulation and anti-government. Indeed, Carter himself seemed to adopt their ideas when he took certain deregulatory actions, including abolition of the Civil Aeronautics Board, which regulated airlines' routes and fares. And his administration's inability to control inflation—in 1980 it was roaring along at a 13 percent clip—and yearlong failure to rescue the hostages held by Iranian revolutionaries seemed to demonstrate that the government could not solve problems.

The growing acceptance of conservative ideas was spurred by several social and political developments of the 1970s. Some religious Democrats were disturbed by the assertion of women's rights and, even more, of gay rights. Many were also offended by the combination of sex, dope, and rock music that seemed to be a lasting effect of the counterculture, as well as by media reports that practically every celebrity in America was flocking to a nightclub in New York called Studio 54 where that effect was on conspicuous display. Other issues emerging in the 1970s may have had greater influence on the rise of conservatism. In fact, they were important enough that they will be examined more fully later in this book, but they merit a brief acknowledgment here. They include abortion and gun rights, with the pro-gun and anti-abortion causes becoming emotional fuel for right-wing activism. Fear of black violence and increased black crime drove many whites to the right. Two remedies for the injustices of segregation—busing and affirmative action—helped turn Democratic working-class whites into potential Republicans, and, for many of them, the man who would complete their conversion was waiting in the wings.

## B. The Rise of the Right: Ronald Reagan

Ronald Reagan was the perfect person to lead the nation's political conversion to a conservatism that would justify the greed, selfishness, and self-absorption that was launched with his inauguration in January 1981. It was as if the great casting director in the sky had chosen him for the role. Here was a man who saw himself as an average guy playing other average-guy heroes of the FDR era. In 1942 he explained to an interviewer that he regarded himself as a "plain guy . . . Mr. Norm is my alias. . . . Nothing about me stands out in any way." Because Reagan saw himself that way, he could bridge the gap between the politics of generosity of the FDR era and the politics of selfishness that was launched with his presidency. He had been a New Dealer himself, and his father an unemployed shoe salesman who was rescued by the New Deal and given a job. When Reagan was a sportscaster in Des Moines in the mid-1930s and Roosevelt came to town, Reagan was part of the crowd that cheered the president as his car passed by. In Hollywood, Reagan had been an active member of his union, and it was not until FDR died that he became a conservative. How can we account for Reagan's conversion?

In the mid-1940s, some of Hollywood's unions were mob dominated. Some were infiltrated by Communists, who had been harmless during the Soviet-American friendship of the war but who in 1946 offended Reagan and other members of the union by insisting on prolonging a strike that kept actors out of work. Reagan's brother, Neil, who shared his background in Dixon, Illinois, was already a conservative by 1945, and warned Reagan about the dangers of Communism. In 1951, Reagan met Nancy Davis, an actress whose political views were influenced by her strongly conservative stepfather, Dr. Loyal Davis. And in 1954 Reagan went to work for

General Electric as host of a television show. GE at the time had a very conservative president, and Reagan was encouraged to voice conservative views as he toured cities around the country where GE plants were located. By 1964 he had become so thoroughly conservative that he made the most persuasive speech of Barry Goldwater's campaign. That speech, along with the celebrity he had gained in his film career and on television, made him the new darling of the American right.

But the essential thing to remember is that he always spoke in language designed to appeal to that average guy back home in Dixon, and he had a gift for striking the conservative chords that have been an eternal part of the American character. In his youth, Reagan had studied the speeches of Franklin Roosevelt. He knew the language that would appeal to the average man, and he used down-to-earth, easily understandable examples to make his points. To illustrate his oft-repeated contention that "government is not the solution, government is the problem," he would say in his standard speech: "Since the beginning of this country the gross national product has increased by 33 times. In the same period the cost of government has increased 234 times." On the subject of welfare, he said, "Recently a judge told me of [a woman who] came to him for a divorce. By divorcing her husband she could get an $80 raise in her welfare payment. She had been talked into the divorce by two friends who had already done the very same thing."

Of course, what Reagan failed to discuss was what the federal government was doing that needed doing to justify its growth, but there is no question that he was effective in making the fact of government's expansion seem alarming. And it was true that a weakness of the welfare program was that it encouraged divorce and single motherhood. But Reagan did not mention that many single mothers desperately needed the welfare payments. Another "fact" mentioned in Reagan's description of this welfare mother who wanted a divorce was that she was "pregnant with her seventh child." At the time, he knew that there was a racial association in the minds of a large part of the public regarding single mothers with a large number of children—that many saw it as a particular problem among African Americans. There was something disingenuous about Reagan's use of the statement about the seventh child.

Reagan was never explicitly anti-black, nor in his personal life is there any evidence that he was a bigot. Indeed, while he was a student at Eureka College in Illinois, when a fellow football player who was black was denied lodging at a local hotel, Reagan asked his family to take the player in, which they did. But the fact remains that Reagan often in his career conformed to counsel once articulated by Lee Atwater, a young South Carolinian who worked in the Reagan campaign in 1980, obtained more influence and power in 1984, and then ran Vice President George H. W. Bush's campaign in 1988 to succeed Reagan. In 1981, Atwater gave an anonymous interview to a political scientist that did not become public until many years later. In it, he described his strategy for dealing with racial issues:

> You start out in 1954 by saying, "Nigger, nigger, nigger, nigger." By 1968 you can't say "nigger." That hurts you. Backfires. So you say stuff like "forced busing," "states' rights" and all that stuff. You're getting so abstract now you're talking about cutting taxes, and all these things you're talking about are totally economic things and a by-product of them is blacks get hurt worse than whites. And subconsciously maybe that is part of it. I'm not saying that. But I'm saying that if it is getting that abstract, and that coded, that we are doing away with the racial problem one way or the other. You follow me—because obviously sitting around saying, "We want to cut this," is much more abstract than even the busing thing, and a hell of a lot more abstract than "Nigger, nigger."

His mention of 1968 is interesting, because that was the year Reagan launched his first effort to gain the presidency. In fact, it could be said that Reagan developed the Atwater strategy before Atwater did. According to Reagan biographer Lou Cannon, Reagan in 1968 "cultivated Southern support by refusing to criticize George Wallace's segregationist advocacies." In any event, he followed the Atwater strategy in that campaign and again in 1976, when he ran unsuccessfully a second time but came much closer, and finally in 1980, when he won the presidency. The most notorious example was his constant repetition of a story about a welfare "queen" driving around in a Cadillac, which did not exactly raise the image of the queen mother of England.

To an amazing extent, Reagan was able to reverse the appeal of the Roosevelt message, which to many had been the politics of generosity, of helping people who needed help, and of not looking down on those in need but respecting them. He not only got away with it but was extremely effective in delivering the countermessage that sold the politics of selfishness, the promise to cut your taxes and get the government off your back, with all its regulations and spending. A big part of his success was that he delivered his message with the same sort of sunny optimism that lay behind FDR's appeal, radiating faith in the future—the faith that Reagan often said would create that "shining city on a hill." He was the most effective public speaker and seller of a message to occupy the White House since Franklin Roosevelt.

There were some similarities between 1980 and 1933. There was a recession in 1980—not as bad as the Depression, but still enough to shake many people's confidence in the future. The country was upset and depressed by the Iran hostage crisis, which did not resolve itself until the moment of Ronald Reagan's inauguration. The terrible inflation of the 1970s had done great harm to the economy, and Paul Volcker's efforts to fight it by a radical raising of interest rates had helped bring about the recession. The country needed a renewal of the kind of confidence that FDR brought in 1933. Reagan, by radiating his own confidence, helped restore it during his time in office.

In a sense, every good actor has to believe in the role he is playing. It was true of Reagan as actor, thinking of himself as the average man whom he was portraying. It was absolutely clear on the night of October 17, 1980, when he returned in the midst of the presidential campaign to Eureka College, where he had loyally remained on the board because of his great affection for the school. The scene was right out of a '30s movie. There was a pep rally at which Reagan lit the bonfire. He introduced his old coach with a tear coming down his face. He and Nancy held hands while the school song was played. There was something real that was communicated to the American people that said he was one of them, that he was one of *us*. Reagan had the power to move us emotionally as a country. I remember his speech at Normandy on the D-Day anniversary in 1984: Although I was firmly against everything Reagan stood for, I found myself choking up during that speech. There was no question that he had a power to speak to people's hearts. And there is no question that his "Mr. Gorbachev, tear down this wall" was one of the memorable moments in modern American history.

There is little doubt in my mind that Reagan's good side gave what I regard as his bad side the impact it had on his countrymen, so that his anti-tax, anti-government message became gospel for many of them.

## C. The Rise of the Right: Rush Limbaugh

The Reagan administration paved the way for the next great deliverer of the conservative message, Rush Limbaugh, when its Federal Communications Commission revoked the Fairness Doctrine in 1987. That doctrine had required broadcasters to air opposing opinions on public issues. Repeal made it possible for Limbaugh and the many other right-wingers who followed in his wake to voice only conservative opinions, with the stations that carry them under no obligation to give the other side.

Limbaugh did not have Reagan's ability to touch emotions. Nonetheless, he was second only to Reagan in his persuasiveness in setting forth conservative dogma. Like Reagan, Limbaugh was born in the Midwest—in a small Missouri town on the banks of the Mississippi. His family, however, was more prosperous than Reagan's. He came from the country club branch of the Republican Party. His grandfather was a successful lawyer, as was his father, both staunch conservatives. The grandfather had been a delegate to the 1936 Republican convention, which nominated Alf Landon to run against Roosevelt. Thus, although Rush did not become politically active and begin to focus on the conservative message until the 1970s, his views were implanted early. Reagan and Limbaugh were similar in that neither got into politics early, and both started out in radio. Reagan was a sports announcer before going to Hollywood and getting into movies. Limbaugh was even more focused on a career in radio; many of his friends from early in his life recall his fascination with the medium, even in high school. Like Reagan, he attended a small college, but he left after less than a year to set out on his career in radio.

Limbaugh has preached a doctrine familiar to me from my childhood as the opinions voiced by some of my father's country club Republican friends. One of the basic statements of his philosophy is this: "I'm convinced that a lot of people simply don't know what's available out there, and how it is possible to find a job and work your way up if you're willing to accept responsibility for your life. I know what it's like to be on the bottom. I've been broke. I've been fired seven times from jobs, and I don't even have a college degree. But I don't blame anyone else for my problems. I knew if I didn't try to solve them on my own, or with the help of friends and family members, no one else was going to take care of me." But the country club Republican of my youth typically did not realize exactly how much he *did* rely on the help of friends or family members, on the money he inherited, the base they gave him in life, the connections they afforded him.

In Limbaugh's case, his prospects were enhanced by a family that was not only prominent and prosperous but full of lawyers—not only his grandfather and father, but an uncle and cousin, as well, both of whom became federal judges. Their skills at argument undoubtedly helped hone Limbaugh's gift for polemics. Family connections certainly played a part in launching his career in radio. His father helped him get his first job at KGMO in his hometown. And when he lost a job in Pittsburgh, Pennsylvania, he did not, like so many other people in similar circumstances, have to take the next position available. He could retreat to the comfort of his family and home, where he stayed for seven months, taking his time to appraise possible job openings.

There's no question he got his politics from his family. He rails against Roosevelt just as his father and grandfather did. He calls the New Deal the "Raw Deal," and refers to Obama as "the black FDR." As Obama's presidency began in January 2009, Limbaugh expressed the hope that he would fail: "I know what his politics are; I know what his plans are as he has stated them. I don't want them to succeed. He's talking about the absorption of as much of the private sector by the U.S. government as possible, from the banking business to the mortgage industry, the automobile business to healthcare. I do not want the government in charge of all these things."

By 2010 Limbaugh was telling his Republican friends, "Don't be afraid of the media calling you the 'party of no.' We need to be the party of no; we need to be the party of hell no."

Limbaugh does not suffer from an excess of modesty. He says, "I have become the intellectual engine of conservatives in America." He has every reason to be immodest. As early as the 1994 campaign, Mary Matalin observed, "I would go to political meetings all over the country and hear conservatives speak the way he speaks, saying the things he says."

Ronald Reagan was Limbaugh's favorite president. Limbaugh's friends include Karl Rove, Roger Ailes, and Clarence Thomas (who presided at his third wedding). He was a White House guest of George H. W. Bush, attended a Medal of Freedom ceremony under George W. Bush, slept in the Lincoln Bedroom, and was toasted by Dick Cheney at a dinner party. He knows how to appeal to the patriotism of America, and once said of Ronald Reagan: "Reagan rejected the notion among liberals and conservatives alike who, for different reasons, believed America was in a permanent state of decline. He had faith in the wisdom of the American people. . . . He knew America wasn't perfect, but he also knew it was the most perfect of nations. Reagan was an advocate of Americanism. . . . America is the solution to the world's problems. We are not the problem."

Limbaugh managed to combine elements of two media figures who helped give liberalism a strong media voice in the FDR era. From Walter Winchell he learned to coin new words that encapsulated his message. One of Winchell's favorite terms was "communazis." Limbaugh subsequently came up with "feminazis" to describe the advocates of women's liberation.

From Will Rogers he took humor. One of Limbaugh's great appeals is that he is often very funny. But his humor lacks the warmth and humanity that Rogers possessed. Indeed, it can be downright mean, as in "Feminism was created to allow unattractive women easier access to the mainstream of this society."

Whatever Limbaugh's faults, critics have found it dangerous to question him on issues of fact. For instance, he once said that President Obama's real aim with his health program was to establish a single-payer system. The White House denied it: During the 2008 New Hampshire primary campaign, when Obama was asked whether he favored a single-payer system, he replied, "I have not said that I was a single-payer supporter because frankly we historically have had an employer-based system in this country." But Limbaugh was able to find a recording of an AFL-CIO conference in 2003, when Obama was campaigning for a seat in the U.S. Senate, in which he said, "I happen to be a proponent of a single-payer universal healthcare plan."

Senate Democratic leader Harry Reid provided another case study of what the embarrassing result can be of challenging Limbaugh on the facts. A man named Jesse Macbeth had been featured at a rally protesting the Iraq War, describing himself as a former U.S. Army Ranger and testifying to atrocities committed by American soldiers in Iraq. Limbaugh called him "a phony soldier." Reid then proceeded to denounce Limbaugh on the Senate floor, declaring he had "crossed the line by calling our men and women in uniform who oppose the war in Iraq 'phony soldiers,'" adding that "this comment was so beyond the pale of decency" that he had written a letter to the president of Clear Channel Communications, the syndicator of Limbaugh's radio show, asking him to repudiate the words and requiring Limbaugh to apologize. Reid enlisted forty Democratic senators plus the independent Bernie Sanders to add their signatures to the letter. The facts were, though, that Macbeth had been in the army—for forty-four days—but was never in combat to witness the horrors he claimed to have seen. Limbaugh auctioned off Reid's letter on eBay, raising $2.1 million for the Marine Corps–Law Enforcement Foundation and matching it with a generous contribution of his own.

But it should be noted that Limbaugh has a way of putting untruths into circulation without being technically guilty of asserting them as fact. Here's an example of his coverage of Vince Foster's suicide: "Okay, folks, I think I've got enough information here to tell you about the contents of this fax that I got. Brace yourselves. This fax contains information that I have just been told will appear in a newsletter to Morgan Stanley sales personnel this afternoon. . . . What it is is a bit of news which says . . . there's a Washington consulting firm that has scheduled the release of a report that will appear, it will be published, that claims that Vince Foster was murdered in an apartment owned by Hillary Clinton and the body was then taken to Fort Marcy Park." Later in that same broadcast Limbaugh referred to the story as "a rumor" that said, "Vince Foster's suicide was not a suicide."

Later Limbaugh would be able to claim, on a show hosted by Ted Koppel, "never have I suggested that this was murder." Well, wait a minute: He hadn't said it was murder, but he had certainly put the suggestion in his listeners' minds. And if you have any doubt that the suggestion was thoroughly implanted in the minds of Limbaugh's audience, you only have to know that eleven years later, Limbaugh was able to say, in relation to an antiwar protester named Cindy Sheehan, who had criticized Senator Hillary Clinton for her support of the Iraq War but recently seemed to be shutting up: "Somebody has gotten to [Sheehan] and said, 'Do the words "Fort Marcy Park" mean anything to you?' I will guarantee you, my friends, that by the time all is said and done—if she calls Clinton out one more time, that's it for Cindy Sheehan."

The next day, Limbaugh said that Sheehan "will not mention [Clinton] again, ladies and gentlemen, unless she wants to end up in Fort Marcy Park. Mark my word on it." In other words, Limbaugh knew that, eleven years later, the accusation that the Clintons had Vince Foster murdered and his body transferred to Fort Marcy Park would come back to his audience if he just mentioned the name of the place.

This story also illustrates the lengths to which Limbaugh will go to find negative news about the Clintons, Obama, and Democrats in general. Notice that he is quoting a newsletter to Morgan Stanley sales personnel that has this bit of news: "A Washington consulting firm has scheduled the release of a report that claims Vince Foster . . ." Limbaugh knew that his listeners would be prone to believe the ugly implication that the Clintons had something to do with Foster's death because Foster was known to have had custody of all the Clinton papers relating to Whitewater; his suicide ignited renewed interest in the Whitewater story that Jeff Gerth of *The New York Times* broke in 1992. Some Republicans speculated that Foster was murdered to cover up what he knew about Whitewater—speculation that was, in fact, fanned by Limbaugh.

In stirring up ugly feelings among his listeners, Limbaugh is doing something truly wrong. It reminds me of the days when I was a politician in the late 1950s and early '60s. A common experience would be to encounter a voter whose favor you sought and to hear him say something that was trending in an ugly direction, perhaps on the matter of race. You could either let him go on and develop that feeling so you could express agreement with the ugly direction he was going in—or you could try to turn the conversation in a more positive direction and make him see that where he was headed was someplace he didn't really want to go. You wouldn't always succeed—sometimes he was determined to go there. But sometimes you could appeal to his better angels, and that's what good politics was about to me.

Sometimes it's a pretty close call between the good and evil in a person's mind, and it may be you can tip the balance toward good if you try. There is a great example of this truth from John McCain in the 2008 presidential campaign. A woman in his audience said to him, "I can't trust Obama. I have read about him, and he's not, he's a, uh, he's an Arab." McCain took the microphone and said, "No, ma'am, he's a decent family man, a citizen that I just happen to have disagreements with on fundamental issues, and that's what this campaign is all about." Another time, when a voter said he was "scared" of the idea of Obama as president of the United States, McCain said, "I have to tell you, Senator Obama is a decent person and a person you don't have to be scared of as president of the United States."

### D. The Rise of the Right: Roger Ailes

The 1988 presidential campaign, pitting Vice President George H. W. Bush against the Democratic governor of Massachusetts, Michael Dukakis, provided a blatant example of the reverse of what John McCain had done, in other words, of how to appeal to men's lesser angels—this time arousing racial fears. Massachusetts had a law permitting furloughs for prisoners. The state legislature passed a bill denying furloughs to murderers, but Dukakis vetoed it. Subsequently, a murderer, Willie Horton, while on furlough, kidnapped an engaged couple, knifed the man, and raped the woman twice. Willie Horton was black.

The furlough policy would have been a legitimate campaign target, but Lee Atwater, who by now had risen to be Bush's campaign manager, declared that he would "make Willie Horton [Dukakis's] running mate." It is thus hard to credit his claim that he had nothing to do with the television commercial telling the story of Horton's crimes and displaying his picture. Explicit racial commentary was not necessary—recall Atwater's explanation of how not to say "nigger" and still say it. There was no better example than this commercial. The photograph of an especially fierce-looking black man was enough to stoke white fear of sex-crazed black murderers running free in the land because of liberals like Dukakis.

The hollowness of Atwater's claim of innocence became clear when his pal Roger Ailes, the campaign's media manager, told a reporter for *Time* magazine: "The only question is whether we depict Willie Horton with a knife in his hand or without." Ailes never denied the quote, but later claimed he was joking, and that he would not have said it had he known what the future had in store for him: "Hell, I had no idea I would be running a network someday."

The network, of course, is Fox News, founded by Ailes with Rupert Murdoch's financial backing in 1996. It ranks alongside Reagan and Limbaugh as one of the major influences in the rightward tilt of American opinion after 1980.

Roger Ailes, like Ronald Reagan and Rush Limbaugh, did not grow up wanting to go into politics; he wanted to go into communications, into the media, and he started out in radio, as had both Reagan and Limbaugh. At Ohio University, which he attended after growing up in Warren, Ohio, his girlfriend, a senior, got him involved in student radio during his freshman year. Later, after she became his wife, she helped him get a job in Cleveland that led to his success producing *The Mike Douglas Show,* an early television talk-show program originating from Cleveland and later broadcast in Philadelphia and elsewhere.

While Ailes was in Cleveland, one of the guests on the show was Richard Nixon. This was the beginning of Ailes's involvement in politics. He gave Nixon some advice about using television that impressed the former vice president and led to an invitation to New York to meet Nixon's law partner, Len Garment. Ailes ultimately landed a job running the media for the 1968 Nixon presidential campaign, which proved to be much more television savvy than the 1960 Nixon campaign, in which John F. Kennedy had clearly outshone Nixon on TV. At the Republican National Convention in 1968, the television cameras somehow always found the pretty young daughters of Richard Nixon sitting in the family box as speeches droned on and Nixon won the nomination. Often appearing with the daughters was David Eisenhower, the charming grandson of Dwight Eisenhower, who was Julie Nixon's fiancé and who had won the nation's affection years before as a young boy in cowboy garb brandishing a toy six-shooter and playing with his grandfather, the beloved 1950s president and hero of World War II.

After Nixon's successful campaign to win the nomination—during which, by the way, he defeated Ronald Reagan—Ailes's media strategy was to avoid debates with Hubert Humphrey, the Democratic nominee, and instead arrange a series of town meetings in which Nixon would appear with prescreened audiences so there would be no hostile questions that Nixon couldn't handle with ease. Interestingly enough, the Nixon campaign may have co-pioneered the Lee Atwater strategy (along with Ronald Reagan in his unsuccessful campaign for the nomination) by avoiding saying anything that would upset southern conservatives. And Nixon did carry five southern states: South Carolina, Florida, North Carolina, Virginia, and Tennessee. But despite the success of the Nixon campaign and of Ailes's handling of the media, Ailes was eventually eased out by White House insiders. Bob Haldeman in particular did not like a description of Nixon that Ailes gave to the writer Joe McGinniss:

Let's face it, a lot of people think Nixon is dull. Think he's a bore, a pain in the ass. They look at him as the kind of kid who always carried a bookbag. Who was forty-two years old the day he was born. They figure other kids got footballs for Christmas, Nixon got a briefcase, and he loved it. He'd always have his homework done, and he'd never let you copy.

Now, you put him on television, you've got a problem right away. He's a funny-looking guy. He looks like somebody hung him in a closet overnight and he jumps out in the morning with his suit all bunched up and starts running around saying, "I want to be president."

The quote may have proved that Ailes was young and inexperienced enough to be imprudent in his comments to reporters, but it also illustrated how intelligent and insightful he was and remains.

A Long Island politician running for senator from New York, Al D'Amato, came to Ailes for advice. D'Amato was a singularly unprepossessing candidate, and, in fact, most voters perceived him as nasty or just a jerk. Ailes said to him, "Jesus, nobody likes you. Your own mother wouldn't vote for you. Do you even have a mother?" When D'Amato told him that indeed he did have a mother, Ailes proceeded to feature her instead of D'Amato in the candidate's campaign commercials, showing a nice elderly woman with a bagful of groceries talking about the inflation that was a great problem for middle-class people at that time. At the end of the commercial she identified herself and said to viewers that if they wanted to change things they should vote for her boy Al. The commercial worked and D'Amato won.

Another key to Ailes's success was his ability to face the facts, no matter how unpleasant. For example, in D'Amato's Senate race against Chuck Schumer, Ailes suggested that he abandon the race because he couldn't win. D'Amato continued his candidacy and lost. And then there was the famous episode the night of Barack Obama's reelection in 2012 when Megyn Kelly interrupted Karl

Rove's declaration that the Republicans still had a chance to win Ohio by saying, "Let's go down and check with our own experts." It turned out that she was instructed to do just that by Ailes.

In 1991, Rush Limbaugh, whose show was already a tremendous success, was living in New York. He was having dinner one night at 21, as was Roger Ailes. Ailes came over to Limbaugh's table and introduced himself. They quickly became friends, and soon Ailes was suggesting that they do a television show together. There were a number of similarities between the two men. Both had demanding fathers who had been tough in their criticism of their sons. Limbaugh's friends remember his father sometimes berating him in front of them. Both went to schools that definitely were not Ivy League: Ohio University for Ailes and Southeast Missouri State for Limbaugh. Perhaps not surprisingly, both have had a lifelong aversion to Ivy League schools—and their graduates. And both, of course, had an early interest in the media that preceded their interest in politics. Their television show lasted only four years, not because it wasn't successful—indeed, it did quite well—but because Limbaugh simply didn't like the television format. But the friendship between the two proved to be lasting.

Ailes's school, Ohio University, was a small college in the small town of Athens. When the army sent me there in 1944 I found myself quickly becoming fond of the school and the town. More than sixty years later, when I revisited Athens, it looked exactly the same, although the university had become much larger, thanks in part to sizable donations by its alumnus Roger Ailes. But his attitude toward elite universities was less charitable: a mixture of envy and dislike, which was communicated by Fox News and its views on Barack Obama and others.

Ailes's biographer Zev Chafets recalls that a few years ago he and Ailes were discussing boyhood friends. One of Ailes's was a man named Austin Pendleton, who was from a wealthier local family and went to Yale, then into the theater, where he had a successful career. When Chafets asked Ailes if he had seen his old friend recently, Ailes said, "I hear he lives in New York, but I haven't seen him in years. I imagine his friends think I'm the devil. I wouldn't want to embarrass him by getting in touch."

Chafets then looked up Pendleton, who told him he'd be delighted to see Ailes. The two got together and had an affectionate reunion, but what is revealing is Ailes's assumption that the Yale man from the Warren, Ohio, elite would not want to see him. Another telling statement that Ailes made to Chafets about the Ivy League: "If I get a job application from someone who went to Princeton or Harvard, they have a harder time selling me. I'd rather hire state school kids. They hustle. They're not entitled. They have a work ethic, a desire to win and practical intelligence."

He once told another interviewer, speaking of his success at Fox News, "I built this channel from my life experience. My first qualification is I didn't go to Columbia Journalism School. There are no parties in this town that I want to go to." Certainly no one can deny he has been successful at Fox News. The network makes more in profits than CNN, MSNBC, and the evening newscasts of NBC, ABC, and CBS combined. He attributes that success to the values he learned growing up in Warren: "God, country, family."

Joe McGinniss says of Ailes: "Success has never made that chip on his shoulder go away. He holds on to what he envisions to be the values of the heartland and is suspicious of people on either coast."

Ailes proved to be a genius at peopling Fox News with journalists, such as Bill O'Reilly and Sean Hannity, who were gifted at exploiting those chips on shoulders.

He had always emphasized his working-class background, but there are some different strains worth noting. His paternal grandfather was a physician, according to one biographer, or a public health official, according to another, and the family lore was that he had been killed in World War I. The truth was that he had deserted Ailes's grandmother and gone off to Akron to set up a whole new life. Ailes's mother had not gone to college herself, nor had her parents, but she could be called aspirational. For instance, she had been

raised a Pentecostal Christian but left that church for the First Pres-
byterian Church, locally considered more respectable. She had her
children take elocution and piano lessons, and even made young
Roger take ballet and tap-dancing classes. (Imagine Roger Ailes in
tights!) And his mother tried to emphasize the importance of good
grades in school, though Ailes, like Rush Limbaugh, was never interested in academics. She later deserted Ailes's father and married
a man named Joe Urban, who had been a New York newspaper
reporter. Interestingly enough, Roger Ailes's one book was dedicated to his wife and mother and to Joe Urban, but not to his father.

Ailes's background may help to account for Fox News' amazing
ability, which was shared by Ronald Reagan and Rush Limbaugh,
to have an appeal across the whole middle class, from the factory
worker to the country clubber, even though their economic interests
were often very different. For example, there was little self-interest
for factory workers in cutting income taxes. The tax that fell most
heavily on them during the years of Reagan and Limbaugh was the
payroll tax, and if Limbaugh or anyone on Fox News ever railed
against that tax, I am unaware of it. (To his credit, Reagan at least
signed a bill in the early '80s that brought some mercy to the
lower-income taxpayer in the form of the Earned Income Tax
Credit.)

The appeal to the factory worker had to be largely based on
values and class resentment. The emphasis on God, country, and
family values, and the exploiting of the snobbery of the meritocratic
elite (successfully depicted as the "liberal elite") were their techniques for reaching the lower middle class. And there was the un-
derlying appeal to racism. It was never voiced openly. But that was
also true among the upper middle class in the country club during
my childhood in Charleston, where the word used was "colored"—
the nice word for black people in those days—and the n-word was
carefully avoided. And, like Rush Limbaugh, the country clubbers
could fondly remember warm and affectionate relationships with
black servants. But they could get very upset with servants who

became at all assertive of their rights and began to ask for better wages. I remember hearing housewives blaming Eleanor Roosevelt for "uppity" behavior by their maids.

Of course those in the country club set then and now have had a strong interest in income tax rates, and any message that called for keeping them low has always had an appeal to them. They seemed to become more resigned to paying higher taxes over a period that began with World War II and continued through the Eisenhower administration and even John Kennedy's, when the top rate was cut to 70 percent, where it remained under the Johnson, Nixon, Ford, and Carter administrations. The big reduction did not come until the Reagan administration, when it was cut nearly in half.

Reagan's anti-tax, anti-government message, with Rush Limbaugh and Fox News as its most influential advocates, has become sacred Republican gospel. Its most devoted disciples would unite in 2010 to call themselves the tea party, becoming powerful enough to dominate the House of Representatives and force across-the-board spending cuts, when *more* spending was needed to boost economic recovery and to fill such vital needs as upgrading the nation's infrastructure.

The anti-tax message found additional adherents as the "I could win the lottery" attitude spread among the American public. Spending on gambling has grown immensely in the past thirty years, much of it because of state lotteries. People entertain hopes of becoming a sports or entertainment star and cashing in, or of coming up with another Facebook—a new idea that will make them a fortune. When they think about hitting the jackpot like that, they also think to themselves that they wouldn't want to have all that newly acquired wealth taken away by the government—the money they might make, not the money they have.

The anti-tax, anti-government argument was strengthened by the decline in the quality of government. Most liberals seemed to adopt a defensive attitude in response to conservative attacks on government instead of taking a look at what was wrong with it and trying to find ways to make it work better. There was certainly a decline in quality of the personnel entering the civil service. By the end of the 1980s, a study by the Volcker Commission found that nearly 90 percent of college honors students never seriously considered working in government, in sharp contrast to previous eras—the New Deal, World War II, the New Frontier, and the Great Society—when many of the country's brightest graduates flocked to Washington. What happened was that gradually after 1965 interest in the mission of government, with the exception of new agencies like the Environmental Protection Agency, that appealed to the current idealism, became less and less a motive for joining it.

As for the political appointees, contrast Franklin Roosevelt's service as assistant secretary of the navy around the time of World War I, a job he held for almost eight years, with the records of most assistant secretaries since around 1980, who generally served only a couple of years. Government had come to be looked upon as a stepping-stone toward more lucrative employment in the private sector. Not only did the Abe Fortases and Clark Cliffords proliferate, but even higher level civil servants and staff employees of senators and members of Congress began to look for rewards for their expertise in the form of lucrative jobs in the private sector. Mark Leibovich's book *This Town* quotes one congressional staffer discussing candidly how best to "monetize" his government service.

An example of how to monetize public service comes from the Office of Personnel Management, which is responsible for background checks on people seeking government employment, looking for information on such things as whether they might have criminal records or association with terrorist groups. During the Clinton administration there was what was called a Reinventing Government program, led by Vice President Al Gore, that sounded promising as a means of addressing the many problems that diminished the government's effectiveness.

But after Clinton announced that "the era of big government is over," the new emphasis on downsizing the federal government meant, among other things, that government couldn't focus on its longstanding personnel problems, because no one wanted to argue in favor of hiring a lot of new people. So rather than hiring, the agencies turned to contracting out much of the work the government needed to do. A group of employees of the Office of Personnel Management, seeing that they could use their experience to improve their incomes, soon retired from the agency and formed a private company to carry out the same sorts of investigations they had done while on the public payroll. They may have done them well enough while they controlled the company, but then they sold it to a hedge fund, whose interest was simply profit. The new owners pressed the investigators doing background checks to perform them as quickly as possible and compile as many investigations as possible during a given month so that all of them could be billed to the government, even if they were sloppily done.

The firm, called USIS, was found in 2013 to have been responsible for the clearances of Edward Snowden and of Aaron Alexis, the man who committed the killings at the Navy Yard in Washington. A former USIS employee told *The Washington Post,* "There was this intense pressure to do more and faster." Said another former employee: "When you're giving me a week to interview fifty people, that's impossible." Still another added: "It's very: 'Here's a sheet of questions, ask the questions, hurry and get the answers, submit them, and move forward. There's just not a lot of paying attention to potential red flags and that sort of thing." An investigator for the army told the *Post,* "They don't ask the right follow-up questions. . . . The bottom line is the buck rather than national security."

By the end of 2013, Steven Pearlstein, *The Washington Post*'s veteran financial columnist, was writing a series called "Insiders' Game: Getting Rich in the New Washington." The headline of his concluding article is "The Power of Money: For the Capital's Elite, the Aim Was Once Influence and a Comfortable Life. Today It's More Often About the Big Score: Power and Money."

But to conclude, as Mark Leibovich seems to do, that Washington is unique as the cesspool of the country is wrong. What about Wall Street with all of its sharks and swindlers? In a 2012 survey reported by Andrew Ross Sorkin of *The New York Times,* insiders from dozens of financial companies evaluated their own morality: 23 percent said they had "observed or had firsthand knowledge of wrongdoing in their workplace," and 24 percent said they would "engage in insider trading to make $10 million if they could get away with it." Twenty-six percent believed "the compensation plans or bonus structures in place at their companies incentivize employees to compromise ethical standards or violate the law." An updated version of this survey reported by Sorkin found almost identical results in 2015.

What about the lawyers? In a survey of attorneys conducted by Peter Lattman of the *Times,* "more than half acknowledged that the prospect of billing extra time influenced their decision to perform pointless assignments, such as doing excessive legal research or extraneous document review." At one of the world's largest law firms, DLA Piper, Lattman uncovered a memo from one partner to another: "Now Vince has random people working full-time on random research projects in standard 'churn that bill, baby!' mode. That bill shall know no limits."

And then there are the doctors all over the country who have accepted money from pharmaceutical companies or medical device makers or have prescribed high-radiation CT scans not because patients need them but because the doctors own the CT scanners. What about them?

And what about all those voters who choose Republican candidates simply because they don't want to pay their fair share of taxes, yet mightily resist the reduction of any of their government benefits, or any government programs that serve the interests of their business, however undeserved those programs or benefits might be.

The truth is that Washington is no worse and no better than the rest of the country. Our national problem is that too many of our cultural winds are blowing us in the direction of self-absorption, self-promotion, and making a barrel of money. And despite all that's wrong with Washington and Wall Street, we need them, just as we need lawyers and doctors. It's silly to think that we can do without Washington, as many in the anti-government crowd seem to believe. You want someone to send you your Social Security check, to make sure your plane will land safely, and to inspect the bridge you drive over. But you do not have to assume that the people performing those functions are competent or dedicated, any more than you should assume that bankers, lawyers, and doctors always act in your best interest. You have to keep an eye on them.

In all these cases the key is not automatic hostility to the institution but automatic informed skepticism. Above all, it is our own participation in choosing to work in politics at the local, state, and national levels. If we don't participate, we're not going to get good officials. For too long, too many of us have read books like *This Town,* exposés of what's gone wrong in our politics and government, and concluded that politics and government are bad and that we're above that sort of thing. But if we don't participate, things aren't going to improve. Only our participation can make that happen.

---★---

# CHAPTER 5

# The Price of Glamour

Toward the end of his life, Clay Felker reminisced to his wife, Gail Sheehy, about his first years in New York. He described an early fantasy of his about the city: "I pictured the editors going out dressed in black tie with beautiful women on their arms. They would walk into '21' and into the corridor of glamour and power of New York. . . . I wanted to become part of that world, too. I wanted to be a New York editor."

When he got out of the navy in 1946, Felker took a train from the Bainbridge naval base in Port Deposit, Maryland, to Penn Station in New York and hailed a taxi to take him to Fifty-second Street, where he "ducked into [a club] called the Four Deuces and headed straight for the men's room, where I literally ripped off my Navy blouse and pulled off my bell-bottoms and changed into the one civilian suit I had from college, a gray-flannel pinstripe, because I wanted to be part of New York." He was actually talking about the Three Deuces, a jazz club where Allen Ginsberg and I would be hanging out just a year later, in the spring of 1947. It was on the western end of Fifty-second Street, right next to the Drama Book Shop. On the other side of the bookstore, as I recall it, was a jazz club called Jimmy Ryan's. Toward the other end of Fifty-second Street, which was, at that time, mostly lined on either side by brownstones, was 21, which had been part of Clay Felker's fantasy, and was where Rush Limbaugh and Roger Ailes would later meet.

Why talk about Clay Felker? In 1964 he started *New York* magazine, which was first published as a supplement in the *New York Herald Tribune*. It quickly became so successful that by 1968 it could stand on its own as a newsstand and subscription magazine. *New York* featured "the New Journalism," which emphasized the writer's contribution to the story, in terms of what he observed, felt, and thought. For magazine journalism there was much to be said in favor of Felker's approach, but it meant that the facts would sometimes get obscured by the writer's desire to display flair.

Felker played another key role in postwar America as well. He was a high priest of the consumerism that gripped the country after World War II. There were several different strains to this consumerism. One part of the movement sought the lowest prices and led to the repeal of the fair-trade laws enacted under the New Deal to protect small retailers. This lowered some prices, but it also led to the triumph of the Wal-Marts and the decline of the small businesses that had been the heart of so many of this country's downtowns. Even worse, it led to the loss of American jobs, as the pursuit of low prices led to the lowest cost producers, who in many cases happened to be in Asia, rather than the United States. Another part of the movement sought quality, with an emphasis on safety. This was pushed by the muckraking journalists of the twentieth century's first decade and was revived by Ralph Nader with the publication of *Unsafe at Any Speed* in 1965. The concern for safety led to a concern with quality, which had the effect of increasingly emphasizing items that cost more.

A miniature version of higher quality meaning more expensive is what happened with coffee when Starbucks introduced high-end coffee. Suddenly a cup of coffee that was commonly sold for 50 cents was costing $2 or $3 or $4. It was better coffee, but it also led you to think you had to spend more for your daily coffee. That happened over and over again with one consumer item after another.

But it could only happen if consumers had a way of finding out what the better products were and where to find them, and this is where Clay Felker came in.

FELKER COMBINED GOOD taste in writers with a sure sense of the information New Yorkers wanted on how to spend their money in a time of rapidly rising incomes. Good writing gave Felker's magazine the authority to convince its readers when it said single-malt Scotch was better than the blended Scotch they had been drinking for years—authority that was only enhanced when the advice, as in the case of single-malt, turned out to be sound.

Tom Wolfe was probably the most famous of Felker's writers, who also included Jimmy Breslin, Gloria Steinem, Nicholas Pileggi, and Richard Reeves. It was Wolfe who wrote the two articles that made the magazine's reputation. The first, proclaiming that *New York* was hipper than the hippest, took on an institution that had heretofore been New York's guide to chic, *The New Yorker* magazine. Wolfe's tone was dismissive: "*The New Yorker* was never anything more than a rather slavish copy of *Punch* [the British humor magazine]. Nevertheless, literati in America took to it like they were dying of thirst. The need was so great that *The New Yorker* was first praised and then practically canonized." That was *The New Yorker* under its founding editor, Harold Ross. Wolfe went on to describe what it had become under his successor, William Shawn: "One went to work there, and one—how does one explain it?—began to get a kind of . . . religious feeling about the place. . . . From the first, according to his old friends there, Shawn felt as if he were entering a priesthood. Hierophants! Tiny giants—all over the place—Shawn could look out of his cubicle, and there they were, those men out there padding along in the hall were James Thurber, Wolcott Gibbs and Robert Benchley themselves."

Shawn helped make the article famous by overreacting to it. He actually tried to get the piece suppressed, something that the *Herald Tribune*'s editor, Jim Bellows, was smart enough to see as a business opportunity. Bellows alerted the media critics in and around New York as to what was happening, and Wolfe's article soon became one of the most talked-about pieces in recent journalistic history. Shawn went so far as to write Jock Whitney, the *Herald Tribune*'s owner, begging him, on "his honor as a publisher and a gentleman," not to publish Wolfe's piece.

In truth, Shawn had some reason to be upset. The article did contain some errors of fact and offenses against fairness. But the title, "Tiny Mummies! The True Story of the Ruler of 43rd Street's Land of the Walking Dead!," did capture a truth about at least some of the long articles in *The New Yorker* of that time. Shawn had a weakness for meticulously reported, beautifully written, but memorably dull articles, and for the occasional piece of fiction that, while carefully written, seemed to say nothing. Wolfe touched a nerve, but Shawn would probably have done better not to have protested. Then the media writers might have instead commented on the fact that a few weeks before the Wolfe piece appeared, Lillian Ross had written a parody in *The New Yorker* of Wolfe's style featuring a main character called Pam Muffin. It just so happened that Clay Felker was at that time engaged to an actress named Pamela Tiffin (the beautiful blonde he wanted on his arm), whom he later married. A measure of the impact of "Tiny Mummies" was the fact that ad pages in Felker's magazine doubled, from fifteen pages to thirty, as a result of the article.

The next big *New York* success was Wolfe's "Radical Chic," which described a dinner party given by the conductor Leonard Bernstein and his wife, Felicia, that was attended by a mixture of New York literati and celebrities and some Black Panthers. Recall that the Black Panthers and their aggressive reaction to police brutality were part of the black power movement that began as a critique of the supposed meekness of Martin Luther King, Jr., and the clergymen who dominated the civil rights movement in its early days. The Panthers often threatened violence and sometimes actually used it, which they defended as a response to police violence against them. At the time, it was chic in New York to embrace the black assertiveness movement and to overlook the occasional misdeeds of people such as the Panthers. In any event, by some mistake Wolfe had got hold of an invitation to the Bernstein party and was received as a guest. He proceeded to make delicious fun of it in the columns of *New York* magazine. Having offended the editor of one taste-making New York magazine, Wolfe took on the editors of another in "Radical Chic." Among the guests at the dinner party were Jason and Barbara Epstein, two of the three founders of *The New York Review of Books*. Jason Epstein proceeded to write a piece in the *New York Review* protesting Wolfe's unfairness to Felicia Bernstein. (It should be noted that though Wolfe clearly saw what was wrong with the Black Panthers, he was less clear about the wrongs the police had done them.)

An article that Clay Felker had written for *Esquire* before he founded *New York* provided an important clue as to what his cultural significance might prove to be when he had his own magazine. It concerned the way New York restaurants assigned tables to various guests. It showed how the VIPs were seated in prominent places and, in the words of Tom Wolfe, "the very unimportant people . . . out of sight in the rear of the room. At '21,' they took no chances. They put the poor devils up on an entirely separate floor . . . These dead zones were known in the business as 'Siberia,' . . . the term spread . . . to swell restaurants all over the country. To this day unsteady souls enter such joints in a state of dread, resentment on the hair trigger, fearful lest the wardens, i.e., the maître d's, icy smiles of welcome frozen on their faces, lead them straight to the gulag."

Felker recognized people's desire to be "in," to be hip, to be the hippest, and, as one critic put it, he had the crass but revolutionary notion that you are what you buy. He made *New York* the magazine that told you what to buy. But the consumer advice—Felker called it his "secret weapon"—would not have had authority if it were not for the high quality of the New Journalism that Felker published. Ironically, the New Journalism had been pioneered by Lillian Ross, the author of that *New Yorker* piece about Pam Muffin, and by Truman Capote, whose "In Cold Blood" *The New Yorker* also published. There was a richness to this kind of journalism, but it always carried the danger of the writer's tilting the facts or actually drifting into a falsehood in order to enrich his story. An example occurred with an article in *New York* magazine by Gail Sheehy, whom Felker married after his divorce from Pamela Tiffin. Entitled "Redpants and Sugarman," the article purported to describe the life of one prostitute and her pimp, though in fact it was based on a composite of prostitutes she had interviewed.

Although *New York* was by far the most influential of the city magazines, it was not the first. That distinction belongs to *Philadelphia* magazine, founded in 1962. The city magazine movement quickly spread, in Washington taking the form of the *Washingtonian*, founded by Laughlin Phillips, son of the art collector Duncan Phillips, who established the Phillips Gallery. The *Washingtonian* was not a quick success, largely, I think, because the city in the 1960s was still operating on the economy based on the civil service salary scale. A great change would occur in the '70s with the huge expansion of lobbying in Washington; with it came an expense-account culture that could finance high-price restaurants and salaries that could pay for the more expensive housing, clothing, and everything else associated with higher incomes of the kind that had already come to New York. In the '70s, the *Washingtonian* was acquired by Philip Merrill, who was already publishing a Baltimore magazine. It was under his leadership and that of the editor he hired, Jack Limpert, that the *Washingtonian* came to reap the rewards of the capital's expanding economy.

The new class of lobbyists consisted not just of trade association offices but of new and greatly expanded law firms, primarily devoted to lobbying. And they all required more office space, which helped create a real estate boom that brought forth another new class of wealth in Washington consisting of real estate entrepreneurs. At *The Washington Post,* Ben Bradlee established the Style section, which, along with the *Washingtonian,* furnished the city with a continuing stream of advice on what was hip and what wasn't. Readers began to fear being cast out by Sally Quinn or one of the Style section's other acid-tongued (for those days) reporters.

At the same time, Bob Woodward and Carl Bernstein were endowing journalism with a glamour it had not previously enjoyed. At *The Washington Monthly* we tried to capture the change with a cover showing a photograph of Woodward gradually changing into a photograph of Robert Redford. Woodward had attended Yale; Sally Quinn, Smith; and her editor and later husband, Ben Bradlee, Harvard. They helped influence a new generation of highly educated writers to pursue careers in journalism. Reporters and editors no longer thought of themselves as blue collar, as had previous generations of journalists. They were part of the new meritocratic elite, who shared with their peers the same interest in demonstrating their good taste, which meant they were just as concerned with being hip as their readers were. A Washington writer named Diana McLellan was gifted at exposing the foibles of this new class, including the journalists. She named Ben Bradlee and Sally Quinn "the fun couple," and McLellan's column, "The Ear," became the most popular feature in the *Washington Star,* where it was originally published. In the early '80s, when the *Star* folded, she took the column to *The Washington Post,* but it proved a less hospitable environment. The newspaper's lawyers often toned down her prose, which could be tart as well as witty. McLellan was British, the daughter of an RAF officer who had married an American.

Her influence, however, was pretty much confined to Washington. Another British writer was soon to take America by storm. Her name was Tina Brown. After leaving Oxford, she joined the staff of *The Sunday Times* in London and married its editor, Harold Evans, who encouraged his staff to practice the New Journalism. She then edited the British publication *Tatler,* which was devoted to coverage of royalty and chic London with a clever, gossipy touch. Indeed, whatever her faults, she had the gift of liveliness, and in 1984 it earned her the editorship of a revived *Vanity Fair*. The magazine had been famous in the 1920s and early '30s for its coverage of glamorous society, but had faded from sight over the years. Tina Brown would make it glamorous again with a combination of well-written articles by respected writers and gossipy profiles of celebrities. She was less gifted, however, at turning a profit, and *Vanity Fair,* while becoming the talk of the town in the '80s, was not financially successful.

The feat of turning it into a money-making operation—greatly increasing its circulation and advertising pages—was performed by Graydon Carter. Carter, along with Kurt Andersen, cofounded *Spy* magazine, and had a couple of things in common with Clay Felker. Both had worked at *Time* magazine before they became editors, and both had a fascination with seating plans. The article that launched Felker on his career was the one he wrote for *Esquire* on restaurant seating plans. Carter owns two restaurants, the Waverly Inn and the Monkey Bar, and controls the seating plans at both of them, even though he is now the very successful, extremely well paid editor of a major magazine. He is also said to obsess over the seating plans at *Vanity Fair*'s two big annual parties: one held after the Oscars are awarded in Hollywood, the other after the White House correspondents' dinner in Washington.

At *Spy,* Carter displayed a gift for exploiting the anxieties of the glamour classes. They feared being named on *Spy*'s 100, a list of the "most alarming, annoying and appalling people, places and things in New York and the nation." Or being identified in the magazine, as certain figures were, as a "mummified boulevardier" or "beaver-faced mogul." *Time* magazine described *Spy* as having "a prevailing tone of backhanded derision and inside irony borrowed from Britain's *Private Eye*." *Spy* could in fact be quite clever, but from time to time drifted into nastiness, and it disdained middlebrow taste. Florsheim shoes were scorned for no other reason than that they were the shoes favored by middle-class men.

As for his political views, Carter says, "I find both parties to be appalling and okay at the same time. I find it harder for anybody as they get older to be 100 percent strongly behind one party. There's a lot more gray than when I was younger. I'm a libertarian." Libertarians are usually on the side of the angels when it comes to issues such as human rights and sexual and racial equality, but they tend to be far less interested in economic equality.

At *Vanity Fair,* Carter has succeeded in selling an incredibly diverse mix of advertising. Many of his ads come from high-end retailers such as Gucci, Rolex, Armani, Dior, Prada, and Cartier. But he also attracts ads for television shows and the kind of skin care and makeup products that can be bought at the corner drugstore. An indication of the mix that he has succeeded in putting together is the October 2013 issue of the magazine, which begins with four pages devoted to Ralph Lauren and ends with four pages given over to the coming NBC season.

The editorial contents of the same issue are also a fascinating mix. There is a combination of celebrities and respected writers doing a decade-by-decade history of the past hundred years: Bill Maher, Dave Eggers, Kurt Andersen (Carter's partner from *Spy* magazine), Jan Morris, Daniel Okrent, Laura Hillenbrand, A. Scott Berg, Julian Fellowes, and Lorne Michaels. The entertainment world is covered in articles about Stephen King and Roman Polanski. (The blurb for the latter reads, "Thirty-five years after Roman Polanski pleaded guilty to sex with a minor . . . he's still in the legal limbo of one of California's longest-running court cases. The Oscar-winning director discusses his crime, his punishment, and his art.") There's also a heavy dose of royalty. One article, entitled "King and Controversy," is about Spain's Juan Carlos. ("The king's inner circle talks about his blonde and his blunders.") And "Curious About George" concerns the new son of Britain's Prince William and the duchess of Cambridge. ("The author of a new Kate Middleton biography delivers a behind-the-scenes look at H.R.H. George Alexander Louis's first weeks.") My favorite, though, is "The Raj Duet," which features "the daughters of Britain's last viceroy, Louis Earl Mountbatten of Burma. . . . Lady Pamela Hicks and her sister the countess knew extreme privilege and epic tragedy." Hicks's memoir describes experiences of a lifetime and friendships with Gandhi, Nehru, and the queen. The featured pullout quote from the article is, "You really had to mind your p's and q's when Queen Mary was around." Carter's fascination with royalty seemed to have hit a new height when he hired the duchess of Cambridge's sister, Pippa Middleton, as a columnist, only to be exceeded by the summer 2016 issue dominated by fawning articles about the queen and the royal family accompanied by lush, glamorizing photographs of them by Annie Leibovitz.

What Carter sells is the secret of being in, whether you live in London or, say, San Francisco, a city for which the October issue offers the keys to success in an article entitled "Bluebloods and Billionaires." The blurb reads, "Many of Silicon Valley's elite have moved into Pacific Heights, learning the customs of San Francisco's exclusive enclave. But on one delicate issue, high tech and high society just don't see eye to eye." Further guides to being in are furnished by reports from the worlds of dance—a piece on choreographed romance about the New York Ballet's Tiler Peck and Robert Fairchild—and of art, in a piece entitled "Balthus's Last Muse" describing shows at the Metropolitan Museum of Art and the Gagosian Gallery. There is also the latest information on hot hotels, fashion, and beauty trends from nail colors through "red-carpet hair." Carter also has a feeling for the hip-serious celebrity, so the October issue features an article about Julian Assange, the founder of WikiLeaks.

By 2002, when he was profiled in the British publication *The Observer,* Carter was successful enough to be called the "now legendary editor of the most influential glossy magazine on the planet. Since he took over from Tina Brown, *Vanity Fair*'s sales have soared and its unique mix of pieces has made it popular with intellectuals, celebrities and politicians."

Clay Felker and Graydon Carter were bookends to the consumer chic that reigned from the late 1960s through at least the first decade of the new century. They shared a gift for putting up an impressive front. Carter wore bespoke suits from Anderson & Sheppard in London and custom-tailored shirts. Tom Wolfe's description of Clay Felker's attire when he first met him: "shirt (Turnbull & Asser, Jermyn Street, London), the suit (Huntsman of Savile Row, London), the shoes (John Lobb, also of Jermyn Street, London), as well as the accent," which Wolfe described as the most fashionable accent in America at the time. One of the mysteries of Felker's self-invention is how he acquired that accent, because it was not the one to which his hometown of Webster Grove, Missouri, was accustomed.

He had a duplex apartment on East Fifty-seventh Street in which "The living room was a 25-by-25-foot grand salon with a two-story, 25-foot-high ceiling and two huge House of Parliament–scale windows, overlooking 57th Street, each 22 feet high and eight feet wide, divided into colossal panes of glass by muntins as thick as your wrist," Wolfe wrote.

> There was a vast fireplace of the sort writers searching for adjectives always call baronial. Fourteen status seekers could sit at the same time on the needlepoint-upholstered fender that went around it, supported by gleaming brass columns. When you arrived *chez* Felker and walked out of the elevator, you found yourself on a balcony big as a lobby overlooking the meticulously conspicuous consumption below. Guests descended to the salon down a staircase that made the Paris Opera's look like my old front stoop. Standing on the gigantic Aubusson rug at the foot of the stairs to welcome you, on a good night, would be Felker's wife, a 20-year-old movie actress named Pamela Tiffin. . . . She was gorgeous.

There is something of the same flavor to a description by *The Observer*'s Gaby Wood of a visit to the *Vanity Fair* office that preceded their move to the more elegant quarters they now occupy on Wall Street:

> You arrive at a huge building on the corner of Times Square, as
> if strolling through the set of *The Sweet Smell of Success*. The
> lift reaches the twenty-second floor and opens onto a corridor
> apparently designed by Stanley Kubrick—blinding white, with
> gargantuan, floor to ceiling black letters at either end spelling
> VANITY FAIR. You would have no idea which way to turn
> were it not for a white-haired woman at a white desk who asks
> you to sit down on a white leather bench while you're waiting.
> If you happen to lean back against the wall, it gives: the corridor
> is upholstered in thick white fabric. . . .
>
> Carter's office is heralded by a huge American flag, and
> looks like a shot from *The Fountainhead* come to life. An enor-
> mous corner of glass reveals the city in an almost mythical per-
> spective. Carter's desk is in front of it, looking in. When he is on
> the phone, he swivels round and looks at the world—his world:
> Manhattan, at his feet.

And, of course, Felker and Carter had that shared interest in seating plans. Carter's interest in that area was probably the more intense. *The New York Times* Styles section, in an article by Allen Salkin, describes how Carter goes about putting together the seating plans for his two restaurants. At around four P.M. emails are sent to Jonathan Kelly, an assistant to Carter who "knows his boss's mind so well that Mr. Carter trusts him to rough out the seating plans for the Waverly Inn and the Monkey Bar." Around four-thirty Kelly heads into Mr. Carter's office to complete the seating charts. Carter then spends roughly twenty minutes each day going over the charts, instructing Kelly on where the seating plan should be changed.

But the restaurants are small potatoes compared with the *Vanity Fair* Academy Awards party. Carter is said to devote most of the six weeks preceding the party to the seating plan for the event. "Fifteen thousand people call Graydon Carter's office begging to be invited," according to Toby Young, a young British journalist Carter hired to write for *Vanity Fair*. They even offer bribes to be included among the guests. One is reported to have offered $300,000. All this striving has made the *Vanity Fair* party *the* event for Hollywood on the night of the awards and has provided an amazing amount of publicity for the magazine. The annual Hollywood issue is the most lucrative of the year in terms of advertising. But Young thinks the party is even more important than that to Carter.

He writes that Carter once told him: "Two kinds of people read *Vanity Fair*. Trailer park white trash and everyone who matters." Of course, it's the "everyone who matters" that matters to Graydon Carter. The big party, Young writes, gives Carter "leverage over some of the biggest players in the media-industrial complex. Graydon hasn't created this annual institution to make the job of editing the magazine easier; he edits the magazine so he can throw parties like this."

After leaving *Vanity Fair,* Young wrote a book about the experience, *How to Lose Friends and Alienate People*. In what may well be its most revealing anecdote, he describes how Carter cautioned him:

> You think you've arrived, doncha? I hate to break it to you, but you're only in the first room. . . . It's not nothing—don't get me wrong—but it's not that great either. Believe me, there are plenty of people in this town who got to the first room and then didn't get any further. After a year or so, maybe longer, you'll discover a secret doorway at the back of the first room that leads to the second room. In time, if you're lucky, you'll discover a doorway in the back of the second room that leads to the third. There are seven rooms in total, and you're in the first. Doncha forget it.

The secret to the success of publications such as *New York* and *Vanity Fair* has been their ability to convince their readers that those seven rooms exist, that the reader must always be insecure about whether he's progressed beyond the first room, or has made it from the second to the third and so on. Indeed, it could be said that the entire stable of publications owned by Si Newhouse, including *Vogue, The New Yorker, Architectural Digest, GQ,* and, of course, *Vanity Fair,* all are essentially selling the information that will get you from one of those rooms to another and then another.

# CHAPTER 6

# Main Street Goes Wall Street

As 1970 began, Louis Rukeyser was not a name that was widely known. A former Baltimore *Sun* reporter, he was serving as an economics correspondent for ABC News. When he launched a television show of financial advice called *Wall Street Week*, it was carried by only thirteen stations of the Eastern Educational Television Network.

Ralph Nader, on the other hand, had already become what a cover story in *Time* magazine called "The Lonely Hero" and America's "toughest customer," hailed for his dedication and modest living (he dwelt in an $80-a-month apartment and wore threadbare suits and well-scuffed shoes). He had attracted scores of the brightest young people in America to his side with his crusade for product safety and consumer rights. He had already forced General Motors to withdraw the Corvair, a car that he had exposed in his book *Unsafe at Any Speed,* and was credited with having brought about the enactment of five different health and safety laws. *Time* described him as having "shown that one persistent man can actually do something about the forces that badger him—that he can indeed even shake and change Big Business, Big Labor and even Bigger Government." The article was but one of many major pieces praising Nader for all he had done for the consumer to protect public health and safety. For the years 1970–75, *The New York Times* index shows 140 entries for Ralph Nader. But by 1980–85, the number was down to 40, and in the next five years it was down to just seven.

Meanwhile, Louis Rukeyser's fame was growing. By the early 1980s, *Wall Street Week* was on more than three hundred stations. It had become the most popular show on public broadcasting, one featured in its fund-raising efforts. It was, in fact, so popular that it spawned new television networks devoted entirely to financial news, beginning with the Financial News Network and culminating in the one that proved to be most popular: CNBC. Apparently a good many people who had been attracted to a lonely crusader against corporate malfeasance were now seeking to find out how they could maximize their share of the profits of those corporations. In 1969 the Harvard Law School newspaper had called Nader "the most outstanding man ever to receive a degree from this institution." Of the thirty-nine Harvard Law Review editors in the class of 1970, none intended to join a Wall Street law firm. By the early '80s the situation was dramatically different: Most of the editors were planning to take positions with Wall Street or large corporate law firms.

In a curious way, however, *Wall Street Week*'s popularity was based in part on an appeal to Nader-like sentiment, in that it was concerned with advancing consumer rights: the rights of the Wall Street consumer, which is to say the individual stockholder. As the influence of *Wall Street Week* grew, so did the emphasis the financial press gave to shareholder value as a measure of corporate success and fairness. And that emphasis, as we shall later see, was not a total blessing.

*Wall Street Week* gave its viewers tips on what stocks to buy and sell—mostly buy. It also explained how the stock market worked, and did so in easily understandable ways that made it possible for neophytes to feel that they were becoming insiders. The show would begin with Rukeyser reciting, in a lighthearted, friendly way, the financial news of the week. Then there would usually be four panelists sitting at a table, each of whom would offer tips on which stocks to buy. The panelists, largely unknown at the time and drawn from the Baltimore financial community—the show was televised from the Baltimore suburb of Owings Mills—included Frank Cappiello, Carter Randall, Mary Farrell, Robert Nurock, and Gail Dudack. In the show's first decade they became names that any regular viewer could easily recite. There was also a weekly guest, and as the show grew in popularity, that slot came to be occupied by ever more prominent members of the financial community, among them Peter Lynch, the guru of the Magellan fund, the most successful mutual fund of that time. The guests were escorted onto the set by an attractive mystery woman (her name was never given) clad in an evening gown and apparently having no other role in the show. The guest slot became so desirable that when one Wall Streeter was asked what his colleagues would do to appear on the show, he answered that it could be spelled with four letters: K-I-L-L.

By 1987, *Wall Street Week* was so influential that it was credited with helping quell the panic after a precipitous 500-point drop in the market in October of that year. It was a significant contributor to the stock market boom that began in 1982 and continued through occasional hiccups to 2007, only to be briefly interrupted before taking off again in 2010. It inspired many of his millions of viewers to make their first hesitant call to a stockbroker and buy a few shares of a stock that had been recommended by one of the panelists the previous week. In fact, Wall Street sharpies did the best they could to figure out which stocks panelists might recommend so they could buy low before the Friday night show and sell high on the following Monday.

It also seems reasonable to say that no one did more than Louis Rukeyser to encourage the view that what's good for Wall Street is good for America. Indeed, it is hard to remember an episode of that program that focused on the sins of Wall Street. Rukeyser was a Republican and a firm believer in Reaganomics. His distaste for taxes extended to advocacy of a zero levy on capital gains. *Wall*

*Street Week*'s assumption that whatever increased shareholder value was good contributed mightily to public indifference to the cost to workers of firms' closing plans, shedding employees, and suppressing wages, all in the name of increasing shareholder value.

*Wall Street Week* turned out to be a perfect example of America's growing interest in making money. One of the more amusing, or appalling, signs of this interest came from the world of espionage. In the Roosevelt era, spies such as the Rosenbergs and Alger Hiss did it because of their commitment to an ideology. In the 1980s and '90s, the two spies who did the most damage, Aldrich Ames in the CIA and Robert Hansen in the FBI, both did it for the money.

In Washington, D.C., the change was particularly marked among those who, in the 1960s, had seemed devoted to lives of service to liberal causes but who, by the 1980s, had become devoted to making money. Some examples:

In 1968, Fred Dutton, a California lawyer, was running Robert Kennedy's presidential campaign, one of the more idealistic of modern times. Before that he worked for the liberal California governor Pat Brown and then in John F. Kennedy's administration as secretary of the cabinet and later assistant secretary of state for congressional relations.

Harry McPherson, a Texan, had come to Washington in 1956 to serve on the Senate staff of Lyndon Johnson and later worked for Johnson in the White House, where he was known to Washington insiders as one of the more liberal members of the staff. He not only supported Johnson's advocacy for civil rights but tried to moderate the president's hawkishness on Vietnam.

Anne Wexler, having become active in Connecticut politics working for an antiwar congressional candidate, got involved in the 1968 antiwar candidacy of Eugene McCarthy and was selected as a delegate to the Democratic National Convention, where she served on the rules committee and wrote a minority report that ultimately led to the adoption of proposed party rules greatly increasing the influence of women and minorities in the selection of candidates and emphasizing the role of primary elections over party bosses in picking nominees. Those proposed rules, which were only a minority position in 1968, became (through the McGovern Commission, one of whose members was Fred Dutton) the actual rules of the party for 1972. Wexler, in 1970, ran another antiwar campaign, for Joseph Duffey, who was seeking a U.S. Senate seat from Connecticut. Duffey, who would later become Wexler's husband, won the Democratic nomination but lost in the general election.

Wexler moved in and out of Washington in those years, working in the antiwar movement. In 1971 she took a job with the public interest group Common Cause. That year *The Washington Monthly* was putting on a conference on corporate responsibility; we had arranged for a combination of liberal reformers and corporate spokesmen to appear. At the last moment, about a week before the conference, we heard rumors that the liberal participants were being urged to withdraw because they would be "co-opted" by the corporations, or would appear to be if they attended. So, anxious to keep our liberal speakers, we dispatched Taylor Branch and John Rothschild, who were then young editors, to meet with a group of the liberals who were threatening us with the label of co-opters. Among them was Anne Wexler. Ultimately Branch and Rothschild were able to use their own liberal antiwar credentials to win over the group so that our liberal speakers did appear. But I would remember that episode in terms of Anne's later career choices.

Vernon Jordan in 1971 had just become president of the United Negro College Fund, having spent the 1960s working in the field of civil rights. He was with the Atlanta law firm that desegregated the University of Georgia, and he personally escorted Charlayne Hunter, the first black woman student there, to the university's admissions office. By 1981, he was a Washington lobbyist, as were McPherson, Dutton, and Wexler.

I met them all during my years in Washington, and can attest that each was a charmer. You could understand why they became such effective lobbyists, and how their example helped to attract so many others to the field of lobbying. They were so well liked by the media that reporters and editors were reluctant to criticize them. At the *Monthly,* we ran articles at one time or another that were critical of Wexler and McPherson, but it was painful for me to do it because I liked them so much.

The first to go to the lobbying world was Harry McPherson, who, after Lyndon Johnson left office in January 1969, joined the law firm that would become Verner, Liipfert, Bernhard, McPherson and Hand. In the late 1990s the firm represented tobacco companies in the negotiations that led to the settlement of the lawsuits brought by various state attorneys general. His firm's fee was reported by the *National Journal* to be $200,000 a month. McPherson justified his representation of the tobacco companies by saying, "We agreed to do it because we thought it was in the public interest and, second, because it was very handsomely compensated work."

But it is hard to see how the public interest could have been best served if the legal duty of Harry McPherson and his talented partners was to get the best possible deal for the tobacco companies. And that was indeed their legal duty as counsel to the companies. McPherson's justification for his work was employed by many of my friends who became lobbyists. They really did think of themselves as still trying to serve the public interest, and I think they really did try. Unfortunately, their idea of the public interest was required to coincide in just about every case with their clients' best interests.

Fred Dutton was the next to go. He said that for him, the light had gone out when Bobby Kennedy was killed. By 1971 he was representing the Mobil oil company, and by 1975 he was a lawyer for Saudi Arabia. As a lobbyist he excelled in the skill that Clark Clifford so conspicuously displayed: flattery. Consider this letter to a top official of the oil cartel Aramco. Dutton expressed his admiration for the Saudi oil minister, "who I sense is about as fascinating an individual as John F. Kennedy, whom I came to think while his Secretary of the Cabinet was about the most interesting political figure (even with his faults) I would ever come to know." As Dutton had every reason to suspect it would be, the letter was passed on to the oil minister himself, and soon after Dutton was awarded the lobbying contract.

Dutton's human relations skills were exercised not only on American and foreign officials but, perhaps even more, on members of the Washington media, whom he cultivated at frequent dinner parties at his homes in Northwest Washington and on Martha's Vineyard. As a result, he was rarely criticized in the media, even though he represented a government that was known for its stifling of free speech and women's rights, its beheadings and stonings, and its outright encouragement and subsidization of Wahhabism, a theology that has become one of the foundations of Islamic extremism. What is ironic about this is Dutton's background as an associate of Robert Kennedy who had been part of RFK's embrace of the rights of Native Americans and Mexican immigrant farm workers, and as a member of the board of regents at the University of California, where he had lent the most sympathetic ear to the students in Berkeley's Free Speech Movement.

I once had lunch with Dutton, who knew enough about me to know that I would be suspicious about his relationship with Saudi Arabia and that I also shared his admiration for Robert Kennedy and felt that his assassination had been a tragedy for American liberalism. He explained one reason why he may have developed an interest in furthering understanding between Arab and American societies. In June 1968, on the Saturday before Robert Kennedy was assassinated, he was debating Eugene McCarthy. In the course of the debate, Kennedy made a remark that struck a number of people, including me, as obviously courting the Jewish vote in California. Dutton thought that it may have influenced the Palestinian Sirhan Sirhan's decision to kill Kennedy. The story didn't convince me that Fred was justified in representing Saudi Arabia, but he had chosen an argument that showed a real understanding of me. It helps explain why he had such great success as a lobbyist.

Vernon Jordan and Anne Wexler took longer to become lobbyists, but looking at their history in the 1970s, one can see how they developed the connections that smoothed the way for their entrance into the field in 1981. With Jordan, it was, first, his position as head of the UNCF and then, later, as head of the National Urban League. The Urban League, as the most moderate of the civil rights organizations, was a favorite of big business. Jordan, in seeking funds for black colleges and then for the Urban League, was meeting one corporate leader after another, making contacts that were to serve him well when he turned to lobbying and began taking on clients.

Wexler, in 1976, worked on Jimmy Carter's presidential campaign and became so influential she was named to his transition team, where she suggested Juanita Kreps for secretary of commerce. Kreps, in turn, made Wexler undersecretary of commerce—a job that, like those of Vernon Jordan, was rich in its possibilities for making connections in the business community. In 1978, Carter brought her onto the White House staff, where she was put in charge of building relationships with the private sector, a job that had even more potential for enriching her Rolodex.

The day after Carter left office in 1981, Wexler opened her lobbying office. Apparently her earlier fears of being co-opted by corporations had been allayed. She was soon representing clients such as New England Electric System, General Motors, and Aetna Life and Casualty, not to mention the National Association of Business Political Action Committees. She was shrewd enough to realize that it would help if she had access to Republicans as well as Democrats. One of her early partners was Nancy Clark Reynolds, who happened to be a close friend of Nancy Reagan. Later she would add Craig Fuller, who had served as Vice President George H. W. Bush's chief of staff, and a former influential Republican congressman, Robert Smith Walker of Pennsylvania.

One of Wexler's early assignments illustrated the compromises she would have to make with her liberal beliefs. She represented a pipeline company that had persuaded Congress to authorize the building of a natural gas pipeline, with a promise by the company that the cost would not be passed on to consumers. Then the company decided it wanted to pass the costs along after all, and, with Wexler's help, persuaded Congress to let it do so.

What happened in the country that changed all of these people during the transition from the late 1960s to the early '80s? One factor, the importance of which cannot be overestimated, was simply the end of the Vietnam War. With it ended one of the great causes that drew people to the liberal banner. Moreover, in 1970 a lottery was established for the military draft, which reduced the pressure on a good many young men and dampened their motivation for opposing the war and the administration. In 1972, draft calls were ended, and the following year saw the withdrawal of all U.S. forces from South Vietnam, whose government fell to the North Vietnamese in 1975.

Some of the self-righteousness that had characterized many of the young antiwar activists was drained away in 1975. During the collapse of the South Vietnamese army and the evacuation of Americans that followed, we left behind many South Vietnamese who did not want to live under Communism. This was contrary to a conviction that had been firmly held by the left: that the Vietcong and North Vietnamese regime enjoyed the support of practically the entire country with the exception of a few corrupt officials in Saigon. In fact, hundreds of thousands of South Vietnamese were so desperate not to live under the Communists that they escaped by any means possible, often on boats so rickety that many sank in the South China Sea. Then, too, there was the gradual facing of the fact—as Jim Fallows did—that they had evaded service only to leave it to the less privileged to do the dying. This led before long to many opponents of the war supporting the construction of the Vietnam Memorial in Washington. In 1976, activists who had been waving the banner of North Vietnam at antiwar rallies waved the Stars and Stripes in celebration of their country's bicentennial. Their new patriotism, however, did not include any willingness on the part of the educated elite to do military service. Although the country appeared to be united in patriotism, it was still divided in regard to who was willing to serve and who wasn't.

Consumerism and inflation also influenced the huge changes in culture during the 1970s. Because of inflation and, later, high interest rates, people felt they needed to make more money. Moderate inflation was a constant problem in the 1970s, but two severe spikes were especially harmful. The first came in 1973, when the Organization of Petroleum Exporting Countries, angered by U.S. support for Israel in the Yom Kippur War, declared an embargo on oil shipments to the United States. At the time oil was a much more important factor in the U.S. economy than it is now, and the jump in prices that resulted from the embargo quickly spread throughout the economy, boosting inflation to double digits. Another round of oil-related inflation came in 1979 with the Iranian revolution that overthrew the shah. The sudden rise in prices led to long lines at gas stations and had immense consequences for the economy, driving many small businesses and gas station owners out of business.

Double-digit inflation lasted through 1982, and when it was finally ended, the remedy caused problems of its own. Paul Volcker, who had been installed as head of the Federal Reserve, decided that the best way to deal with it was to wring inflation out of the economy with high interest rates. The result was double-digit interest rates on top of double-digit inflation. Thus, you paid an inflated price for your house and inflated interest on the money to buy it. The average cost of a new house in 1970 almost tripled by 1980. The Consumer Price Index also grew dramatically, from 37.8 at the beginning of 1970 to 90 in 1981. In Washington, D.C., new-house prices increased more in the '70s than in any other decade in the century. On top of that came mortgages with interest rates of 12, 13, 14 percent, and more. (I bought a car in 1982 with a loan requiring 18 percent interest.) So there was a realistic need for people to make more money.

What was the role of consumerism in these developments? Remember that the Nader movement, because of its interest in quality for consumers, had, as we have seen, the unintended consequence of causing people to want things that cost more. The best car, the best wine, the best restaurants were more expensive—sometimes a lot more expensive. Over and over, elite members of society were making choices that involved a lot of money—borrowed if need be. Use of credit cards increased dramatically during the 1970s. In Washington, D.C., the *Washingtonian*'s circulation increased from 17,000 in 1970 to 80,000 in 1980. One article noted that in the '60s Washington had been a "culinary backwater," but by 1978 a typical issue of the magazine devoted fourteen pages to food and wine, including an article on the "blue chips of Bordeaux." The culinary backwater was now worthy of a cover story on "the 50 finest" restaurants, "from matchbooks to maître d's." When I came to Washington in 1961, there were hardly fifty restaurants in all. One ad the *Washingtonian* ran for itself said a lot about what has happened to Washington since then: "The nation's capital is tops when it comes to income growth and potential sales. Washington's upscale market is an intelligent and urbane group of individuals, people who are politically as well as culturally oriented. This affluent market is ready to buy the very best that life has to offer: travel, entertainment, wining and dining, fashions, decorating, investments." As for another measure of wealth and taste, an article in the magazine noted that real estate prices appeared headed for "stratospheric heights."

A Washington that wanted to think of itself as "intelligent and urbane" with people who are affluent enough to "buy the very best" was to become more and more preoccupied with money and how to get it, and in doing so would begin to separate itself from the average American. In 1980, if Washingtonians weren't watching *Wall Street Week,* they were glued to the television watching *Dallas,* which dealt with the life of a rich Texas family. The city of Dallas was a pioneer in the art of conspicuous consumption. In 1976 the city constructed the first football stadium with climate-controlled luxury suites that were available only to rich individuals or corporations. Football, a game where fans once submitted themselves to the same weather conditions—if one person suffered wet, cold, or heat, so did everybody else in the stadium—now had separate climates for those who could pay the high prices required to separate themselves from the crowd. Soon the luxury boxes were showing up in baseball, basketball, and hockey stadiums all over the country, serving as obvious examples of the class divide that was steadily increasing.

CHAPTER 7

★

# The Issues That Divide Us

## A. Race, Religion, and Crime

The black power movement that emerged in the late 1960s was a totally justified expression of anger at the outrages of slavery, segregation, and all the other mistreatment of blacks by the white world. When Ta-Nehisi Coates argues that America's blacks deserve reparations, thoughtful whites have to concede that he makes a powerful case. But as many of us have learned in our personal lives, the fact that an expression of anger may be justified does not necessarily mean that it is guaranteed to produce the desired reaction. Unfortunately, the angry assertion of black power and the threat of violence that sometimes accompanied it, whether implied or stated openly, played into the hands of the Nixon-Reagan-Atwater-Ailes strategy that began developing in 1968 and was intended to exploit white fear of black violence.

That fear had long been an undercurrent in white society. The emphasis on nonviolence by Martin Luther King, Jr., and other traditional civil rights leaders was effective because it helped allay these fears. But beginning with the riots in the Watts neighborhood of Los Angeles in 1965, and continuing with the Detroit riots of 1967 and in Washington, D.C., the following year, the fear came back, and it came back strong. Stokely Carmichael throwing a brick through the window of a Washington drugstore represented a shocking new direction for the civil rights struggle. Here was a man who had stood at the side of Martin Luther King, Jr., but was now turning to violence. It is worth mentioning here that a new sense of assertiveness was also coming into play in other movements for change, especially for women's rights. It was evident in the Jewish community, as well, where rising consciousness of the Holocaust horrors created a new kind of self-assertion, as reflected in the popular 1960 movie *Exodus* about the founding of the state of Israel.

But it was the edge of violence in the black power movement that set it apart from the others and aroused the fears of white people. "If America don't come around, we're gonna burn it down," proclaimed H. Rap Brown, who in 1967 had become the new head of the Student Nonviolent Coordinating Committee. Black Panthers actually invaded the California legislature, armed with guns and wearing bandoliers across their chests. Then came two efforts to right the wrongs of the past that served to alienate many whites even more, particularly working-class people. One was forced busing for school integration. The other was affirmative action. Both seemed justified, but nonetheless the anxieties stirred by the two developments seemed almost designed to advance the cause of those who wanted to stir up racial antagonism. (Imagine yourself as a working-class parent of a child who has been bused out of a better school in his neighborhood, a school that gave his son a better chance, to one where his prospects would not be as good. Imagine having your daughter denied admission to the college of her choice because of affirmative action.) Added to these factors was the growth of welfare in the 1960s and early '70s, with the number of recipients increasing threefold. It lent some credence to Ronald Reagan's picture of "welfare queens." There was a widespread impression that practically all welfare recipients were black. That wasn't true, but unfortunately black women dominated demonstrations staged by the National Welfare Rights Organization in 1970–71.

Thanks to Lyndon Johnson's determination to see it imple-
mented, the Voting Rights Act quickly resulted in the registration of
black voters throughout the South, and led to the election of blacks
to a large number of public offices. But unfortunately it also encouraged gerrymandering to create safe black seats in Congress. This
technique was noted by Republicans, who turned it into a fine art,
isolating blacks and creating more congressional districts that
whites could control, particularly conservative whites. Black members of Congress tended to go along with this development because
they wanted to protect black seats, and the black power movement
too often supported them, even though gerrymandering wasn't in
their long-term interest.

The old all-white juries of the American South that put black
men in jail regardless of innocence or guilt found echoes in black
juries that freed black defendants without regard to the evidence of
guilt. My wife served on one such jury in Washington, D.C. Perhaps
the most spectacular example of it was the O. J. Simpson trial in the
mid-1990s in Los Angeles, where a mostly black jury's verdict of
not guilty, despite DNA and other incontrovertible evidence, was
viewed as an outrage by everyone but the black community.

Indeed, the Simpson verdict could be understood only if you
knew that just three years before, in the Los Angeles suburb of Simi
Valley, a white jury found white policemen not guilty of beating a
black man named Rodney King, even though videotape clearly
showed they had administered a beating. If the Simpson trial was
influenced by the black power movement, the Rodney King trial
was influenced by the 1988 Willie Horton ads and similar Republican tactics. The problem that emerged in the late 1960s and early
'70s was a new kind of racial feeling in the country, one that was
not expressed in openly racist terms by whites but was nevertheless
felt. For blacks, anger that may previously have been only felt was
now being openly expressed to whites.

The change in feeling is illustrated by two experiences my wife
had while working in political campaigns. In 1960 I was running

the Kennedy presidential campaign in my county and running for a seat in the state legislature at the same time. Because I was so busy with the Kennedy campaign, my wife did a lot of my campaigning for the legislature. Among the places she visited was an all-black area of Charleston, where she was welcomed in almost every home and treated with great courtesy. I got my highest vote totals there of all the precincts in the county. I suspect that from 1970 on she would not have encountered as much courtesy and that there would have been some doors slammed in her face. By 2008, when she went back to West Virginia to campaign for a black man, she was heckled by whites, one even threatened to sic his dog on her—an incredible change for a state where in 1960 I had proudly pointed out to John Kennedy that the student population of West Virginia State College consisted of equal numbers of peacefully coexisting blacks and whites.

In the mid-1970s hope emerged of overcoming the revival of racial animosity brought about by Nixon's coded racism and fueled by the excesses of the black power movement. Jimmy Carter campaigned as a representative of the New South, a movement of moderate progressives who opposed racism. Another member of this movement was the young Bill Clinton, who managed Carter's campaign in Arkansas.

When Carter was inaugurated as governor of Georgia in 1971, replacing the outright segregationist Lester Maddox, Carter declared, "I say to you quite frankly that the time for racial discrimination is over." Carter was a born-again Southern Baptist who, like Martin Luther King, Jr., appealed to the Christian values he had in common with most—indeed, nearly all—white southerners. But at the same time, he appealed to southerners' pride. He was a graduate of the U.S. Naval Academy who had risen to command a nuclear submarine before returning to Georgia to take over his father's peanut farm and business. Then he had served as governor of Georgia, and was successful enough to have appeared on the cover of *Time*. Carter managed to turn his appeal to pride in the New South to victory in the 1976 presidential election. He carried ten of the eleven states of the old Confederacy, the first Democrat to do so since Franklin D. Roosevelt in 1944. He also carried the border states of Missouri, Kentucky, and West Virginia, the last of which produced his third-highest majority of all the states.

Although Carter's subsequent history would show him to be the most committed to good causes of all the presidents who have followed him, and definitely the least interested in amassing big bucks, he was unable to inspire the American people as president. A dull speaker who was far too detail oriented, he often failed to convey the big picture. But his presidency was not without accomplishments, the most notable being the Camp David Accords, which brought peace between Egypt and Israel. Still, his countrymen blamed him for failing to quell inflation, which was probably the most persistent and politically damaging problem of the 1970s. Then came his inability to free American hostages taken by Iranian revolutionaries in the fall of 1979, climaxed by the botched attempt to rescue them in the operation known as Desert One in the spring of 1980. By the end of his term, Carter was no longer a source of pride for the New South; indeed, it could be said that he was disrespected by much of the country, including the South and the border states that were once such a strong part of his coalition.

All of this, however, cannot erase the significance of his 1976 accomplishment in winning the election as a son of the New South. In a way, it reminds me of West Virginia's 1960 triumph over anti-Catholic sentiment in voting for John F. Kennedy. Both demonstrated that an appeal to people's pride could actually alter their behavior. Bill Clinton, having learned the strategy from managing Carter's Arkansas campaign, replicated it in his own run for the presidency in 1992. In that election, Clinton carried Georgia, Florida, Tennessee, and Arkansas in the old Confederacy and the border states of Kentucky, West Virginia, and Missouri. No Democrat has matched that since. One reason why Clinton's southern successes were considerably more modest than Carter's was that the coded racism of Nixon's time had returned to Republican politics in full force from Reagan's 1980 campaign on.

The most dangerous thing about the new racism was that it was hidden—strongly felt by people, white men in particular, who could be fans of black entertainers and athletes and never express overt racism, never use the n-word, but who were nonetheless convinced that far too many blacks were freeloaders or criminals. If they had not been Republicans before, they increasingly tended to join the Republicans, whom they regarded as taking a much harder line on welfare and crime than the Democrats. Tendencies toward conservatism were strengthened by the economic developments of the '70s—inflation, high interest rates—by fear of crime, which did increase; by the Supreme Court's decision in *Roe v. Wade* legalizing abortion; and by their reaction to the sexual revolution and the growing use of illicit drugs. There was a tilt toward selfishness in a society that, from the 1930s all the way into the early '60s, had tended toward the sharing of benefits and burdens, and a willingness to do one's part in helping the national community—from paying the necessary taxes to serving in the military.

Jimmy Carter's best address to the country, made in the summer of 1979, came to be known as the "malaise" speech, although that word did not appear in the speech. He warned of the nation's drift toward selfishness and self-absorption, a phenomenon that he was one of the few political leaders to recognize. He then called for voluntary sacrifice to fight inflation by driving less, adjusting thermostats, and taking other simple steps to conserve energy. In the end, the speech fell on deaf ears, testimony to the fact that the country as a whole was no longer much interested in sharing the burdens. This became more obvious in the 1980 campaign when Ronald Reagan sought to inspire voters with his promise to cut their taxes. Selfishness and self-absorption ("What's in it for me?") have always been part of America. It's just that from the 1970s on they became ever more widespread, to the point where they were held by a clear majority.

FOR PEOPLE TO change as much as they did in the years beginning back then, they needed a philosophical basis and justification for what they were doing—actually what they were doing for themselves as opposed to what they were doing for the rest of the society. This came in the form of a revival of conservative thought and the growing influence of the evangelical movement on American Christianity. Evangelicalism dominated Christianity from the 1970s on. It emphasizes what Jesus can do for you—personal salvation—not what you can do for Jesus. FDR's Christianity, with its call to help our fellow man, was largely forgotten, along with his frequent references to driving the money changers from the temple. Indeed, the money changers and moneymakers are now admired.

Two of the most prominent evangelicals of the 1970s were Pat Robertson and Jerry Falwell. Falwell founded an organization called the Moral Majority, and Robertson created the Christian Broadcast Network, predecessor of the ABC Family Channel. Both men were strong Republicans. In 1988 Robertson ran for the Republican nomination for president, and in the Iowa caucuses he outpolled George H. W. Bush. Falwell became so dedicated in his opposition to Democrats that in 1994 he distributed a documentary called *The Clinton Chronicles: An Investigation into the Alleged Criminal Activities of Bill Clinton*. It connected the president of the United States to a murder conspiracy that involved Ron Brown, the chairman of the Democratic National Committee; James McDougal, who had been involved in the Whitewater real estate venture with Clinton; and Vince Foster, who had been Clinton's deputy White House counsel and a law partner of Hillary Clinton. When Ellen DeGeneres came out as a lesbian, Falwell called her "Ellen DeGenerate."

The revival of conservative thought that had begun with Friedrich Hayek, William F. Buckley, Jr., and Barry Goldwater was accompanied in the mid-1960s by the development of a new ideology called neoconservatism. Its main spokesmen were Irving Kristol, editor of *The Public Interest,* and Norman Podhoretz, editor of *Commentary.* Kristol described neoconservatives as liberals who have been "mugged by reality." The expression reveals much about the movement. It began in 1965, the year of the riots in the Watts area of Los Angeles, which were followed soon after by the riots in Detroit in 1967 and Washington, D.C., in 1968. These all had the effect of stirring white fear, which was heightened even more by the increase in black crime that followed in the late '60s and into the '70s. None of these neoconservatives were overt racists. Nonetheless, there was a hint of racism, or at least a fear of blacks, conveyed by the word "mugged."

In the late '70s and early '80s I was sometimes suspected of being a neoconservative, enough so that I was invited to a few of their conferences. At one of them, a man who later became the head of a neocon think tank came up to me after a discussion of social problems and said, "It's too bad we can't talk about the real problem," with a wink, wink, nudge, nudge that made it clear to me he was talking about blacks. The first article to gain national attention for the group was one by Daniel Patrick Moynihan on the disintegration of the black family. Moynihan would mostly remain in the liberal camp, but in general, neoconservatives, including Kristol and Podhoretz, gradually became more and more conservative.

At first their emphasis was largely on social issues such as crime, the subject of an influential article by James Q. Wilson. But more and more in the '70s their emphasis turned to anti-communism and a strong pro-Israel stance. Podhoretz, for instance, tended to see any enemies of Israel as enemies of *Commentary,* which was known to exaggerate the threat of such enemies to the world. I remember one cover in the '70s that showed a vast armada proceeding out of Iran to attack the world: planes filled the sky, tanks covered the land, and ships crowded the sea. The irony was that soon after that cover appeared, the Iranian government collapsed, the shah had to flee, the revolutionaries took over, and the shah's military power was revealed as a paper tiger. Later, in both U.S. military conflicts with Iraq, Podhoretz was leading the cheering section for war well before the United States intervened. More recently, he has been beating the drums for war with Iran. Kristol is not quite as bellicose, but nevertheless is strongly pro-Israel. The group gradually adopted ever more conservative economic doctrines, too. Kristol became a supporter of Ronald Reagan's supply-side economics and the Reagan tax cuts. A later publication, the *City Journal,* published by the neoconservative Manhattan Institute, is a strong advocate for the merits of the market economy, and only rarely a critic.

Both Kristol and Podhoretz had been identified with a group called the New York Intellectuals, made up of people who were mostly liberal in the 1930s, '40s, and '50s. If there was any split in the group it was between those who were anti-communist and those who were more anti-communist. There were divisions, for example, over the degree of guilt of Alger Hiss and the proper punishment of the Rosenbergs. Some of the intellectuals, such as Irving Howe, were socialists, none were communists, and the rest remained left of center.

When I was at Columbia, Podhoretz was a fellow student, one who was considered quite brilliant. Although we were not friends, I did have a class with him where he was very generous in offering his opinions. I remember nothing conservative about any of them.

By coincidence, in the late 1940s Kristol and I shared the same subway stop, Broadway and Ninety-sixth. When I exited the subway I often stopped for a beer at Neary's bar, which was directly beneath Kristol's apartment. Our paths did not cross, however, until many years later. But I did read Kristol's memoir, and in it I saw a clue as to why he ultimately became conservative. It relates to an experience that was common to both of us—military service—but with important differences.

We were both in the army during World War II, Kristol for much longer than I. My experience was good; Kristol's was bad. He was a victim of physical and verbal abuse from his fellow soldiers because he was Jewish. You can imagine how in some basic way that must have shaken his faith in democracy. Perhaps I should explain here that the wartime army was totally democratic, so that one's experience in it might tend to either reinforce or undermine that faith. In my case, there was an experience that considerably reinforced my faith. One day in the quarters I shared with fifteen or twenty other soldiers I discovered that my fountain pen had been stolen and asked around as to whether anybody had seen it. Shortly afterward we went out for training and I was delayed in getting back to quarters. When I did, I found thirteen crumpled dollar bills on top of my bunk, approximately the well-advertised price of my pen. In this and other ways, my faith in the democratic idea was, if anything, heightened by my experience with my fellow soldiers.

Kristol's son, William, has succeeded him as the main spokesman for neoconservatism through his publication *The Weekly Standard*. Interestingly enough, the positions of the old conservatives and the neoconservatives pretty much merged in the 1980s, and in turn, as the Republican Party became more and more conservative, both movements identified more and more with the GOP. For Bill Kristol, wanting Republicans to succeed meant wanting Democrats to fail. There was irony in his advocacy of this kind of policy. One of his father's leading causes had been anti-communism; he was prominent among intellectuals resisting Stalinist influences.

Irving Kristol was well aware of the history of the Bolshevik seizure of power, and of one of Lenin's most cynical and effective tactics: Refusing to give any help whatsoever to the new, democratic Kerensky government in Russia. Communists were instructed to sabotage a government that was clearly trying to do some good things so that it would fail, and the Communists could take power. The irony is that Bill Kristol and his allies have used much the same tactics against Bill Clinton and Barack Obama: Do anything to make them fail, even in what might be generally regarded as good causes, in order to bring Republicans to power. Republican leaders

Newt Gingrich during Bill Clinton's administration and Mitch McConnell during Barack Obama's have followed Kristol's advice, as have Rush Limbaugh, Roger Ailes, and the great majority of Republicans in both the House and Senate.

By March 2010 the trend had gone far enough that Norman Podhoretz was able to write in *The Wall Street Journal,* "I hereby declare that I would rather be ruled by the Tea Party than by the Democratic Party, and I would rather have Sarah Palin sitting in the Oval Office than Barack Obama." It is hard to think of anything that has done more to divide the country than this automatic opposition to the Democrats that the Republican Party has adopted. The neoconservatives also contributed to this division with their advocacy of war against Iraq, of which they were the most influential architects and propagandists.

Another negative effect of the neoconservatives was seen in the excesses of the war on crime that began in the 1970s. There was no theme of the neocons that had more impact on liberals than their "mugged by reality" message. It resonated in the late '60s and early '70s because real muggings were happening as the rate of violent crime soared. The murder rate alone rose more than 50 percent between 1965 and 1970, and 100 percent by 1980. The neoconservative and conservative answer for this problem was to get tough on crime in general.

At *The Washington Monthly* in 1976, we published an article that made a distinction between the treatment of violent and non-violent crimes and recommended tough sentences for cold-blooded violent criminals and lighter sentences for nonviolent ones, especially first offenders, for whom we recommended probation. Giving in to an editor's weakness for attracting attention with a cover headline, we ran one that read "Criminals Belong in Jail," in big, bold letters. I remain embarrassed by that headline and feel guilty about it, because even though the article was reasonable and right, the message in the headline was exactly the one adopted by neocons and conservatives generally—and indeed many liberals. And so more jails were built for the nonviolent as well as the violent. Indeed, these days the majority of inmates in federal prisons are there for nonviolent offenses. In recent decades, too much of the wealth of the nation has gone to building, maintaining, and staffing prisons instead of to schools, roads, and other, more important, public needs.

By the twenty-first century we had more than two million people incarcerated. In the meantime, crime had dropped dramatically. By 2000 the murder rate was back down to what it had been in 1965, and it would drop even further by 2012. Conservatives stuck to their tough-on-crime message and incitement of public fears, regardless of the evidence of a decline in crime.

Along with the extravagant expenditures on penal facilities went excessive generosity in appropriations to police departments. As a result, many departments began to look like they were preparing to invade Iraq. Small cities and even sheriffs' offices in rural counties were fielding SWAT teams of helmeted officers, usually clad in black and armed with an intimidating array of weaponry. It was in some ways a comic spectacle, but at the same time it was dangerous to have heavily armed police teams battering down the doors of minor drug offenders, creating too many situations where somebody could get shot.

Radley Balko, in his book *Rise of the Warrior Cop,* published in 2013, reported that 80 percent of towns with a population between 25,000 and 50,000 have SWAT teams that collectively have carried out some 50,000 raids nationwide. During one nighttime raid by a SWAT team in Ogden, Utah, Mathew David Stewart awoke to the sound of his front door being battered down. Thinking he must be under attack by criminals, he grabbed his handgun, and in the resulting exchange of shots, Stewart was hit twice, as were six officers, including one who was killed. The only evidence of crime police found in Stewart's home were sixteen small marijuana plants. While Stewart was in jail awaiting trial, he hanged himself.

Shortly after I read the Balko book, I saw an article in my hometown paper, *The Charleston Gazette-Mail,* describing the activities of a West Virginia SWAT team. It had killed a disabled man named Richard Kohler, whose only alleged crime "was giving away pills prescribed for him in exchange for stolen items." The police said that when they pried open his door at 6:05 in the morning, he aimed a rifle at them. The only problem with this explanation was that the outside of the door was riddled with bullets. Police did not even have an arrest warrant for Kohler, whose daughter described him as a nonviolent man with no criminal record who required a cane to get around and needed help getting out of bed.

The wildly excessive use of imprisonment and SWAT teams as solutions to crime does not in any way minimize the fact that fear of crime was a strong element in the country beginning in the late '60s and that this fear was particularly strong in white America. Ironically, most of the violence was black against black, not black against white.

### B. Guns, Abortion, and the Environment

A bold assertion of gun rights became an example of how the civil and women's rights movements of the 1960s spawned new claims to rights that would deepen divisions along liberal and conservative lines in the '70s. The National Rifle Association, a group that had been largely concerned with marksmanship and gun safety, turned into a gun rights lobbying organization. After the assassinations of John F. Kennedy in 1963 and Robert F. Kennedy and Martin Luther King, Jr., in 1968, Congress passed the Gun Control Act, which was, for the most part, supported by the NRA. But not all of the association's members were pleased. Perhaps the increase of crime in this country during the late '60s was a factor. In any event, by 1970 gun rights advocates were considered a significant factor in the defeat of Senator Joseph Tydings of Maryland, who had introduced gun control legislation that year in the Senate.

By the mid-1970s the NRA had established its own lobbying

arm and was plunging into the political arena as a strong advocate of gun rights. And as it became more involved in politics, it tended to ally itself more and more with Republicans. It endorsed Ronald Reagan in 1980, and by 2012, 88 percent of the Republicans in Congress were getting contributions from the NRA's political action committee, as opposed to only 11 percent of Democrats. The NRA's power has grown to the point where it has even been able to defeat gun control legislation introduced after such shocking events as the mass murders of schoolchildren at Columbine and Sandy Hook and the attempted assassination of Representative Gabrielle Giffords of Arizona. In 2013 it engineered the recall of two state legislators in Colorado—senators John Morse and Angela Giron—who had helped pass a gun control measure. More disturbing gun violence occurred at a Charleston, South Carolina, church in 2015 and in San Bernardino, California, and Orlando, Florida, in 2016.

There is no better illustration of the power of lowest-common-denominator lobbying than the National Rifle Association. The most extreme members gradually came to dominate the organization. They were the ones most capable of causing trouble for the leadership at annual meetings, and the leadership found they could avoid that kind of trouble by expressing the views these members advocated. These same tendencies help explain the rise of extremist groups in the Republican Party as it has become more and more the voice of the far right.

ANOTHER EXAMPLE OF rights being aggressively asserted was abortion. In the 1950s, abortion was hardly ever discussed openly in America. In fact, it was generally only whispered among friends when a young woman was "in trouble." But as an outgrowth of the women's rights movement, abortion became a public issue, leading eventually to the 1973 Supreme Court decision in *Roe v. Wade* that established the right to an abortion. The ruling brought the issue to the forefront of national politics, dividing much of the country between Right-to-Lifers and supporters of the right to choose. Their views were represented on one side by the National Right to Life Committee, and on the other by the National Abortion Rights Action League (NARAL). At the same time, a wide political division on *Roe v. Wade* became clear. Republican president Gerald Ford opposed it. Jimmy Carter, his opponent in the 1976 election, favored it. The divide between parties on this issue would remain a constant in American politics, with abortion rights advocates heavily represented among the Democrats and opponents being mostly Republicans.

The anti-abortion cause had an early victory in the passage by Congress of the Hyde Amendment (offered by Republican representative Henry Hyde of Illinois), which prohibited the use of federal funds in the Medicaid program to finance abortions. For me this remains one of the more outrageous acts of the anti-abortion movement, because the poor women who depend on Medicaid for their healthcare are the most likely to have limited access to or knowledge of birth control techniques, devices, and medications.

But despite the ongoing controversy, most of the public seemed to accept *Roe v. Wade* in the 1970s. In the '80s, however, the anti-abortion movement gained a new ally in science. One has to note the irony of conservatives' disdaining science on environmental issues yet showing such eagerness to make use of scientific advances in detecting when a fetus becomes viable. Nevertheless, the ultrasound techniques and developments in the recording of fetal brain and heart function caused many people to realize how much earlier a child began to be formed than they had previously thought. A physician, Bernard Nathanson, who had been one of the earliest advocates of abortion rights and had helped found the National Association for the Repeal of Abortion Laws, was, by the mid-1980s, showing a film he had made called *The Silent Scream*. Nathanson, who had himself terminated some five thousand pregnancies in his career, narrated: "We see the child's mouth wide open in a silent scream. For the first time, we are going to watch a child being torn apart, dismembered, disarticulated, crushed, and destroyed by the unfeeling steel instruments of the abortionist." Needless to say, this movie intensified the emotional support of the anti-abortion movement. Norma McCorvey, who had been the original Jane Roe of *Roe v. Wade,* became, by the 1990s, a confirmed right-to-lifer.

Another factor in the debate was the disappearance of the shame once associated with unwed motherhood. Certainly, through the 1950s, an unwanted pregnancy was usually a cause for shame. Frequently there would be some attempt to cover things up. If a woman was affluent, she might take a long trip to Europe and have an abortion in Switzerland or give birth to the child there. The Catholic Church had many homes for unwed mothers, and in a number of places Florence Crittenton Homes served much the same function for young women. There was one such home near my house in Washington, but by the end of the 1970s it had closed because unwed mothers no longer felt they had to get out of town or hide their condition.

In 1996 a movie called *Citizen Ruth* starred Laura Dern as a feckless unemployed woman who has become pregnant for the fifth time. She is convicted of a drug offense and is offered a shorter sentence by a judge if she agrees to have an abortion. She then falls into the hands of a pro-life group, whose primary intention seems to be to use her for public relations purposes to score points for their side. Next she gets involved with a pro-choice group that is similarly motivated. Both sides want to use her for their political purposes. The movie illustrates the problem of communication between the two sides on the abortion question. The pro-choice people are not eager to acknowledge the moral dilemma, and the pro-lifers are equally unwilling to face the compelling real-life reasons why a woman may need to have an abortion. One of the most maddening positions of anti-abortion groups is that most of them oppose not only abortion but contraception as well. You would think that they'd want to prevent the pregnancies that lead women to consider the possibility of abortion; if the pregnancy is prevented, then the issue of abortion never arises.

The growth in intensity of the anti-abortion feeling is illustrated by the growing size of the demonstrations, and by Republican legislatures (for example, in Texas and Mississippi) that have been active in passing laws radically restricting access to abortion. Some 250,000 people participated in the annual March for Life in Washington in 2010. In the next three years the number grew to 650,000. But most Americans, though by a dwindling majority, continue to feel that the decision should be left to the woman to make and that it must be a legal right, even though more people also felt that it was a moral choice. Nevertheless, the increase in the intensity of feelings against abortion unquestionably contributed to a similar increase in the moral fervor of the right, particularly among the religious right. The many Catholics and evangelicals who had come together following *Roe v. Wade* to oppose abortion became even more ardent in their opposition.

There was a comparable and growing intensity among defenders of gun rights. Many in the NRA seemed to think that the government actually wanted to take away their guns—that it was just itching to disarm them. In fact, no one in the gun control movement wants to take from a hunter the right to possess a shotgun or deer rifle, or from anyone else the right to possess a handgun, as long as that weapon is registered and the person is shown not to have a criminal record or a mental illness. Still, episodes such as the tragedy in Waco, Texas, where a federal siege of a compound held by members of the Branch Davidian church began with a raid to investigate reports of illegal weapons and ended with a fire that took the lives of seventy-six men, women, and children, lingers in the minds of gun rights proponents. Many of them, including NRA people, saw the Waco tragedy as a sign that the government really does want to take away their guns.

THE ENVIRONMENTAL PROTECTION Agency, established in 1970 through the combined efforts of Republican president Richard M. Nixon and a Democratic Congress, led to another conservative-liberal split during the decade that followed, even though the EPA's first leader, William Ruckelshaus, was a Republican. Many American rivers, such as the Kanawha, which flows through my hometown of Charleston, had become so obviously polluted that there was no denying the seriousness of the problem. The same was true of the air we breathed. I remember walking down Madison Avenue, in the early '50s at five P.M., with buses belching exhaust and endless lines of cars idling, and wondering what all the stuff in the air was doing to my health. The smog over Los Angeles had become so obvious that it was the butt of one comedian's joke after another. More seriously, in Donora, Pennsylvania, smog actually killed people.

So there was a lot of support for the EPA in the beginning, as indicated by its bipartisan origins. But gradually, as Reagan conservatives began to dominate the Republican Party, the image took hold on the right of the EPA representing the government, which meant, of course, that it had to be bad. Conservatives increasingly took sides against the EPA. A notable illustration of this trend was the appointment by Ronald Reagan of Anne Gorsuch as head of the EPA in the early 1980s. Gorsuch's mission, as far as outsiders could tell, was simply to emasculate the agency.

This was certainly the case in the conservatives' denial of the evidence of pollution. I had an experience with this attitude when I appeared on Brian Lamb's early morning show on C-SPAN in the early '90s, along with Cal Thomas, a prominent conservative commentator. As we were talking in the green room before the broadcast, Thomas, who knew I was from West Virginia, mentioned to me how clean he found the Ohio River (which makes up much of the state's western border) to be compared with his last visit there twenty years before. Several minutes later he was on the air condemning the EPA, which had certainly had something to do with cleaning up the Ohio, as an example of government overreach. The conservatives, as Thomas illustrated, were becoming automatically anti-EPA, regardless of its accomplishments.

   The earliest evidence of the harm that the EPA was doing to liberalism came in coal-producing states, where both miners and mine
owners felt threatened by the environmental movement. The owners, of course, had always been Republicans, but most miners had
been on the liberal Democratic side. An early result of their movement to the other side was Jay Rockefeller's defeat in his 1972 campaign for governor of West Virginia, during which he opposed strip
mining. Wyoming, the nation's number-one coal producer, had two
Democratic senators in 1960 and reelected one of them by a comfortable margin in 1970. After the EPA came into existence late in
that year, the state, where coal mining had gradually become the
major industry, never again elected a Democratic senator. Over the
years, miners in such states became increasingly conservative, with
a large number of white males and their families moving away from
the liberal side and gradually changing the electoral results in Kentucky, West Virginia, Wyoming, and other places where extraction
industries, including oil and natural gas, are important.

   Unfortunately, environmentalists tended to dismiss the concerns
of the miners and did not face the demoralization that would be
caused by the loss of their jobs, especially older miners who could
not see a realistic prospect of other employment paying nearly as
well. It was a mistake similar to that of those who were right to be
free traders but wrong not to feel the pain free trade was causing
those whose jobs in manufacturing were lost as a result.

   Opposition to the EPA now extends well beyond those who fear
that it threatens their jobs. It has become an article of faith in the
Republican Party that the EPA must be opposed. And the agency is
hampered by young people's ignorance of its past accomplishments.
Millennials may be opposed to global warming, but they have no
memory of black smoke pouring out of factory stacks, the choking
exhaust of buses and trucks, or of rivers clogged with filth and dead
fish. In short, many of them have no understanding of how much
the EPA has cleaned up. They only hear now of the apparent failures of the agency. For example, when discharge from an aban-

doned gold mine recently polluted a river, the media generally reported it as a failure of the EPA without noting that the gold industry had left the task of cleaning up its mess to the agency, totally ignoring the responsibility of the gold industry for the problem. Furthermore, Republican opposition to the EPA now includes complete denial of climate change, which almost every respectable scientist concedes is real.

On all these issues—race, crime, guns, abortion, and the environment—I tend to the liberal side. In every case, however, I find myself troubled by many of my fellow liberals' failure to understand the legitimate concerns of the other side. Similarly, I am dismayed by liberals' willingness to cede Christianity to the evangelicals and to abandon the faith of Roosevelt and King, with its great potential for bringing us together under the banner of the Golden Rule.

---
★
---

# CHAPTER 8

# The Education Wars

nother major issue dividing America from 1970 on was the
decline in the quality of public schools, especially those attended by the less privileged. The poor quality of teacher
education had been apparent for some time, but there was one thing
that kept bad teacher training from having too much impact on the
quality of schools, and that was the fact that until the 1960s teaching was one of the few professions open to women. Smart women
thus tended to go into teaching, so even if they were badly prepared,
they were talented enough to be good teachers anyway.

My first exposure to this truth came the summer after I heard
Lionel Trilling's pointed criticisms of Columbia's Teachers College.
That year, 1947, I attended summer school, one of the few places at
Columbia where people from many different parts of the university
were thrown together. Quite a few of the students, maybe a third,
were from the Teachers College. I found that despite Trilling's disdain, a lot of these women—and they were almost all women—
were very smart.

From 1961 to 1968 I worked for the Peace Corps as head of the
evaluation division, a job in which I must have visited at least thirty
teacher-training programs and edited reports about many others.
Generally the problem was that teachers' colleges and the education

departments of universities wanted to give our teachers generalized courses in methodology. But most of our teachers were going to teach in secondary schools. What we primarily needed to know was whether they had the subject knowledge. Unfortunately, teachers' colleges were very poor at communicating such knowledge. Another thing we needed to know was whether the Peace Corps volunteers had an aptitude for teaching and for the classroom. And it was surprisingly difficult to get the teacher-training institutions to arrange the practice teaching that would reveal that aptitude. If we wanted methodology courses, it was not generalized methodology but how to teach the specific subject our teacher was going to be responsible for in the secondary school where he or she would be assigned. Fortunately, throughout the 1960s, the quality of people coming into our teacher programs was high enough that they could do a good job overseas.

But this was going to change, if not for the Peace Corps, for the rest of the country. What changed it was one of the large but mostly unacknowledged problems of American public education. With new jobs in many fields opening up to women throughout the country, teaching was no longer one of the few careers that smart women could pursue. Now women could be lawyers, MBAs—do almost anything. The number of women in professional schools skyrocketed in the 1970s and '80s. The result was that there was much less talent going into teacher-training institutions, many of which provided the kind of third-rate instruction only a very talented student could overcome. Moreover, the best teachers tended to be recruited by the suburban school districts, which generally had more money and fewer problems to deal with. Meanwhile, the states maintained certification requirements for teachers that were heavily influenced by the political power of teacher-training institutions. These requirements emphasized education credits, not knowledge of subject matter to be taught. In 1984 *The Washington Monthly* took note of this reality with an article entitled "Yes, but Where Are Your Credits in Recess Management 101?"

The difficult challenge for public education posed by the declining quality of people entering the teaching profession combined with the pressures of racial integration in the schools to produce a flight from city public schools by people who could afford to send their children to private schools or to move to suburbs where the public schools were still good. This movement was dramatic in places such as Washington, D.C., and New York City. My son's experience in the Washington public schools illustrated the problem. When he entered Hardy Elementary School there were too few black children, only one in his class. After busing for racial integration was instituted, things changed so dramatically that by fifth grade, he was the only white student in his class. Some of his classmates carried knives. We moved him into a private school, and then my wife got a job there to pay his tuition.

There was another factor at work, too: declining teacher dedication. By the time my son left his public school, a visitor there would find the teachers' parking lot empty by three-thirty. At his new private school, Georgetown Day, the teachers' lot was still full an hour later. Georgetown Day had been the first school in Washington to integrate, having done so at its founding in 1945. It remained integrated and provided a high quality of education. One reason for this was that the school could hire teachers without regard to whether they had education courses; it could hire them solely on the basis of ability and knowledge of the subject they were to teach. Yet at the time my wife joined the staff, beginning teachers were paid less than those in public schools, even though they were, on the whole, better teachers.

Another indication of what was happening to the public schools was provided by three outstanding older teachers at Hardy in my son's first years there. When the federal court ruling by Judge J. Skelly Wright came down it not only ordered busing but required teacher reassignments. Three teachers were required to move to schools in deprived areas across town. It is certainly true that those schools desperately needed such teachers, but faced with the prospect of traveling all the way across the city every day, all three retired. Those good teachers just quit teaching, a considerable loss for Hardy with no gains for the inner-city schools.

This story was repeated over and over again in big cities across America. The problem was exacerbated by prejudiced white parents who would withdraw their children from a school simply because it became integrated—and by middle-class black parents who fled the growing crime, thus depriving black youth of role models. But teachers' unions and schools of education contributed to the problem by refusing to see the need for improvement in the quality of teaching and by resisting changes in certification requirements and other reforms.

A movement to reform the public schools has been going on for many years; *The Washington Monthly* became an early participant in its first year of publication, 1969. But progress has been painfully slow because of entrenched resistance. One problem for the reform movement was that it attracted conservatives who were generally against labor unions of any kind. Thus the teachers' unions could make a plausible argument that the reform movement was coming mostly from enemies of organized labor. This argument gained strength in recent years as liberals showed increasing concern about the country's growing inequality of wealth, and argued that the decline in the power of unions had a lot to do with it.

The decline in the quality of public schools, city schools especially, was particularly threatening to members of the white working class, for whom education is a precious means of upward mobility for themselves and their children. Indeed, about the only people unharmed by failing public schools were those fortunate enough to live in upscale suburban areas and in attractive small towns of the kind that teachers might wish to live in. And, of course, the many parents who could afford to send their children to private schools.

When children from different neighborhoods and backgrounds no longer went to the same school, the result was a separation of social classes. When I was in public school in Charleston, the schools were not yet racially integrated, but they had a wide variety of white students, so that I got to know people from all walks of life and to respect them, just as other Americans did who attended similar public schools, especially those of which were racially diverse. The separation of people from different circumstances caused by the decline in public schools was a real tragedy. The affluent elite and many seniors grew indifferent to the fate of public schools because they were no longer sending their children to them. Why should they pay the taxes needed to support good schools? Why not vote for California's Proposition 13, which, by putting a ceiling on real estate taxes, the major support for public schools, devastated the state's excellent system of public education?

The teaching reform movement gradually began to take shape in the 1970s, but it had difficulty gaining traction because liberals were afraid of being seen as hostile to teachers and their unions, both of which they'd long regarded as the good guys. Conservatives' idea of reform was to provide vouchers paid with public school funds that would allow students to attend private schools, rather than attempting to reform the public schools. In 1994, when I was a fellow at the conservative Hoover Institution at Stanford University (I was the token liberal), I had a chance for an extended conversation with the resident education expert. But every attempt I made to talk about ways to improve the public schools elicited only a yawn and another statement of his advocacy of vouchers as the answer.

There were two other problems that the reform movement faced. One was the common understanding that we wanted "qualified" teachers in our schools. The trouble was that "qualified teacher" had come to mean, in effect, one who was certified by the state, and state certifications were based on passing education courses as mandated by the teachers' colleges. (If you don't recognize the term "teachers' colleges," most of them have changed their names to Something or Other State.) The second problem was that in urban areas such as Washington, D.C., many of the public school teachers were black, and so any reform movement that threatened their livelihoods was seen as inimical to black progress. This was one of the problems—as was her gift for tactlessness—Michelle Rhee ran into in her efforts to reform the Washington schools, and was one of the reasons why the mayor who had sponsored her, Adrian Fenty, was defeated for reelection, after which Rhee resigned.

In 1979, soon after Marion Barry was elected Washington's mayor, we had lunch. He asked what I thought was the city's number-one problem. I immediately said schools. "Jesus, man, don't you realize it's jobs?" he replied. Both of us had a point. Washington's black youth needed jobs; they also needed the education that would get them those jobs. This clash of two legitimate points of view is still another obstacle reformers face.

Still, Bill and Hillary Clinton were able to overcome union opposition and get modest reforms, including a test of teacher competence, passed by the Arkansas legislature in the early 1980s (more about their effort later).

The reform movement took a major step forward in 1989 when Wendy Kopp, a graduate of Princeton University, founded an organization called Teach for America, which placed graduates from some of the country's best colleges and universities in two-year teaching assignments in urban and rural areas where there were shortages of good teachers. These young teachers brought enthusiasm, intelligence, and a strong educational background of their own to the job. The only weakness of Teach for America was that the five weeks of training teachers received in the summer wasn't as good as it might have been. It has gradually improved over the years, but there is no question that while schools of education greatly overemphasized teaching methodology, a certain measure of it is desirable, if only to learn methods for handling a classroom. And, of course, some subject-related methodology is always desirable. In any event, Teach for America grew from five hundred teachers in its first year to more than six thousand in 2013, with fifty-seven thousand applicants from the time of its founding. An indication of the quality of schools that they come from is the fact that the greatest number of graduates for 2012 were from the Berkeley campus of the University of California.

In 1994, two alumni of Teach for America, Dave Levin and Mike Feinberg, founded KIPP—short for the Knowledge Is Power Program. KIPP ran charter schools that admitted public school students on an open-enrollment basis. These schools became so popular that they had to go to a lottery system for admissions, but otherwise the admission remained totally nondiscriminatory. As a result, KIPP schools had wide ranges of abilities and backgrounds in its student population, just as public schools do. KIPP became a model for the charter school movement. It has now spread to twenty-nine states and the District of Columbia, where the results have been outstanding. Unfortunately, not all charter schools have been as good as KIPP—John Oliver has revealed how hustlers and con men have been awarded charters in Ohio and Pennsylvania— but on the whole, in large cities such as New York and Washington, D.C., they have done considerably better than the public schools.

In Dale Russakoff's impressive dissection in her book *The Prize* of why the effort to reform the Newark public schools undertaken by Mark Zuckerberg and the city's then-mayor Cory Booker was, on the whole, a failure, she found a bright spot in the 30 percent of Newark's public schools that are charters. For example, though 71 percent of charter school students in Newark passed third-grade language-arts tests in the 2013–14 school year, only 41 percent of students in Newark's traditional public schools passed those tests.

The high point of the reform movement may have been the release in 2010 of Davis Guggenheim's *Waiting for "Superman,"* a documentary that exposed the problems of public education. But almost immediately there was a counterattack, led by Diane Ravitch, a well-known education writer. In early 2012, *The New York Review of Books* published two articles by Ravitch in back-to-back issues, in which she argued:

The "no excuses" reformers maintain that all children can attain academic proficiency without regard to poverty, disability, or other conditions, and that someone must be held accountable if they do not. That someone is invariably their teacher.

Nothing is said about holding accountable the district leadership or the elected officials who determine such crucial issues as funding, class size, and resource allocation. The reformers say that our economy is in jeopardy, not because of growing poverty or income inequality or the outsourcing of manufacturing jobs, but because of bad teachers. These bad teachers must be found out and thrown out. Any laws, regulations, or contracts that protect these pedagogical malefactors must be eliminated so that they can be quickly removed without regard to experience, seniority, or due process.

Ravitch's argument is a misstatement of the position of many reformers. At *The Washington Monthly*, for example, we have criticized the unions for protecting bad teachers, but we have never said that teachers alone should be held accountable for the failures of public education. We have never contended that poverty and disability have nothing to do with these failures. We have also criticized second-rate administrators and clueless school boards. Indeed, Ravitch's portrayal has only a smidgen of truth, in that it describes the Johnny-Come-Lately Republicans who have recently joined the school reform movement, because they are indeed out to destroy unions.

The counterreform movement, however, gained another important ally in 2012 when *The New Yorker* ran an admiring profile of Ravitch. One could conclude that the meritocratic elites as represented by a couple of influential magazines were turning against the cause of school reform. These publications were joined by many liberals in New York, as indicated by the 2013 mayoral election in which Bill de Blasio, campaigning on an anti-school-reform platform, won by a substantial margin. Another sign that the cause of reform is losing its appeal to the meritocrats is that, according to an April 2016 article in *The Washington Post,* the applicant pool at Teach for America has been shrinking since 2013.

What is troubling about this counterattack is that it is based on a false premise: that because the overall efficacy of education is dependent on many factors, including the student's family life and environment, teacher quality alone isn't worth all the fuss the reformers have been making. But the truth is that there is substantial evidence that while all those other factors do influence the educational outcomes for students, the quality of the teacher by itself makes a very substantial difference. A research study reported by Annie Lowrey of *The New York Times* in 2012 tracked 2.5 million students over twenty years. It found that, even taking full account of environmental factors, good teachers "will have a wide-ranging, lasting positive effect on the students' lives, beyond academics, including lower average teenage pregnancy rates and greater college matriculation and adult earnings."

There are at least a few hopeful signs for reform. Some Republicans have gone from simply favoring vouchers to offering support for public charter schools. Even Ravitch concedes that better teacher training is necessary. And a task force appointed by Randi Weingarten, president of the American Federation of Teachers, recently recommended basic qualifications for teachers: a year of practice teaching, a test of subject knowledge, and a requirement that they enter and graduate their teacher-preparation programs with a 3.0 grade point average. Unfortunately, largely due to pressure from teachers' colleges and unions, as Weingarten surely knows, no state requires all of these.

A recent report by the National Council on Teacher Quality awarded my home state of West Virginia a D-plus grade because it gave tenure "virtually automatically," and its teachers were "almost impossible to fire." It said there was no way to determine whether a teacher had mastered the subject. In California a judge recently struck down the teacher-tenure law on the basis that it denied students the right to a good education. The judge found that California granted tenure after less than two years' service, required that lay-offs be entirely by seniority, and had an appeals process that could take up to ten years and cost a school district $450,000 to dismiss one teacher. Needless to say, the judge's reasoning did not impress the teachers' union, so it appealed and won a reversal.

In short, the quality of public education remains a serious ob-stacle to equal opportunity in this country. The nation is divided between those who can afford a good education and those who can't. And, sadly, it is also divided between those who want to im-prove the schools and those who don't, or who differ in crucial ways on how to fix the schools. Still, there is hope. Both Ravitch and reformers agree that teacher training must be improved. Ravitch and reformer Amanda Ripley urge that Finland's rigorous teacher training should be used as a model for this country. And most liber-als would agree that pupils from families and neighborhoods strug-gling to keep their heads above water need help from the rest of us to make the struggle less daunting. Perhaps most important of all is that those in the entertainment industry with influence over the opinion of young people make sure that they never suggest that tak-ing school seriously is uncool. The students themselves, though they have excellent excuses for not giving school their best effort, should consider whether it is a good idea to use those excuses to wreck the rest of their lives.

★

# CHAPTER 9

# A Cynical Age

As for the political life of the nation, and specifically how it affected the federal government in Washington, the 1970s saw a growth of cynicism about politics and government. The main factors were Lyndon Johnson's lies about Vietnam and Richard Nixon's lies about Watergate. (Another factor was certainly disappointment with Jimmy Carter.) In the case of Vietnam, the extent of the deception gradually became clear to Americans, despite the repeated assurances by military and Johnson administration officials that there was light at the end of the tunnel, and that victory would be the ultimate outcome. What people saw was that more and more American troops were being sent to Vietnam and more and more of them were dying. The growing sense that we were being lied to was confirmed by the release of the Pentagon Papers in 1971 by a whistleblower named Daniel Ellsberg. He gave *New York Times* and *Washington Post* reporters copies of a report created by the RAND Corporation for the Pentagon. It revealed that civilian and military officials had known that the United States was not doing well in Vietnam. Evidence to this effect had been repeatedly put before them even as they continued to promise success in the war.

As for Watergate, suspicion that Nixon and his aides were involved mounted after *The Washington Post* revealed that a White House employee was implicated in the break-in and that a former CIA official had led the burglars. Then came the Senate hearings conducted by Senator Sam Ervin and the disclosure of the White House tapes, which contained Nixon's conversations with his aides about the developing scandal and revealed that the president was not only in on the cover-up but was the author of it. The combined effect of Vietnam and Watergate was thus to inspire disillusionment and cynicism on the part of the American public about Washington and the government.

Another contributor to cynicism about institutions was the movie *The Godfather,* which appeared in 1972. In the first scene, while the wedding of the godfather's daughter is being celebrated outside, Don Corleone (Marlon Brando) is in his office with his lawyer, Tom Hagen (Robert Duvall), who tells him: "The senator called. He apologized for not coming, but said you would understand. Also some of the judges. They've all sent gifts." In a later scene, in which the heads of the Mafia families of New York are meeting, one says of Don Corleone: "He has all the judges and the politicians in his pocket." In *The Godfather: Part III,* Michael Corleone says, "The higher I go, the crookeder it becomes."

Francis Ford Coppola, the films' director and cowriter, said he meant *The Godfather* to be a critique of capitalism. If so, he failed as spectacularly as Oliver Stone later did with his intention to disillusion people about Wall Street with the movie of that name. By not showing the evil that the godfather's family did—the prostitution, the gambling, and the rackets in action—Coppola actually succeeded in making the viewer identify with the godfather and his son and successor, Michael, played by Al Pacino. By the time Michael orders the climactic murders of the family's competitors, the viewer has come to the conclusion that those guys really deserved what they got. For an idea of how the country had changed, try to imagine a movie in which Judge Hardy is in the pocket of a Mafia don.

In 1972, the same year *The Godfather* was released, Robert

Redford starred in a movie called *The Candidate,* in which he plays an idealistic young man running for governor who is corrupted by what he has to do to win. Near the end of the movie he turns to the camera and says, "I am a politician," words clearly intended to indicate to the audience that this meant he had lost his soul. In the years since 1972 there have been few portrayals of politics and government that made them attractive. Two of the exceptions were the television series *The West Wing* and the movie *The American President,* both of which appeared in the 1990s. But the overall tone has been typified by the more recent television series *Scandal* and *House of Cards.*

One result of this cynicism has been a decline in voting. Another has been a declining interest in serving in the government, which means that the ablest people in the country are not flocking to Washington the way they did during the New Deal, World War II, the New Frontier, and the Great Society. Increasingly, civil service positions go to people who are simply looking for a nice secure job or a way to turn their government experience into more profitable pursuits, a path that is also taken by many who go into politics. Such people are entering government for reasons of self-interest, not the public interest. But talented people have not stopped coming into government entirely. There continue to be idealistic men and women devoted to public service.

One example is Timothy Geithner. In 1988 Geithner was a young graduate of Dartmouth and the Johns Hopkins School of Advanced International Studies who, after a brief stint working as a consultant with Henry Kissinger's firm, decided he wanted to follow his father's footsteps into the civil service. He joined the Treasury Department, where he remained for the next twelve years, explaining, "I wanted to serve my country." He would later head the Federal Reserve in New York before joining the new Obama administration in 2009 as secretary of the Treasury.

That we continue to have people like him in the civil service is illustrated by the recipients of the annual awards, nicknamed Sammies, given by the Partnership for Public Service to recognize out-standing bureaucrats. A dozen or so public officials have earned these awards each year for more than a decade. The 2016 recipients include Paul McGann, Jean D. Moody-Williams, and Dennis Wagner of the Centers for Medicare and Medicaid Services, who developed a program to decrease hospital acquired infections that in four years saved an estimated 87,000 lives.

Unfortunately, since the 1970s, there have been fewer of these outstanding civil servants. And this has contributed to a decline in the quality of government agencies that fostered a sense that government was the problem not the solution, and to the election of Ronald Reagan and the triumph of anti-government conservatism in the Republican Party from 1980 on.

What happened with the civil service was similar to what happened with the schools, where many of the very able women who had once been drawn to teaching careers left education for more lucrative professions. In the civil service, when the supply of talent dwindled, there was a tendency among liberals not to want to face the problem just as they had not done with the public schools. A tenet of liberalism has always been that the civil servants and the teachers are the good guys, and it was hard to give up automatically defending them. For conservatives, the declining quality of government only reinforced their anti-government attitude. The result was that too few people were thinking about how to make government better.

IF IT'S HARD to fire bad teachers, it's almost impossible to fire bad civil servants. The rate of discharge for inefficiency at the end of the '70s was one-seventh of 1 percent, and so it has remained. The focus on job security led government agencies to be more concerned with the size of their budgets than with the performance of their missions. The Rural Electrification Administration, for example, which was founded to bring electricity to rural areas, had largely gotten that job done by the early 1950s, so it began seeking out new things to do, including financing improvements in country clubs, just so that the agency could survive. In the civil service generally, pay and benefits became a major concern, as did the size of one's office. The emphasis on getting promotions resulted in an estimate by the Civil Service Commission in 1977 that 150,000 workers were "overgraded"—they had managed to get higher levels of salary and rank than their level of work required. This was accomplished by the rewriting of job descriptions. As Leonard Reed, a former civil servant, observed, "Anybody who's ever worked at a government agency knows that job descriptions would endow a file clerk with responsibilities before which a graduate of the Harvard Business School quails."

Furthermore, job descriptions were used to restrict the entry of outsiders to those who fit descriptions that had often been created solely to fit them. Thus new people who came into the civil service tended to be friends of people already there—the buddy system.

As for office space: In the 1970s, federal employment in the Washington area grew by 25 percent, while the amount of government-leased office space grew by 47 percent. A friend of mine gave me a letter that had been written to him by one of his friends who'd been assigned to the USAID mission in Saigon. The entire letter is concerned with budget matters, personnel, and the view from his office, as well as its square footage and floor covering. This was at the beginning of March 1975, just six weeks before the fall of Saigon.

The evacuation of Saigon and South Vietnam by the Americans was a discouraging display of government ineptitude. Secretary of State Henry Kissinger, Ambassador Graham Martin, and CIA Station Chief Thomas Polgar had, like the USAID official, refused to face the fact that the South Vietnamese army was collapsing. They had therefore neglected to make plans for the evacuation of large numbers of South Vietnamese whom we had urged to rely on us, who had committed themselves publicly to our side, and who were to be put in grave danger by the North Vietnamese takeover. We were able to evacuate only a handful of these people, amid tragic scenes of South Vietnamese desperately reaching for the struts of helicopters and being left to the mercy of the North Vietnamese. Another episode that contributed to the impression of government ineptitude was the botched attempt to rescue Americans held hostage in Iran.

As time went on, other government failures exacerbated the anti-government feeling in the country, especially among Republicans. Two episodes in the early '90s—one known as Ruby Ridge, which occurred in 1992, and the other, a year later, named for the nearby city of Waco, Texas, are powerful examples. In the Ruby Ridge incident, the unarmed wife of a man named Randy Weaver was killed by an FBI sniper during a standoff at the Weavers' home in northern Idaho, although she was innocent of any wrongdoing. Their son was also killed during the two-day siege, even though there was evidence that negotiations to end it could have been successful.

In the Waco case, the Bureau of Alcohol, Tobacco and Firearms decided to launch an armed attack on the Branch Davidian compound. The only crime the Davidians were accused of was storing illegal firearms. There was no evidence that they had used the firearms to do anyone any harm. Nonetheless, after they refused to allow a search of their compound, they were attacked by armed federal agents. After the first raid failed, at the cost of the lives of several agents and Davidians, and after a siege of nearly two months, federal agents, employing helicopters and nine armored vehicles, punched holes in buildings and launched an assault on the Branch Davidians. Fires broke out—it was unclear whether they were set by the Branch Davidians or the federal agents—and seventy-six people died, many of them children.

The effect these two incidents had, coming very quickly one after the other, was to convince members of the National Rifle Association that the government really was out to seize their guns. In Waco, it appears that the Branch Davidians were known as friendly and were well regarded, which the ATF could have found out if it had consulted with the local sheriff before the initial raid. The final assault seems to have been a matter of convenience for the FBI: The agents, tired of conducting the siege, wanted to go home. But, in fact, their negotiators thought the talks with the Branch Davidians had an excellent chance of succeeding, and they were opposed to the attack. Nevertheless, agents convinced Attorney General Janet Reno of the need for an assault, and she took the matter to President Bill Clinton. According to Clinton, she told him that there was evidence of sexual abuse of children in the compound, although the FBI later denied having made such allegations. Clinton, much to his later regret, told her to go ahead if she thought it was the right thing to do.

One has to be careful not to overstate the decline in government's performance. There are still some parts of agencies doing a good job, or trying to. Despite the ineptitude of their superiors in Saigon and Washington, several career diplomats and military officers made heroic efforts to successfully evacuate more than a hundred thousand Vietnamese. The negotiators at Waco were smart, able people who were giving the right advice, but unfortunately, they were overruled by their superiors. Despite the recent scandal at the Department of Veterans Affairs, many VA hospitals give outstanding care to the veterans who can get in. One problem has been the startling, and unanticipated, number of brain injuries inflicted on our troops in Iraq and Afghanistan by the improvised explosive devices (IEDs) used by insurgents. But, unquestionably, bureaucratic ineptitude played a part in the failure to provide timely services to veterans, and in the attempts to cover up that failure.

Ironically, a good many of the scandals that Republicans complain about were at least partially caused by inadequate funding for which Republicans were largely responsible. Budget cuts at the IRS have reduced a once-proud agency to the point where it cannot answer taxpayer phone calls, and its enforcement powers have been emasculated. In the years since 2010, Congress has cut the IRS budget by 17 percent in inflation-adjusted terms, resulting in a loss of one-fourth of its enforcement budget. As for the Environmental

Protection Agency, its average budget under Obama has been $8.8 billion in today's dollars, compared with $9.7 billion under George W. Bush and $10.6 billion under Bill Clinton. Today the EPA has fewer employees than it did in 1989, and yet it has more responsibilities than ever before. A Republican congressman, Scott DesJarlais, said, "It's clear that the EPA cannot currently handle the issues on its plate." But who other than the Republicans is responsible for the EPA not having the budget to carry out its responsibilities?

Democrats, for their part, have tended to be equally uninterested in improving the government. This may be because they have been so busy defending the government against unfair attacks that they have automatically adopted a defensive posture and have not done nearly enough to take on the issue of making the government work better. The only president who has taken any significant action in this direction is Bill Clinton, and, unfortunately, his Reinventing Government initiative, which showed considerable promise in its beginnings, became largely a downsizing effort that did not face the important need to attract new talent to the civil service.

THE TWO MOST frequent causes of cynicism about government in recent years concern gridlock and immigration. As for gridlock, "they can't get anything done in Washington" is the constant refrain. The permanent cause of this problem is, of course, the separation of powers ordained by the Constitution; thus, whenever voters choose to elect a president and a Congress of different parties, action becomes more difficult. And in the last six years of the Obama administration, they chose a Democratic president and a Republican House of Representatives dedicated to making him fail and ably assisted in that mission by a Republican Senate in the final two years. So it would seem that voters who blame Washington might better blame themselves.

The other most frequent complaint against government has been that it cannot control its borders, by which the critics mean one border, ours with Mexico. It is true that Border Patrol agents have sometimes been overwhelmed by the sheer number of illegal immigrants trying to cross that border, but it is also true that prejudice against Mexicans plays a considerable role in the critics' concern. That prejudice has existed for the past two centuries of American history, the most recent example being an unanticipated consequence of a Great Society reform, the Immigration Act of 1965.

Ted Kennedy was its floor manager in the Senate, and Lyndon Johnson signed it at the foot of the Statue of Liberty. Johnson said of the previous immigration policy, which had been especially unfair to Asians, Jews, and southern and eastern Europeans, "It violates the basic principle of American democracy, the principle that values and rewards each man on the basis of his merit as a man. It has been un-American in the highest sense, because it has been untrue to the faith that brought thousands to these shores even before we were a country." The bill that Johnson signed changed the face of America. Before 1965 the majority of immigrants had come from Europe. Since then, 53 percent have come from Latin America and 30 percent from Asia. The white population of the United States had decreased from over 80 percent to 63.4 percent by 2011, and by 2050 the country is projected to no longer be a majority white nation.

The 1965 act reversed the terrible exclusions of the immigration policy that had come into effect in the 1920s. At the same time, it has to be conceded that the relative unity of the Roosevelt era, for which I obviously have considerable nostalgia, may have been partially based on the reduction in immigration—the fact that society had time to assimilate the great wave of immigrants that arrived on our shores before World War I. There weren't stories of thousands and hundreds of thousands and even millions of illegal immigrants. But after 1965, the number of legal and illegal immigrants began to rise steadily, until it hit a peak in 1995, when roughly half the immigrants were illegal.

By the 1970s, the problem was beginning to cause a liberal-conservative split. When the 1965 bill was passed, it enjoyed considerable Republican support: 74 percent of Democrats voted for it and 85 percent of Republicans. But with the increase in both legal and illegal immigration from 1965 on, the Republicans changed. In 1976, a conservative publication, *Reader's Digest,* which happened to have the largest circulation of any magazine in America, published an article entitled "Illegal Aliens: A Time to Call a Halt!" By 1994, California was actually passing a measure, Proposition 187, intended to deny illegal immigrants access to public schools and social services, including healthcare. It got the support of 60 percent of the voters. The proposition was ruled unconstitutional by a federal judge, but it was a sign of the state of public opinion at that time. The Republican governor, Pete Wilson, was a leader of the anti-immigrant campaign.

By 2006, the Republican Pat Buchanan was declaring, "If we do not get control of our borders and stop this greatest invasion in history, I see the dissolution of the U.S. and the loss of the American Southwest." The conservative media have fanned the flames of anger to the point where a bus carrying women and children who had arrived illegally from Central America was attacked by an ugly mob recently in California.

Anger on the right prevents any solution to the immigration problem that involves a path to citizenship. We can't deport twelve million people. To be sure, there are those on the left who almost irrationally oppose any limitation on illegal immigration, but the fact remains that the most irrational are those on the right who stir up anger. After the Republican defeat in the 2012 presidential election, several moderate Republicans spoke out about the need for Republicans to accept reasonable immigration reform, arguing that otherwise they would permanently alienate the Hispanic vote. But the fact remains that during the Republican primary debates preceding that year's Republican National Convention, when Rick Perry dared to defend the admission of sons and daughters of illegal immigrants to Texas universities, he was attacked by all the other candidates and compelled to make a quick retreat. And not long after Republican leaders suggested reform following the 2012 defeat, they were soon quieted by the defeat in 2014 of the House Republican leader Eric Cantor by a tea party anti-immigration hard-liner. One year later Donald Trump was not only urging building a wall along our southern borders but actually proposing a ban on all Muslim immigration and deportation of all twelve million illegal immigrants already in this country. After he won the Republican primaries and the party's presidential nomination in 2016, Trump moderated his position, but his nomination confirmed the lesson for other Republican candidates that they can win primaries by being hard-liners on immigration.

As for my own feelings, obviously I disagree with the hard-liners and on the whole am sympathetic to the liberal policy on immigration. But as with abortion, guns, crime, and the environment, I understand the feelings of the people on the other side. It is not irrational to fear that Syrian refugees might include a few terrorists, as indeed they did in the case of those admitted to Europe who took part in the Paris and Brussels attacks. People on the other side can have views we regard as deplorable without being deplorable themselves. If we don't understand their side, how are we going to persuade them to see our side?

CHAPTER 10

★

# Fashionable Trouble

nnual lists of what's in and what's out did not become common until the 1970s, but there was one part of our culture where they had long reigned: the world of fashion. The importance of fashion grew steadily after World War II, beginning in 1947 with the introduction of Dior's New Look. Recall that in the 1950s, a fashion editor, Diana Vreeland of *Harper's Bazaar,* became enough of a celebrity that the 1957 movie *Funny Face* featured a character resembling her. By the third millennium, when another movie, *The Devil Wears Prada,* was made with a fashion editor at the center (a character much like Anna Wintour), the fashion industry had risen to become a major influence on the development of the nation's luxury economy, both a product of and an incentive for all of the money being made by those at the top.

The magazine Wintour edits, *Vogue,* publishes a September issue so packed with ads that a reader risks back injury just picking it up. In 2014, Wintour was named artistic director of all Condé Nast magazines. The editors of those magazines came like knights to a royal court to attend a party she gave at La Scala opera house in Milan. They included David Remnick of *The New Yorker* and Graydon Carter of *Vanity Fair.* At another event in Wintour's honor, this at the Metropolitan Museum's annual Costume Institute Gala, it was announced that the institute (founded, by the way, by Diana Vreeland) would be renamed the Anna Wintour Costume Center. The event was attended by movie stars, a flock of prominent designers, and, of course, all the Condé Nast editors. Michelle Obama was also present, prompting one guest to comment to a reporter for *The New York Times*: "Two first ladies in one room at the same time."

Obama's presence was one example of the importance the fashion industry has attained. At a recent party for another designer, Oscar de la Renta, the guests included a former first lady, Hillary Rodham Clinton, and her husband, Bill. Another sign of the industry's standing in the new millennium came in 2007 when a Pulitzer Prize was awarded to Robin Givhan of *The Washington Post* for her reporting on fashion. Givhan's coverage helps explain why the fashion industry has attained its current power. Here's her description of Michelle Obama's attire for a hike in the Grand Canyon: "Obama was wearing play shorts—the kind of casual cotton fare that a woman might choose for a family outing when her itinerary includes hiking around the rim of the Grand Canyon on a hot summer day. . . . But it does American culture no favors if a first lady tries so hard to be average that she winds up looking common."

What does Givhan admire? Well, clearly it's not looking common. As for what she finds worthy of praise, here's what she wrote about Hillary Clinton's staffer Huma Abedin: "When Abedin posed for *Vogue* in 2007, she established herself as a Washington power personality. Last year she made a return appearance in her wedding gown, a succinct pronouncement that her social currency had only risen." In other words, Givhan sees fashion as bestowing status, and that indeed is what fashion reporting does.

*The New York Times*, undeniably the nation's best and most influential newspaper, devotes more and more space to coverage of fashion. In 2004, it launched *T*, its style magazine. *T* is largely devoted to photographs and editorial copy that extol the virtues of designer and other luxury brands. It has become a great success, packed with ads for the same products shown in its photographs and described in its editorial copy. The *Times* also publishes Thursday and Sunday Styles sections that reflect similar points of view—namely that designer and luxury brands are essential. Consider a typical spread in *T*: One page features a model wearing a Dolce & Gabbana coat that sells for $3,145; the facing page offers a Chanel dress for $10,345. Looking at these alluring photographs—artworks themselves—of beautiful models clad in the latest designer apparel makes readers want to have these clothes, meaning either they or their spouses have to make enough money to buy them.

The effect on the reader was captured by a "What I Wore" column in one of the *Times*' Styles sections in which a reader is asked to tell what she wore in one week. In this example, the reader is Muffie Potter Aston, described by the *Times* as a "mainstay of the city's charity circuit" living on the Upper East Side with her husband, plastic surgeon Sherrell Aston:

> Dressed for a lunch at Le Cirque. . . . I put on a creamy white Dolce & Gabbana sleeveless turtleneck dress and draped a cream Christian Dior silk and lace sweater over my shoulders. I added cream Manolo Blahnik heels and a cream snakeskin Lambertson Truex bag. . . .
>
> At night, I was a co-chair for the opening-night gala of the American Ballet Theater. . . . I wore the most divine Badgley Mischka Couture silver sequin mermaid-style dress with double tulle overlays. I carried a light and dark silver Judith Leiber minaudière with this Art Deco design. My daughters each said I looked like a stunning princess.

Ms. Aston managed to drop designer and luxury brand names twenty-eight times in her seven-day diary.

Another Styles article reflected, if once again unconsciously, snobbery about fashion, while also throwing in a couple of other ways to look down one's nose. It described how the twenty-nine-year-old Audrey Gelman lured chic New Yorkers into participating in the political campaign of a candidate for the decidedly un-chic office of comptroller of the city of New York:

"Working in an arena—city politics—where it passes for 'style' if you manage to keep the mustard off the lapel of your Poly-blend suit, Ms. Gelman cuts a striking figure." For a fund-raiser, she "wore a sleeveless white Dior cocktail dress" and later "popped up in *Paper* magazine's 2013 list of 'Beautiful People,' wearing a Mod-inspired Vuitton shift. . . . She liked the idea of rolling up the sleeves of her Jil Sander blouse and delving into politics as practiced at the street level."

There is probably no other place where meritocratic and celebrity cultures are so intertwined as New York City. The *Times* story on Gelman notes that the able fund-raiser attended Oberlin College, one of the acceptable non-Ivies, with her friend Lena Dunham of *Girls*. How did Gelman and Dunham meet? "My mom was Lena's shrink for eight years," Gelman explains. They would run into each other in her mother's waiting room. Gelman's then-boyfriend, Terry Richardson, is described by the *Times* as a photographer "known for his pornography-chic portraits of skin-baring celebrities."

So politicians consume their hot dogs carelessly and wear—horror of horrors!—polyester suits, which everyone knows have been out since publication of *The Official Preppy Handbook* in 1980. But politicians can be okay if they wear Dior, go to the right school, have a best friend who is a celebrity, especially one they met in a way that makes a neat anecdote, and—better still—have a boyfriend who is known for pornography-chic.

Fashion's demand for luxury brand names extends even to children. One Fashion and Style section featured a child on its front page wearing a $1,570 taffeta coat from Barneys. Barneys, by the way, is an example of how New York retailers often followed the path from appealing to Everyman to appealing to the high-enders. In the early 1950s, I can remember, Barneys was advertising men's gray flannel suits for only $19.

Men have not been exempt from the high-end trend. Indeed, *T* has devoted entire issues to male fashion, and, of course, fashionable menswear also costs money. In one issue Bruce Pask, the *Times'* men's fashion editor, said, "The suit should properly contain the body. It's a very empowering thing to wear a jacket that hugs the torso, a shape that you fill completely and appropriately." The next paragraph of the *Times* article suggested this means you need "a skilled tailor." Custom-made suits usually start at around $2,000 and often go considerably higher, depending on the fabric and the identity of the tailor. *The Wall Street Journal*'s fashion page—by the way, the *Journal* publishes its own fashion magazine as well—featured a made-to-measure suit from the Italian tailor House of Kiton costing $40,000. But apparently a lot of men want to be empowered. Even male journalists, a type formerly known for their rumpled suits, now have personal tailors. After all, they can't risk a wrinkle if that cable news producer happens to call.

Of course, there's absolutely nothing wrong with wanting a suit that fits and is made of good material. But there's also nothing wrong with wearing an off-the-rack suit that fits, or one that does not bear a designer label. After all, the regular sizes were determined by what would fit most men.

The Scottish economist Robert Giffen determined that higher prices increase desirability rather than suppress demand. Indeed, according to *The Wall Street Journal,* the price of a basket of luxury goods rose 13 percent in 2013, while the regular consumer price index increased only 1.5 percent. Louis Vuitton raised the price of its monogrammed Speedy bag by 15 percent that year; its chief financial officer explained to the *Journal* that "the client base is used to that type of price increase." Such is the demand for things that are in.

*The New York Times* has become increasingly dependent on high-end advertising. In 2014 and again in 2015, the *Times* actually held something called the International Luxury Conference presided over by the editor-in-chief of *T,* Deborah Needleman, and its fashion director, Vanessa Friedman. Its concern: "How does the luxury market expand whilst maintaining a commitment to authenticity and innovation?" The *Times,* by the way, now accepts ads on the lower right-hand corner of its front page. Typically they come from firms such as Cartier and Tiffany. On page 3, the right-hand column is probably the next most desirable advertising space. A typical display was that of February 16, 2016. At the top is an ad for an "exquisite" diamond engagement ring by Tiffany, in the middle one for a suit by Dior, and below that a Van Cleef & Arpels ad for a diamond necklace. Tiffany has become a major *Times* advertiser, sometimes taking an entire page or section in addition to its space on pages 1 and 3.

The taste for luxury extends all the way from the $77 million apartments in Manhattan and $147 million Hamptons estates of hedge fund managers to university dorms for those who "want to send their sons or daughters to college campuses but give them all the luxuries of home." Today's pictures of students arriving at college often depict jammed SUVs or U-Hauls being unloaded by students and their parents. It's hard not to recall that in the 1930s, '40s, and '50s, a single suitcase would do the job. Certainly when I went to Columbia in 1946 that was the case, although my parents did send me a small radio, too, after I arrived. My wife tells me that when she went to college in the 1950s she carried a typewriter and a small footlocker, nothing more.

In general the contrast between the things people buy today and what they bought in the Roosevelt era (which I treat as the years between 1933 and 1965) is dramatic. In housing, the immense mansions that CEOs and hedge fund executives are putting up today stand in sharp contrast to the 1950s, when a *Fortune* article reported, "The executive who feels, as apparently Robert R. Young does, that to be completely happy he needs a forty room 'cottage' in Newport and a thirty-one room oceanside villa in Palm Beach is a rare bird these days." This same *Fortune* article said a typical '50s executive lived in a seven-room house.

In the '50s, women rarely paid more than $50 for a handbag or a pair of shoes, and usually less than $25. Today a four-digit price for either is practically required in the fashionable world, a price far greater than can be explained by inflation in the economy as a whole. A *Times* Fashion and Style section featured a Balenciaga calfskin satchel for $1,735. And, of course, Birkin bags, such as the one that Martha Stewart carried into the courtroom during her legal troubles, will get you into five-digit prices. As for shoes, even the simplest flats can command more than a thousand dollars.

Though the *Times*' *T* magazine covers subjects other than fashion strictly defined, it's worth noting here that fashion is always its real subject in letting readers know what's in and what's out. An article on the decorator Stephen Sills in the fall 2014 issue, devoted to design, illustrates just how this is done:

> Perhaps no pied-à-terre since Billy Baldwin's aubergine-lacquered studio on the Upper East Side has wielded so much influence as that of the Manhattan penthouse of Stephen Sills and his then-partner in business and life, James Huniford. The Sills style, which mixed innovation with a deep regard for history, attracted clients like Vera Wang and Tina Turner as well as supporters like Bill Blass and Anna Wintour. Even the French were impressed. . . . [Sills and Huniford's] prominence came at a moment when the received style of American decorating—embodied essentially by Parish-Hadley, Mario Buatta and McMillen—was winding down, and the question lingered as to what would come next. . . . The answer arrived in the form of the work of Sills Huniford.
>
> Sills, now 63, recently completed redecorating the space, the third reimagining of this environment since he moved here in 1988. . . . The surfaces have been bleached, limed and white-washed, creating a ghosted-over version of its former self. The one exception is a chic new dressing room, which has been veneered entirely in dyed-green satinwood paneling that suggests the first-class compartment of some mysterious European train.

"I just can't live with color anymore," the designer says, and while he means it in a general sense, he doesn't mean it the way Richard Meier or John Pawson would. Sills's love of color runs deeply through his work, as the green room attests. He uses color for its potential to introduce an element of the exotic to rooms—a feeling of otherworldliness, not unlike what Wes Anderson does with his movie sets. The new apartment, with its bleached parquet floor made in Poland, monumental Hellenistic lion sculpture and daybed by Jean-Michel Frank—improbable as these contents may make it seem—is about the future. "I want it to be very Cubistic," Sills explains enigmatically, possibly referring to the angular 1930s French armchairs posed in the living room.

The idea behind such writing about taste is to make the reader feel at once more sophisticated and at the same time insecure about what he still doesn't know, so that he'll keep coming back for more. *T* keeps its readers coming back by both satisfying their need to feel in, in this case by assuring them that Sills is definitely in and their rooms should be pale. At the same time it leaves them nervous about what they don't know—namely, does that accent of color have to be a whole room or can you get by with a red pillow or two? And the reader is left wondering, What about Huniford? The article says that Huniford and Sills have now split and that Huniford is operating on his own, but does not tell us whether Huniford is still chic.

I'm afraid that the part of the Sills message that has registered most strongly is "I just can't live with color." Much of recent interior decorating seems relentlessly bland, with kitchens that look so sterile one expects a patient to be wheeled in for surgery.

THOUGH THE *TIMES* and the Condé Nast publications are among the guiltiest parties in spreading the what's-in gospel, there are exceptions among their writers. Neil Irwin of the *Times* exposed the absurdity of the in and out lists with a list of trendy foods as determined by *New York Times* food critics. Quiche, which reigned from 1967 to 1980, is no longer mentioned; fried calamari (1980 to 1996) has dropped out. Two of the longest-lasting items were radicchio and goat cheese, which were in favor from 1980 to 2010. The briefest reign belonged to tuna tartare (1994 to 2000). The latest champion appears to be kale; the most frequently mentioned of all, it has been going strong since 2002.

Another version of the what's-in, what's-out preoccupation is the restaurant list. Daniel Riley wrote in *GQ* describing how he had eaten in five of *Bon Appétit*'s Best New Restaurants in America and at all of the Best New Restaurants in Cambridge, Massachusetts. He confessed that he has seen this practice as the best way to demonstrate conversational "with-it-ness." He writes that for him and his friends, "there are lots of dinners where the conversation centered solely on what other places we've been to and which we plan to try. For every restaurant we checked off we added two until that game became unwinnable and exhausting." He came to realize that his fascination "had nothing to do with anticipation of tasting the entrée that had been recommended or the drinks that would be served but rather with the validation of crossing the thing off the list and knowing full well that I have a new 'Yep, I've been there' to wield."

The old elite distinguished itself by social class, so that if two of its members encountered someone lacking that status, one would whisper to the other what sounded like "knock" but was, in fact, "NOC," meaning "not our class." Today they might note instead that the person in question does not seem to know the difference between Parish-Hadley and Sills Huniford. Taste has become the way that class is proved. But taste has also become very expensive. Looking back at my most pretentious days at Columbia in the late 1940s, I recall how cheap it was to be a snob, at least the cultural one I aspired to be. My income through most of my time at Columbia was $105 a month, and that was enough to afford weekly trips to a concert or the theater or ballet, for which the prices were usu-

ally $1.20 or $1.80 for the cheapest tickets, maybe $2.40 for the
Metropolitan Opera. I could impress my girlfriend simply by knowing the difference between red and white wine, or with my knowledge of which were the good inexpensive restaurants. Barbetta in
those days served cheap—and wonderful—Neapolitan food, not
the high-end Northern Italian cuisine that has been offered there
since the 1960s by the Vassar-educated daughter of the original pro-
prietor.

Taste had become firmly established as the measure of class by
the 1980s. At the same time, much larger numbers of people began
wanting to be rich. Since then, taste as a signifier of class has become so intertwined with the desire to be wealthy that it's hard to
know which comes first or which causes the other. Nowhere was
this more evident than in the world of art. In the 1940s or '50s, if
you wanted to display your knowledge of art, you would have a
print of a work that you admired on your wall for an investment of
a couple of dollars. But somewhere in the '70s it became important
to have some kind of original work on the wall, and that meant
money—more and more of it as the price of art escalated. In 1967,
a new record was set for the highest price paid for an artwork when
a Leonardo da Vinci painting sold for $35 million. By 1987, that
price had been eclipsed by a Van Gogh that sold for $82 million.
And in 2011, a Cézanne went for $259 million (all prices in current
dollars).

Of course, if you discover an artist before he's become in, you
can prove your taste for far less. And you can still have the right
posters on the wall, but today the right posters can cost several hundred dollars.

One very good thing that's happened to the country in this regard is that knowledge of art has improved dramatically since the
1950s. A section devoted to art in the new season in the Sunday
*New York Times* recently ran to twenty-seven pages in a paper
where, in the 1940s and '50s, there might have been one given over
to art. The growth in attendance at museums has been equally im-

pressive. If you go to a major show these days you may not even be able to get near the better-known works because the crowd around them is so great. I remember attending a Turner exhibit at the Metropolitan Museum in New York in late 1946 or early '47 and encountering only a handful of people for what was a major show. Today it would be mobbed.

There is a nagging question, however, about this great surge in museum-going: How many people are going for the same reason that Daniel Riley was going to all those restaurants—to check them off a list of in things? Certainly, if you have made the effort to see the more popular works in the more popular art shows, you know that the experience is not exactly a magic one as you try to view the works through the scores of bobbing heads of other viewers. It is hard not to suspect that at least one of the motives for going to those museums is, in fact, the same as eating at in restaurants, getting into the right schools, scoring well on the SATs, and being accepted by the right university.

AFTER GRADUATING FROM an A-list college, with all As, the next step is picking the right graduate school. For most of the meritocratic elite in the late 1970s that meant institutions that issue either law degrees or MBAs. At first the law degree was to get them into a top law firm that was advising large businesses or Wall Street, while the business school was to prepare them for the elite job. In the late '70s, that was management consultant. They went to work for firms such as McKinsey. One was my friend and former Peace Corps colleague Julien Phillips. Julien remained with the firm for his entire career, but he tells me that in the early '80s, many of his colleagues began to look at how much money was being made by the people they were advising and decided they needed to make some of it themselves. How much did that desire to make more money have to do with their growing perception of the need to prove their class by demonstrating their good taste, and with their realization that this process created the need for more and more money? Money that, of course, could be obtained by reaching the higher peaks of the corporate and financial world.

Another factor in the growing desire to make money was simply the growth of selfishness in the country, the tilting from a society concerned with community and generosity and a willingness to share burdens and benefits, which characterized the Roosevelt era, to the "Me" decade of the '70s and beyond that became more and more concerned with satisfying selfish desires.

Probably the most widely publicized source of large incomes is the compensation of the stars of the sports and entertainment world and the owners and producers of the franchises and studios behind their work. Equally important are the fortunes earned by the entrepreneurs of Silicon Valley, and even more important are the salaries and bonuses earned by CEOs and other corporate executives, most of which have steadily become more excessive since the early 1980s. These have been compounded by awards of stock that the CEOs themselves have cashed in through stock buybacks that the CEOs have been principals in deciding upon.

Wall Street is home to the more conspicuous and influential moneymakers. They are conspicuous because, like many of their fellow rich of today, they like to flaunt their wealth. (The 2001 Broadway production of *The Producers* featured a song entitled "When You've Got It, Flaunt It.") They are both conspicuous and influential for another reason: They live in New York, a major molder of American tastes and values. Wall Streeters fueled the real estate industry that builds the offices, apartments, and mansions where they work and live. They also finance much of the art, music, dance, theater, and other entertainment in the city, as well as most of its fine restaurants, private schools, charities, and good causes—Lloyd Blankfein of Goldman Sachs became a cochair of Human Rights Watch. Indeed, they are the principal funders of the luxury industry, which, in turn, has become the most prominent advertiser in *The New York Times*. The paper's fashion reporting is the most obvious example of the influence of the city's wealth, but even one of the *Times'* most thoughtful opinion writers can unconsciously show its influence. In a recent column, David Brooks wrote:

> I've been living in and visiting New York for almost half a century now. One thought occurs to me as I walk around these days: the city has never been better.
>
> There has never been a time when there were so many places to visit, shop, and eat, when the rivers and parks were so beautiful, when there were so many vibrant neighborhoods across all the boroughs.

If you can afford it. The rivers and parks are free, but those shops and restaurants aren't, nor are the vibrant neighborhoods. I remember walking around Manhattan and Brooklyn during the late '40s and thinking that one neighborhood after another could, with some spiffing up, be made quite attractive. That has happened, but almost without exception, those neighborhoods have become expensive places to live.

Wall Street has become so essential to the economy of New York that it reminds me of the role that the coal industry played in West Virginia. The question is, Will Wall Street's influence be as baleful as the coal industry's? In West Virginia, coal has always had its courageous critics, but fear of killing the goose that seemed to be laying the golden egg kept most people quiet. Indeed, it has prevented many from even being able to face the harm the industry is doing. One has to wonder how many New Yorkers have similar fears about facing what is wrong with Wall Street.

———————★———————

# CHAPTER 11

# Clinton and Beyond

In 1977, Hillary Clinton moved with her husband, Bill, to Little Rock, where he was assuming the office of Arkansas attorney general. Heretofore she had rejected what she had described in her Wellesley graduation speech as the "acquisitive and competitive life of the corporate world." She had demonstrated that rejection by working at the nonprofit Children's Defense Fund in Washington and for the House Judiciary Committee during the Nixon impeachment hearings, as well as by heading the legal aid clinic at the University of Arkansas. But now she would join the Rose Law Firm, the major corporate law firm in Arkansas, representing the state's three leading companies: Wal-Mart, Tyson Foods, and Stephens, the state's largest investment firm.

For her, the position meant a substantial income and the prestige associated with working for the town's leading legal firm. For the firm, having the wife of a high state official as a partner would suggest to potential clients that it was not without influence in the public sphere. That impression would become even stronger when her husband was elected governor in 1978. Her acquisitive instincts were further honed by her association with her friend Jim Blair, a Tyson Foods executive who had become a prominent and successful player in the commodities futures market, specifically concentrating on cattle futures. In just six months, she turned a $1,000 investment into $100,000, and was then smart enough to get out.

Her success in the market did not go unnoticed by critics, who found it interesting that she didn't have to pay up when she lost on trades, as most traders did. And from time to time during the months when she was in the market, she did suffer losses. It seems probable that her not being required to pay up when those losses occurred had some relation to her friendship with Blair and with the fact that she was the governor's wife. She went on to profitable relationships with the corporate world, soon becoming a director of Wal-Mart and, by 1991, of several other corporations.

But one of her ventures into moneymaking definitely did not work out: when she and her husband got involved in the Whitewater land development project. The Clintons lost money on that deal, and it is hard to see how they committed any significant wrongdoing in connection with it, as a long 1992 article in *The New York Times* implied. Whitewater became the first of a series of "scandals" with which Hillary Clinton's name is often linked in the media and by right-wing critics to suggest that she is either untrustworthy or, as Donald Trump contends, downright crooked. Whitewater, however, is an illustration not of her untrustworthiness or crookedness but of her defensiveness.

In December 1993, as *The Washington Post* was demanding that the Clintons release all Whitewater documents, practically the entire White House staff supported handing over the papers. Only Hillary opposed doing so, and her intransigence led to the appointment of a special prosecutor and ultimately of Ken Starr. He was unable to prove the Clintons guilty of anything in regard to Whitewater but managed to torment them with other accusations, culminating in Bill Clinton's impeachment by the House of Representatives.

Her continued defensiveness is understandable in light of her treatment by right-wingers including Fox News, Rush "Fort Marcy" Limbaugh, and Donald Trump, who actually repeated the rumor about Vince Foster's "murder." Still, it has led her too often to give the appearance of having something to hide, even though that "something" usually turns out to be something not crooked but at worst embarrassing, such as her venture into commodities futures.

The commodities futures deals, her corporate directorships, and her motivation for getting into Whitewater were, however, signs of an acquisitive bent that became characteristic of both Clintons after they left the White House and moved to New York and a life among the rich, chic, and famous, where amassing a fortune in excess of $100 million seemed perfectly natural.

But until Bill Clinton became a former president in 2001, he had manifested little interest in making money—the sole exception being Whitewater, which mostly involved Hillary. His passion was politics, and nobody had more skill than he in practicing that art. His great gift was his curiosity about every human being he met. He seemed truly interested in people, and they in turn ended up liking him and wanting to vote for him. In his book *My Life,* he wrote: "I learned that everyone has a story—of dreams and nightmares, hope and heartache, love and loss, courage and fear, sacrifice and selfishness. All my life I've been interested in other people's stories. I wanted to know them, understand them, feel them."

Bill Clinton was an exception to the rule among baby boomers, the great majority of whom lost interest in politics as a career sometime in the '70s and never regained it. Their interest in politics became sporadic, centered mostly on presidential campaigns and on specific causes such as women's rights or gay rights. Clinton may have been influenced by the excitement of the 1960 presidential race between John F. Kennedy and Richard Nixon, by the New Frontier's call to public service, and by the impressive steps taken by both Kennedy and Lyndon Johnson in support of civil rights, in which Clinton was a strong believer. Clinton enjoyed not only politics in general but the specific political act of governing. Once again, he was the exception. And it was the lack of interest among his fellow baby boomers in participating in government that led to the decline of public service in this country that is so evident today.

Clinton also was highly intelligent and indeed was among the first to detect where the Democratic Party was going wrong in the 1970s. His support for Jimmy Carter in 1976 showed that he understood the need to keep the average white guy in the Democratic Party. In 1980 Clinton made a speech at the Democratic National Convention in which he warned of a "dangerous and growing number who are opting for special-interest and single-interest-group politics, which threatens to take every last drop of blood out of our political system."

Unfortunately for Clinton, all his brilliant political analysis and talent as a politician could not save him from defeat in his 1980 bid for reelection as governor. One major problem was that Carter was at the top of the Democratic ticket, and the president had gone from popular in Arkansas to very unpopular. In addition, Clinton had proposed a tax on license plates to finance increased aid to education. The problem was that the tax rose with the weight of the vehicle, and older cars—the kind driven by the average person—tended to be heavier than newer models. Jimmy Carter, already a burden, did Clinton no favor by sending several thousand Cuban immigrants to Fort Smith, Arkansas. The Cubans had been allowed to leave by Fidel Castro, who'd wanted to get rid of political opponents but had also opened prison doors in his country, so that the flood of immigrants contained a mixture of good people and some murderers, rapists, and other criminals. Carter had to send them somewhere to be sorted out, and he picked Fort Smith. Some of the less desirable immigrants escaped and wreaked havoc on nearby communities. It all added up to a humiliating defeat for Clinton in November 1980.

Clinton could hardly be blamed for Fort Smith; he had opposed Carter's decision to send the Cubans there. But he got the blame nonetheless, a situation somewhat like what had befallen Carter himself when he was held responsible for the Americans taken hostage in Iran. It wasn't Carter's fault, any more than Fort Smith was Clinton's, but both got the blame. Another unfortunate problem with the Fort Smith Cubans: A considerable proportion of them were black, their presence thus contributing to the kind of fears that the coded racism of Nixon and Reagan had helped foster. One of the constant difficulties for figures such as Clinton and Carter, who were trying to lead the South and the country out of its racist past, was the unspoken but clear anti-black message of the Nixons and Reagans.

The Fort Smith disturbances recalled the baleful effect that the riots in Los Angeles, Detroit, and Washington had on similar efforts by Lyndon Johnson in the 1960s. Clinton had the common sense to realize that our better angels are seldom easy victors over our baser instincts; that's why he was so upset when Carter put those Cubans in Fort Smith.

Clinton stood out among Democratic politicians in 1980 for his willingness to think originally. He was absolutely right about the danger of letting special-interest and single-interest groups prevail when their interest is not in the national interest.

Unfortunately, this kind of politics prevailed despite his warnings. Clinton was also one of the first governors to face the problem of the quality of public school teachers. After he won back the governor's seat in 1982, he took on the Arkansas Education Association, the state's teachers' union, on the issue of teacher competence, and with Hillary leading the charge, he fought hard; indeed, he so angered the union that it opposed him in his next election.

The education program he proposed to the Arkansas legislature in 1983 had been developed by a task force headed by Hillary and included many things dear to the teachers' hearts, including higher pay and smaller classes. And to finance their higher pay, he supported an increase in the sales tax, which was not an issue with automatic political appeal. Still, the teachers' unions, in an example of what was and remains their fatal flaw, opposed him solely because he dared to suggest that some of them might not be competent as teachers.

The union fought hard against the bill, with its members crowding the state capitol, heckling Hillary and filling the Senate gallery as the crucial vote approached. It was clear that every vote would count. One state senator, Vada Sheid, told of her experience with Clinton's lobbying on the issue. Her story illustrates how much he relied on friendships he had built up through years of campaigning. Clinton and Sheid had first met in 1974 when he came into her furniture store in the town of Mountain Home to seek her support in his run for Congress. They struck up a conversation, and she sewed a loose button on his shirt. Nine years later she was a state senator planning to vote against his education bill because she needed the support of the teachers' union in her next election campaign.

"Bill Clinton comes to the Senate, he calls me and he says, 'Vada, you're not thinkin' clear, you've forgotten your grandchildren have always had priority with you. . . . You're afraid, Vada, but I have to have one more vote to pass this thing.' "

When she expressed her concern and said, "This will defeat me," Clinton told her he had to have this one vote, and "he was emotional about it." Despite her fears, she then voted for Clinton's education package. Her reward was a vigorous union campaign against her and the loss of her seat in the next election.

But Clinton remembered what she had done and appointed her to the State Police Commission. One might not instantly conclude that her background as a furniture store owner would qualify her to be a police commissioner, but assuming that she was qualified, I would defend the practice of awarding government jobs to people to whom one is politically indebted. Again assuming that the person is qualified, it is the kind of innocent favor that one can do, and innocent favors are important to the practice of decent politics. I see a lot wrong, however, with the ignorance of most of the elite regarding politics and how to practice it decently.

Perhaps the clearest example of this was the widespread criti-

cism from the elites about Clinton's invitation to campaign con-
tributors to stay in the Lincoln Bedroom. The fact is that if you're
trying to practice good politics, decent politics, you have to have a
way to reward people that does not involve selling out on an issue.
That is the wrong response to a campaign contribution. But there's
nothing wrong with finding an innocent favor you can do—like an
invitation to dinner or to stay the night at the White House—for
someone who has helped you in politics.

But back to Clinton and education reform. With Vada Sheid's
help, Clinton's bill passed and education reform became a fact in
Arkansas. It took Clinton more than three years and two elections,
though, to win back the support of the teachers' union. Clinton
made his stand on school reform for two reasons. One was that if
the children of Arkansas were to have a fair chance in life, they
needed a better education than they had been getting, and the right
to that fair chance was more important than an unsuitable teacher's
right to a job. His other reason was the need for America to regain
its competitive edge, which it seemed to be losing as the '70s edged
into the '80s, and other countries, especially Japan and Germany,
were believed to be making better products than we were.

AT *THE WASHINGTON MONTHLY* we were Clinton's allies on both
the need to give students a fair chance in life and the need to improve the country's competitiveness. Throughout the '70s we were
the only publication, liberal or conservative, to consistently write
about the need for more entrepreneurs. But we did make a distinction that Clinton sometimes neglected. We wanted entrepreneurs
who would create new and better products and services, and who
could provide jobs. With Clinton, too often in his career, this interest in entrepreneurialism would simply lead him to side with business on issues, most damagingly in the late '90s when he permitted
a deregulation of Wall Street that was to prove very unfortunate for
the economy.

Others came along in the 1980s to revitalize thinking among

liberals and Democrats. One was a friend of Bill Clinton's from Oxford and Yale, the economist Robert Reich, who wrote that in the 1970s we had gotten used to an economy where the question was how we could divide the existing pie in an equitable manner rather than how we could increase the size of the pie for all. Gary Hart, who had run the McGovern campaign in 1972 and later been elected to the U.S. Senate from Colorado, provided new thinking about national defense. In fact, it could be said that just about any thinking done by liberals on national defense would be new; the prevalence of anti-war sentiment in the late '60s and early '70s had made defense something on which they had pretty much the same attitude: They were against the military.

A writer named Randall Rothenberg wrote a book about some of the new thinking on the left by those he called "neoliberals." I had come up with that name at a tenth anniversary dinner for *The Washington Monthly* because a story had appeared in *The Washington Post* that morning that called us "neoconservatives," and I thought it didn't really describe what we were about. Rothenberg not only saw the merit of what we had been talking about at the *Monthly* and what Gary Hart had been saying on defense and Robert Reich on the economy, he also saw, as the *Monthly* did not, that the element most likely to revitalize the economy was in the realm of technology, with the microchip and an information revolution at its heart.

Unfortunately, these new thinkers were dismissed by the late Joseph Kraft, an influential columnist at that time, as "Atari Democrats." Certainly our thinking did not have much influence on the upper reaches of the Democratic Party in the '80s. The presidential nominee in 1984, Walter Mondale, who had been Jimmy Carter's vice president, was an immensely likable man with a delightful sense of humor. But his thinking tended to be along conventional Democratic lines, and he happened to run in a year when he could have been the most unconventional candidate in the world and still not have had much chance against Ronald Reagan, who carried every state but Minnesota and the District of Columbia. The Democratic candidate in 1988, Michael Dukakis, campaigned on the idea that he would be a competent president, just as he had been a competent governor of Massachusetts. He was not as likable as Mondale and lacked the former vice president's sense of humor; one comedian called him the only colorless Greek in America.

When Dukakis was asked at a debate what he would do if his wife was raped and murdered, Dukakis's answer seemed legalistic and unemotional. In his one gesture toward Democratic reformers, he tried to show his interest in the military by being photographed riding in a tank. Unfortunately, the image of his head poking out of the tank turret in an oversize helmet simply made him look ridiculous. The *Monthly* had just gone to press, carrying a piece in which I congratulated Dukakis for running a skillful campaign. When I saw that picture I figured that anyone who read my words would be laughing as hard at me as at Dukakis.

Needless to say, Dukakis lost the election; George H. W. Bush won forty states. Afterward, Robert Reich observed that "liberalism and, inevitably, the Democratic party, too, appeared less the embodiment of a shared vision and more a tangle of narrow appeals from labor unions, teachers, gays, Hispanics, blacks, Jews . . . fractious Democratic constituencies, each promoting its own agenda." (This was true, but it's also important to remember that the interests of the Democratic groups were a lot closer to the national interest than were those of the groups represented by the Republican Party.)

The stage was now set for Bill Clinton, who depicted himself as a different kind of Democrat, a man who wouldn't automatically be a slave to those interest groups. Clinton had already demonstrated his independence from conventional liberalism by taking on the teachers' unions and requiring competence testing for Arkansas teachers. In the most famous and symbolic incident of his presidential campaign, he rebuked a statement by a black political activist named Sister Souljah, who had said: "If black people kill black people every day, why not have a week and kill white people?" In another statement in a music video, she said, "If there are good white people I haven't met them." Clinton's comment was, "If you took the words 'white' and 'black' and you reversed them you might think David Duke was giving that speech."

Clinton also advocated reforming welfare, requiring that it be coupled with work and job training. He also promised a middle-class tax cut, with the definition of the middle class including the working class.

As a Rhodes scholar from down home, Clinton was able to appeal to meritocrats and campaign as sufficiently racially progressive to become known as "the first black president," yet he was able to win back many of the whites that had been lost to the Democratic Party since Carter's victory in 1976. He did not do as well as Carter in the South. Still, he carried four former Confederate states and all the border states.

Clinton understood that average whites did not like being looked down upon by those who instructed them in what was politically correct. He realized that if he was going to tell them they should not advocate violence against blacks, he had to also say that blacks were wrong to urge violence against whites. Subsequent Democratic presidential candidates Al Gore, John Kerry, Barack Obama, and Hillary Clinton have not shared his gift for speaking to the average white as an equal. This has left the Rush Limbaughs and the Donald Trumps free to suggest that every liberal appeal to the average man's better angels should be scorned as political correctness.

CLINTON WAS THE first baby boomer to become president. He was also the first draft evader to win the country's highest office. Every president from Harry Truman through George H. W. Bush had served in the military—Reagan, of course, ended up being assigned to make movies, but he had enlisted and subjected himself to serving wherever required. It became clear that baby boomers were willing to forgive draft evaders, as they did with George W. Bush, who had gone into the Air National Guard, a sure way of avoiding the draft during the Vietnam War. In 2000, 2004, and 2008, men who had served—Al Gore, John Kerry, and John McCain—all lost presidential elections to men who had not served. And in the 2012 race, neither Barack Obama nor Mitt Romney had served in the military. It was no longer an issue.

According to a 2013 Pew Research Center report, the percentage of Americans who served in the military has been declining since 1970. This means fewer and fewer people have a real sense of what's going on with the armed forces. The number of members of Congress who have served declined steadily from 72 percent in the House and 78 percent in the Senate in 1971 to about 20 percent today. Few Americans were aware that the fighting in Iraq and Afghanistan was done by a relatively small number of people from our relatively small military. From an army of about 500,000 there were slightly fewer than 100,000 combat troops. Because of the demands of the two wars, these combat soldiers were repeatedly called back into the field. By contrast, a draftee served one year in Vietnam, and that was the end of his exposure to danger.

The soldiers who keep getting sent to Iraq and Afghanistan for repeated tours of duty have to get on the planes carrying them back with full knowledge of the terrors that lie ahead of them, and with an awareness that with every day of combat, their chances of being wounded or killed grow. The public does not know how to distinguish between those who deserve our special honor and care, and those to whom less is owed. For example, with regard to former soldiers on the waiting list for care at VA hospitals, it may well be that those with combat-related injuries should have priority. But hardly any of the comment about the recent scandal over treatment for veterans made that point, and almost none of the war reporting dealt with the relatively small number of people who were actually doing the fighting.

The dismaying fact is that more than half of the military serve in bureaucrats' staffs, in the Pentagon, or in places such as CENTCOM headquarters in Tampa, Florida, where we discovered, thanks to the Petraeus-Broadwell-Kelley scandal, that commanders had the kind of entourages that we would expect to find in the court of an emperor. (Photos of the then–CENTCOM commander leaving his base to attend a party given by Jill Kelley show him preceded by a V-shaped escort of a dozen or so motorcyclists reminiscent of a presidential inaugural parade.) There is something truly disturbing about a public that sings the national anthem with such fervor and talks about honoring our veterans while devoting so little effort to either serving or finding out the facts about those who do serve.

Bill Clinton was certainly justified in opposing the war in Vietnam, but one can ask why he didn't do voluntary service in a civilian cause, as his opponent for the 1992 nomination, Senator Paul Tsongas of Massachusetts, had in Ethiopia from 1962 to 1964 as a Peace Corps volunteer. Clinton won a draft deferment by pledging to authorities that he would join the Reserve Officer Training Corps. This enabled him to return to Oxford for the second year of the Rhodes scholarship he had won. During that year the draft lottery went into effect and Clinton received a high number that meant he would not be drafted. He then decided to withdraw his pledge to join the ROTC. As his biographer David Maraniss observed, "Clinton played the draft like a chess player."

As it turned out, with so many of his fellow members of the meritocratic elite behaving similarly, he was not punished at the polls as he pursued his political career. Only a handful from the generations that follow the baby boomers have performed military service, and an even smaller number come from the meritocratic elite.

From 1980 to 1992 America developed into a country that cherished patriotism, but not to the extent of paying taxes for the common good or doing one's part to provide for the common defense. The decline in the number of people willing to join the military was accompanied by a similar decline in the willingness of the country's most privileged to pay anything like the top tax rates that had prevailed prior to Ronald Reagan's presidency. Reagan slashed the top tax rate from 70 percent to 36 percent during his administration, with the largest cut coming in 1981, and it never again rose above 39 percent.

Another factor, often unacknowledged, is the impact on Americans of the payroll tax that finances Social Security. Since 1980 the tax has grown to the point that it constitutes the largest tax burden on those with incomes less than $80,000. Ironically, a good part of the proceeds of that tax goes to finance the retirement of people who are affluent enough to not really need Social Security. So money is taken from those who have come to need it more and more as their share of the economy shrinks and directed to those who need it less and less because their share is steadily increasing.

The growing solicitude for the "haves" found its most extreme expression in what happened to the estate tax between the early 1970s and today. Back then, it kicked in at $200,000. Now the estate has to be more than $5 million.

But perhaps more important was the way that the need to make money grew after 1980, and the influence that desire had in bringing about huge pay increases for top corporate executives and those in the finance industry, with its growing emphasis on making money for its own sake rather than to foster growth in the American economy.

Ironically, Bill Clinton, in so many ways the populist advocate of the average man and woman, ended up serving the culture of moneymaking. In 1998, four of his appointees played a crucial role in sabotaging Commodity Futures Trading Commission chair Brooksley Born's proposal to regulate derivatives. The guilty members of the Clinton team were Robert Rubin, his Treasury secretary; Larry Summers, Rubin's deputy; Alan Greenspan, whom Clinton had reappointed as Federal Reserve chairman; and Arthur Levitt, Clinton's chairman of the Securities and Exchange Commission. And in 2000, Congress passed and Clinton signed the Commodity Futures Modernization Act, which prohibited *any* agency from regulating derivatives. He had already, in 1999, signed the repeal of the

Glass-Steagall Act, the New Deal–era legislation that since 1933 had prevented banks from engaging in risky trading activities.

This was only four years after just one reckless trader, Nick Leeson, brought down Barings, London's oldest merchant bank. It was also just four years after the last of this country's savings and loans were closed as part of the resolution of the S&Ls scandal that had peaked in 1989, a scandal made possible by deregulation that had begun under Jimmy Carter but had become a religion under Ronald Reagan. S&Ls were permitted to engage in activities so risky that more than a thousand were forced to close their doors at a cost to the taxpayer of more than $130 billion. Were these experiences forgotten or their lessons simply ignored by Clinton and the Congress in 1999?

Almost immediately after the repeal of Glass-Steagall, Citicorp merged with Travelers to create Citigroup, a giant financial conglomerate that included Salomon Smith Barney, which, with its risky trading activities, quickly pushed the new organization into deep financial trouble. In 1999 the economy improved, however, and Citigroup survived and prospered until the flaws of its gigantism were finally revealed in the economic collapse of 2008. Interestingly enough, Sandy Weil, the head of Citigroup, hired Robert Rubin in 1999, and he served Citigroup for ten years as an adviser to the chairman. Rubin later said that although he had advised Citigroup to take more risks, he also advised that the risk be carefully managed. Somehow he must have failed to communicate the latter advice.

Just before the market crash in 2007, the bank had $43 billion in collateralized debt obligations (CDOs), the riskiest of all the new financial instruments. The collateral for the debt was a large number of mortgages, some perfectly sound, some worthless, but so long separated from their original lenders that no one who held the instruments could have confidence in their soundness. When the financial meltdown began, they immediately began to unload those CDOs. AIG, the main insurer of the CDOs, nearly collapsed. Rubin refused to accept any responsibility for the financial meltdown that followed in 2008. Earlier, when Rubin was at Treasury, he advised Bill Clinton to avoid using polarizing terms such as "the rich," "corporate welfare," and even "corporate responsibility." When Robert Reich would suggest some populist policy, Rubin would say, "Look, I spent most of my life on Wall Street. I can tell you you're just asking for trouble."

Later, when I read about Barack Obama's Treasury secretary Timothy Geithner and his advice to the president, it turned out to be similar to Rubin's on too many occasions. The problem was not that Geithner wasn't a good and thoughtful man, but that his motto, "First do no harm," led him to fear any action that he thought could possibly lead to another Lehman Brothers, an investment bank that failed in 2008 and shook investor confidence in other financial institutions, leading to the collapse of stock prices and the recession that quickly followed. Thus the fear of upsetting financial markets in some way or other has limited the reformist instincts of Democratic presidents who might otherwise have entertained tougher responses to the abuses of the corporate and financial worlds.

If Clinton and the Democrats were guilty of being too cozy with the rich, the Republicans were consistently much worse, with Ronald Reagan their symbolic leader. To understand the growth of the moneymaking culture and how it separated the society in a way that has 40 percent of the nation's wealth in the hands of 1 percent of the population, while 90 percent are poorer today than they were in 1987, it helps to recall the budget bill that accompanied Reagan's tax cut that Congress passed in July 1981. Taken together, the bills signaled to the haves of the nation that they were not only deserving of a much larger share of the wealth but could also shed some of their responsibility for those in need of a helping hand by cutting the food stamp program and a program designed to give jobs to the unemployed.

Corporate executives among the haves soon afterward got a signal as to where that much larger share of the wealth might come from. During the 1980 campaign, Reagan had not enjoyed widespread union support, but he had sought and won the support of the Professional Air Traffic Controllers Organization. So when PATCO had wage and working-condition demands to make on the administration in 1981, it had reason to expect the administration to be sympathetic. And indeed, Drew Lewis, Reagan's secretary of transportation, did reach a tentative agreement with Robert Poli, the head of PATCO. But when the agreement was submitted to union locals, many of them dissented. Poli decided to call a strike. Although there was a law forbidding federal employees from striking, several federal employee groups had in the past carried out work stoppages and escaped punishment. PATCO itself had staged a "sick-in" just a few years before in which workers called in sick. But this time they did not get away with it. Reagan immediately announced that if the air controllers didn't return to work within forty-eight hours they would be fired. When 11,345 of them did not return, Reagan made good on his threat and fired them.

Curiously enough, the strike was not caused by a feeling on the part of the controllers that they weren't making enough. One union member later recalled, "We certainly couldn't complain at the time of being underpaid." He said they were, however, troubled by "the difference between what we were making and what airline pilots were making." This is an interesting aspect of that controversy, because that is exactly what happened to so many people in the 1980s. It wasn't a matter of whether they were making enough; rather, it was what someone else was making that troubled them. A survey ten years later found that less than half of the controllers who had been fired were making as much as they had made at the time they went on strike.

The controllers had assumed that people would not put up with the delays in airline service that would be caused if they were fired. But there was no great public outcry in support of the workers. The opposite was true: There was widespread support for Reagan, even though air traffic was slowed for a considerable period. The situation was somewhat alleviated by assigning military controllers to temporary duty on civilian airways and by the fact that some five thousand air traffic controllers did not go on strike.

Reagan may have been justified in firing the striking controllers, but he then twisted the knife in a way that, in retrospect at least, seems quite shocking. He prohibited the controllers from seeking any federal employment for the rest of their lives. No wonder they had difficulty equaling their previous earnings.

Reagan's stunning lack of empathy for the worker inspired other employers to feel that they could not only get away with turning the screws on their workers, but that they were justified in doing so. The result was the precipitous rise in the share of the nation's wealth held by corporate executives and investors, and the declining share held by workers. The amazing thing, looking back on this development, was the fact that it went largely unnoticed by the public and even by supposedly informed observers. Several factors help explain it. One is that among the liberals whom one would expect to be sharp critics of this trend, there were a good many, including me, who had begun to feel that the unions deserved some kind of comeuppance, particularly the public employees' unions that would defend tenure even for incompetent employees.

This meant that too many liberals would fail to protest as beginning in the 1980s bosses and investors would no longer share corporate earnings fairly with the workers. The increasing support for the investors' getting a larger share was suggested by a fact noted earlier: The television show *Wall Street Week* was reaching four million households in the 1980s, and the number of investors in mutual funds grew by 500 percent. A lot of these investors had relatively small holdings, but still their investments made them sympathetic to the cause of increasing shareholder value. At the same time the bosses themselves were under pressure to increase shareholder value because they knew their companies might become the targets of corporate raiders such as Carl Icahn, Henry Kravis, or T. Boone

Pickens, who would tell shareholders that the current bosses were not doing enough to create shareholder value and promise that they would do a better job. The CEOs thought that they deserved more money because they saw rock stars, sports figures, and movie actors making huge sums and felt they did more for the economy than those guys.

The CEOs, who had begun giving themselves that self-glorifying title in the 1970s, became obsessed with what other CEOs were making, and a whole new industry of executive consultants grew up to determine what the top people in a company should be paid. And most of these consultants were hired by CEOs or their friends on the board who knew the consultants would recommend higher salaries for the top executives. To create more wealth for themselves and for investors, CEOs began to get that wealth from the worker. Firing workers to increase profits became increasingly accepted. Plant closings were unquestioningly accepted because it was thought they would increase shareholder value. The same for holding down wages. And all this unfairness was encouraged by the emphasis on quarterly earnings, which became the preoccupation of the financial press, *Wall Street Week,* and the financial news networks that followed in the wake of its stunning success.

Two developments made the situation even worse. Corporate boards decided to give CEOs shares of stock on the basis of the CEOs' success in increasing the value of the stock. But this meant that the CEOs were tempted to do things that would increase the value of the stock, even though those actions might not be in the long-term interests of the company. One method that emerged was to buy back stocks—stock repurchase programs—which meant that profits the company made, instead of being devoted to, say, increasing workers' wages or reinvested to grow the company or develop better products, would be used to buy back the stock. That would usually increase their value, at least temporarily, enabling the CEO to cash in.

Finally, of course, there was the challenge of global competition.

As the '80s began, Japanese competition was making inroads on American business, taking a large share of the market from American auto manufacturers and destroying the makers of American television sets. RCA, which had been one of the largest corporations in America, with its name placed at the top of the main building of Rockefeller Center ("30 Rock"), had, by the end of the '80s, disappeared, thanks to Japanese competition.

There is no question that globalization drove companies to become more efficient. But efficiency did not require the large sums they began to devote to the pay of their executives in comparison to what they had paid in the past—or at least from the New Deal through the 1970s. The ratio of CEO pay to factory-worker pay rose from 42 to 1 in 1960 (and it was not much higher in 1980, when it began its steep climb) to over 200 to 1 by the early 1990s, and as high in some companies as 531 to 1 in the year 2000. The pay of the top executives of the country's leading corporations more than doubled from 1980 to 1990. There is no legitimate reason why the money that went to the executives could not have gone to the workers. Indeed, the prevailing attitude among American businesses from the early 1940s through the '70s was that business had to accept, if grudgingly, the New Deal reforms and share a decent portion of the wealth with the workers. It wasn't always the way it has become since the 1980s. There was a better way possible. There was a code word common among businesspeople in the 1950s: "responsible." By that they meant, in part, that they didn't want anybody rocking the boat with extreme views of any kind, either from the left or the right. But enough of them were also saying that they had a responsibility for the welfare of their employees and of the communities in which they were operating.

The growing snobbery of the meritocratic elite also contributed to the indifference to the plight of the worker. The sentiment heard during the Vietnam War about those who bore the brunt of the fighting—"Let those hillbillies go get shot"—had its counterpart in a sentiment that might be stated, "Let those workers lose their jobs or have their wages cut or their plant closed—so long as we're prospering in Silicon Valley or on Wall Street." Of course, nobody would say such things openly, but by their indifference, the meritocratic class in effect said just that. In any event, the bonds that had held America, especially white America, together through the 1940s, and '50s, and early '60s began to fray with the Vietnam War and were finally broken with Reagan's treatment of the air traffic controllers and his tax cut for the wealthy. Add to that the symbolism of Bill Clinton's being elected in 1992 as the first president who had not served in the military since World War II, and those bonds were the willingness to share both the benefits and the burdens of being an American.

When the Clintons moved to New York, they entered a world where Anna Wintour was royalty, an apartment for Chelsea cost $10 million, it was hard to see anything wrong with being paid $250,000 for a speech to Goldman Sachs executives, and the bond that had connected the Clintons to the people of Arkansas through many elections could now be so broken that the state voted overwhelmingly for Donald Trump.

★

# CHAPTER 12

# What Do We Do Now?

I can remember when the worst of the Depression hit my home-town of Charleston, West Virginia. It was 1931. I know because the big event of my day had been when the iceman would arrive at the kitchen door in the morning, lugging a great block of ice over his back. But then he stopped coming because my parents bought a refrigerator. The date was significant because soon afterward other men came, hungry men, showing up at our kitchen door to ask for food. Before long they were coming almost every day—except Sunday. They must have respected the Sabbath.

Sometimes several would come in one morning, so that my mother could not feed everyone and would have to send them to the Union Mission or the Salvation Army, where they would have to do a little praying before they were fed. When we went down-town, men would approach my father asking for spare change. Boys—sometimes even men—would offer to shine his shoes for a nickel or a dime. Women rarely begged, but they would come to the door and offer to sell eggs or corn or tomatoes at pathetically low prices. When things were at their very worst, men would actu-ally set up little stands on the sidewalks offering apples for five cents each. They had bought two for five cents at the grocery store.

We had a series of relatives come from the farm (my parents had both been born on farms) to live with us while seeking work in Charleston.

Then things gradually started getting better—noticeably so in 1934 and 1935. The apple sellers were the first to disappear. The shoeshine price firmed up at ten cents, and the parade of hungry men gradually dwindled to one or two a week and then as few as one or two a month in the next year or so. Around the same time the begging on the streets slowed and soon stopped, except for what you began to realize were a few regular handout artists. By 1937 all the relatives had found jobs. I remember because that is when I got my room back. Soon my springer spaniel and I were conducting daily inspections of the riverfront parkway, a New Deal project that was being built just a half a block from my house. From there we could see the middle span being placed in the South Side bridge, another New Deal project.

It is not hard to see why I was impressed, and why I grew up believing in the possibility of major change. I saw it happen before my eyes. It was change that I came to understand required the action of both individuals and of the government they elected, paid taxes to support, and oftentimes served, either in the military or the civil service—reflecting a willingness to share the benefits and burdens of society that was captured in the New Deal slogan "We Do Our Part."

I am convinced that we need a rebirth of that willingness to do our part—as improbable as that may seem with Donald Trump in the White House, perhaps even the impossible dream of a nostalgic senior citizen. I am convinced that the country is now in a place much like the 1930s, not in the sense that the economy is in such dire straits but that a large number of major changes need to be made that require government action—from reforming policies on immigration, criminal law enforcement, and incarceration, to rebuilding infrastructure, addressing climate change, improving public education, and making higher education accessible and affordable. What may prove to be the toughest challenge may be reforming American capitalism and radically reducing the role of money in politics.

There is something terribly wrong for executives and shareholders to take an unfair share of corporate income. And there is something truly demented about having such a high proportion of Wall Street activity devoted to making money for the sake of making money.

It would be nice to think these changes are going to be made voluntarily, as Seattle entrepreneur Dan Price did with his company. He slashed his million-dollar income in order to give his employees a minimum wage of $70,000. But I am afraid that, if we ask all those super-wealthy executives, shareholders, and Wall Streeters to volunteer to give up their private jets and houses in the Hamptons, not a lot of hands will be raised.

Actually, however, fair tax and fair compensation policies will not take away all those jets and houses in the Hamptons—maybe just the place in St. Kitts. Still, taxes will have to be considerably higher, meaning there will be opposition, not just from the Wall Streeters and executives affected but from all those dependent on the luxury economy. In New York, Wall Street constitutes one-third of the city's economy, contributing much of the income of the real estate, fashion, restaurant, arts, and entertainment sectors. *The New York Times* has become increasingly dependent on luxury advertising. Perhaps nothing symbolizes this dependence more than Condé Nast's recent move of its publications, including *Vanity Fair, Vogue, GQ,* and *The New Yorker,* downtown right next to Wall Street.

As for Washington, D.C., Hermès, the French luxury firm, recently entertained 120 guests at an elaborate dinner party. (It was served by sixty waiters, one for every two guests as in the court of Louis XIV.) The purpose was to celebrate the opening of its new store in CityCenterDC, a downtown area characterized by what *The Washington Post* describes as "its opulence and energy," where it will join Burberry, Salvatore Ferragamo, Hugo Boss, and the soon-to-be-opened Dior and Louis Vuitton stores. Hermès, of course, features the Birkin handbag at ten thousand dollars and up, which may sound like a lot but is small change for K Streeters. For an idea of just how well the local lobbying community is doing, consider the recent divorce proceedings involving two of them. The wife's petition says the couple "spent millions renovating" their home in Kalorama, one of the highest of Washington's high-end neighborhoods, and asked that "they equally divide" their internationally known artworks. His answer says he paid half the down payment on another "multimillion-dollar home" for her and that she earns "many millions" annually.

Because of developments like the *Citizens United* decision, big money is now a powerful force in our political system. This is not to say the rich are always on the wrong side. Warren Buffett is willing to pay more taxes, Bill Gates's foundation has made major contributions to the delivery of healthcare and better education, and even the Koch brothers are funding prison reform. But make no mistake, the normal tendency of big money is to fight any change they see as threatening its power.

Economic royalists fought Roosevelt's reforms in the 1930s but gradually if grudgingly began to accept them. The same was true of the moderates in the Republican Party. In 1954, Dwight Eisenhower wrote, "Should any political party attempt to abolish social security, unemployment insurance, and eliminate labor laws and farm programs, you would not hear of that party again in our political history." That attitude of accommodation to the New Deal would prevail through the 1960s, begin to fray in the '70s, and undergo major revision with the Reagan revolution.

In 2016 the Democrats seemed to be coming together with an agenda that would make us a fairer and more equal society. Unfortunately, their presidential campaign focused more on what was wrong with the opposition candidate and less on what they could do to make a better country. Donald Trump, on the other hand, proved gifted at exploiting both the legitimate concerns and the worst fears of the white working class, while promising to make America great again. The result, with a little help from Vladimir Putin, Julian Assange, and James Comey, was an electoral victory that made Donald Trump president of the United States and retained Republican control of both the House and the Senate. Democrats could remain hopeful because they did win the popular vote in the presidential race. Nonetheless, their road ahead looks challenging. Most of the Senate seats that are up for election in 2018 seem likely to be won by Republicans because the seats are considered either safely theirs or held by vulnerable Democrats. The House has been a challenge for the Democrats since the redistricting of 2011. To explain that, let me take you back to the fall of 2010.

It was a Saturday in October, four days before the elections that would send a conservative majority to the House of Representatives and install conservative majorities in most of the state legislatures and governorships being contested. Jon Stewart and Stephen Colbert were holding their "Rally to Restore Sanity and/or Fear" on the National Mall. They were so highly regarded among thoughtful liberals, particularly the young ones, that two hundred thousand people turned out for the event. Yet, of the many speakers who appeared that day, only one mentioned the upcoming elections and the importance of voting: the eighty-four-year-old singer Tony Bennett, who leaned back and shouted "VOTE!" into the microphone as he was being escorted off the stage.

As it happened, this was the election that drove a stake into the heart of House Democrats, because candidates elected to state legislatures in 2010 were in charge of the congressional redistricting mandated by the 2010 census. The result of the Republican success, and the Democrats' not voting, was that the GOP, which had long been out-gerrymandering the Democrats, was able to gerrymander a sufficient number of additional districts to make it probable that the Republicans will control the House until 2022.

You can blame Stewart and Colbert for blowing a tremendous

opportunity. But you also have to wonder what the Democrats were thinking—or not thinking—when they decided to sit home on Election Day. Barack Obama in his first two years had not only saved the auto industry but also engineered the passage of his stimulus program, the Affordable Care Act, and the Dodd-Frank Wall Street Reform and Consumer Protection Act.

My best guess is that to the extent Democrats were thinking at all, it was about what Obama hadn't done, instead of what he had done. For instance, he had not fought for single-payer instead of the health insurance program that he had to settle for in negotiations with Congress. There is a great tendency among liberals, as former representative Barney Frank has observed, to make the perfect the enemy of the good, and to think that if they just advocate good causes and show up for presidential elections then they have done their duty.

The 2010 election demonstrated that if you don't show up for midterms, bad things can happen. This was confirmed in 2014, when the Democrats lost control of the Senate because their voters once again did not show up in sufficient numbers. And remember what happened to Bill Clinton in 1994, after he engineered passage of an economic program that would make his presidency one of the most prosperous in history, with increased incomes across the board, a balanced budget, and unemployment at a record low of 3.9 percent. Clinton's reward was a great Republican victory that transferred control of both the House and Senate to the GOP.

In contrast, recall that Franklin Roosevelt, in his first midterm election in 1934, was rewarded with an overwhelming victory as Democratic voters gave him even greater majorities in the House and Senate than he had won in 1932.

One explanation may come from the youth vote. Only one-fifth of voters younger than thirty are turning out in midterm elections these days. Even as the Roosevelt era was ending in the 1960s, 50 percent more young people voted. Journalist Ryan Cooper, a twenty-something himself, described this trend in a recent *Washing-*

*ton Monthly* article, adding, "Even though I am, by the standard of my generation, a serious political obsessive, running for elected office strikes me as landing somewhere between 'incomprehensible' and 'I'd rather be thrown in jail.' And if I feel that way, imagine what regular people my age must think!"

And if young people are less than enthusiastic about running for office, they are equally uninterested in working for the government. Lisa Rein of *The Washington Post* wrote in 2015: "The federal workforce under the age of thirty dropped to seven percent this year. With agencies starved for digital expertise and thousands of federal jobs coming open because of a wave of baby boomer retirements, top government officials, including the White House, are growing increasingly distressed about the dwindling role played by young workers."

Another recent study found that only 28 percent of young adults feel an obligation to keep informed about news and public issues. They believe politics and government are either crooked or incompetent. They say that they are "turned off" by the gridlock in Washington. (So, by the way, say a great many people over thirty.)

But, if they don't stay informed, participate in politics, run for office, or work in government, how is the gridlock going to be ended and how are politics and government going to get better?

Republicans understand the potential of the youth vote and fear it so much that the legislatures they control have been busy enacting voter suppression laws designed, among other things, to keep young people away from the polls.

Those laws can be changed only by political action, the same way we can make the other changes in policy that are needed today. Voter suppression laws can be changed by electing state legislatures that will repeal them or by having them declared unconstitutional by the courts. It is obvious that political action may be required to elect the legislatures, but why is it relevant to action by the courts? We elect the president who appoints and the senators who confirm the judges who determine the constitutionality of our laws. After the Democrats lost control of the Senate in 2014, Obama was able to get only a handful of judges confirmed, and even those were for the lower federal courts.

Can changing laws change the behavior of today's economic royalists? The answer is yes—some of them will remain real bastards (a recent book about our wealthiest described "a lot" of them as "rather unpleasant, hard as nails kinds of people")—but what we saw in the 1940s, '50s, and '60s was that most of them, having first fought the laws and regulations enacted by the New Deal, were willing to accept them, albeit grudgingly, and with them a more modest share of the nation's income.

My long life has given me an opportunity to get to know several wealthy people, one of them among America's richest. What struck me was that for many, their major motive in life was to win the game and, if possible, to also be well regarded. Well, think about that for a minute. What it means is that we can affect their behavior by changing the rules of the game and by defining what the game is.

The object of the game now is to maximize profits for the benefit of corporate shareholders and executives. Why not make the object to maximize earnings to compensate shareholders, executives, *and* workers?

This means new laws and regulations that will encourage a more equitable sharing of income between workers, investors, and executives. The SEC made a start in 2015 by requiring companies to publish their ratios of executive pay to worker income. The need for this regulation has been made clear by the results of recent studies. One, by the AFL-CIO, found that CEO pay was 354 times that of the average employee. Of course, the AFL-CIO might not be considered entirely objective. Still, another study by the liberal Economic Policy Institute that is often cited by *The New York Times* found the ratio to be 300 to 1. Bloomberg News, a source not unfriendly to business, says the figure for Fortune 500 companies is 204 to 1.

Even this number represents a 1,000 percent increase from what Bloomberg estimates the ratio to have been in 1950 at a time when the American economy was enjoying perhaps its greatest era of prosperity. It's hard to argue that executives today are 1,000 percent smarter than those back then.

Executive compensation is related to corporate profit, another figure that contrasts dramatically with that of 1950. Then and for the remainder of the Roosevelt era corporate profits accounted for 6 percent of GDP, a fact that has to inspire some doubt that prosperity has to depend on double the amount of profit that is the rate today. Much of today's executive compensation comes from the stock that they have been awarded. This has led them into the practice of stock-buyback programs to increase the value of their shares. Stock buybacks were forbidden by New Deal regulations as an illegal way of manipulating profit, but in 1984 Reagan's SEC abolished that regulation and since then stock buybacks have grown to constitute more and more of corporate profit. Stock buybacks increase the wealth of only the shareholders. They do not help companies grow or provide better products or services, but they do take money that could go to better wages. Between 2003 and 2012, the 500 companies that make up the S&P 500 index spent 54 percent of their profits in stock buybacks. In 2014 alone, they spent seven hundred billion on stock buybacks.

Let's take one company and see the impact of these buybacks on its workers. Over the past ten years Wal-Mart has spent an average of $6.5 billion a year on stock buybacks. This would have been enough to give each of its 1.4 million U.S. workers a $4,642 raise for every one of those years. So Congress or the SEC could make a good start on reforming the system by simply reinstating the regulation that prohibited buybacks.

We need a strong SEC to issue those rules. What has that got to do with politics? For one thing, the commissioners are appointed by the president we elect. For another, the new rule requiring companies to report the ratio of executive to worker pay would not exist had it not first been required by the Dodd-Frank law that was passed by a Democratic Congress in 2010. Finally, the reason the rule was not published until 2015 is that Republicans who have ruled Congress—the House since 2011 and the Senate since 2014—have not only done nothing to push the SEC to adopt the rule, most of them have actually been advocating for the repeal of Dodd-Frank. This has left corporate lobbyists free to use one delaying tactic after another to prolong the SEC proceedings. So, yes, the political choices you make have a great deal to do with what happens at the SEC.

Those choices make a difference in countless other ways. If you want the Food and Drug Administration to protect you from contaminated food and drugs that do more harm than good, or the Centers for Disease Control and Prevention to protect you from dangerous diseases, or the Federal Aviation Administration to keep your plane from crashing, remember that the people you elect appoint the leaders of these agencies, write the laws that determine what they can and cannot do, and oversee their operations. Those operations depend for their effectiveness on capable people being willing to serve in those agencies.

So it is time to stop being disillusioned with government and start doing something to make it better.

I am not asking for a revolution in human nature, such as everyone going into politics or public service for a career. What I am talking about is a lot more people, especially the most talented, serving the public interest instead of their private interests for a portion of their lives. This is not pie-in-the-sky. Between March 1933 and the end of the war in 1945, 2.5 million Americans joined the federal government to participate in the New Deal and the civilian war effort. And they were not all saints. Recall that they included Tommy Corcoran, Abe Fortas, and Clark Clifford, who were, though they may have strayed later, good public servants while they were in the government. And many of their contemporaries did not try to cash in after they left. Harry Truman was noted for his refusal to capitalize on his service. Indeed, when he died, his only asset was his home in Independence. Ben Cohen, Tommy Corcoran's partner in so many of the great accomplishments of the New Deal, left the government but never tried to cash in. Jerome Frank remained in public service the rest of his life. When I came to Washington in 1961, there were so many New Dealers still working in the government that I joked, "Everyone sounds like Eleanor Roosevelt," meaning their views were as liberal as hers.

If serving in government is not for you, perhaps you'd consider teaching in a public school for a few years, or as a career. And, for that matter, you can do any job you enjoy that is not harmful to the public interest as long as you contribute a substantial amount of time to political action supporting the right candidates and the right policies.

There are other public interest jobs you can do. In journalism, there is an immediate and imperative need to restore respect for fact. Unless a political debate can proceed from facts that are agreed upon, there's no chance that one side or the other will be persuaded. The false rumors that Rush Limbaugh liked to peddle have been followed by fake news. It is not just the responsibility of the people who report it but of the people who publish their reports, most notably Facebook, which profits from its status as a source of news but has been reluctant to accept responsibility for the accuracy of that news. A more long-range need of journalism is for reporting about what is right and wrong in government. Unfortunately, most reporters prefer covering the horse race of political campaigns: who's ahead in the polls, what are the strategies and tactics of the candidates and their advisers, who's dominating the news cycle, who committed the latest gaffe, and the biggest prize of all, uncovering a scandal that will dominate the news for weeks. Scandal has been most avidly pursued since Watergate made Bob Woodward and Carl Bernstein famous. The appeal of the horse race was most pronounced after Theodore White's *The Making of the President 1960* became a bestseller. It was even more marked after another bestseller, Mark Halperin and John Heilemann's *Game Change*, was made into a successful movie for HBO and earned the authors six nights a week of their own television show. Indeed regular appearances on television have become a primary career objective of too many political reporters. The absurd result comes when the show's host says "Now let's turn to our panel," and you realize you are doomed to hear predictable opinion, rarely accompanied by a fact you don't know. This has become so obvious that MSNBC's Chris Matthews now has a feature toward the end of *Hardball* entitled "Tell Me Something I Don't Know."

When, after elections, these political reporters are compelled to turn their attention to government, they focus on the White House and the Congress, assuming that none of the executive branch agencies, except occasionally State, Defense, and Justice, are worthy of their time—unless of course some scandal or disaster occurs, which then becomes the Big Story for days or weeks thereafter. I want to see those same reporters devoting their attention to preventing the scandal or disaster before it happens. Consider just one example. Any enterprising reporter could have discovered before the *Deepwater Horizon* explosion that reckless deep drilling was occurring in the Gulf of Mexico and that the Minerals Management Service that oversaw the drilling was inept and tainted by corruption.

Some journalists will argue that the audience for this kind of reporting will be modest until today's attention spans increase, but it seems to me that the challenge for them is to make the reporting lively enough that people's attention spans will grow.

There is also a great need for better teaching about government. It is shocking that someone as brilliant and well educated as Barack Obama could come to the presidency so stunningly innocent of any knowledge about how the bureaucracy under him functions— innocence that he repeatedly demonstrated, from his overly optimistic assurance that stimulus projects were "shovel ready" to the embarrassingly botched launch of the Affordable Care Act. It was as if, wrote Steven Brill, the president and his White House aides "either believed that they were big policy thinkers who were above worrying about making the law work or that they did not understand that effective government does not happen automatically."

And instead of serving in government, writing about it, or teaching it, you might be able to think of a better way for the government to perform its functions. Sometimes new agencies are needed. Franklin Roosevelt frequently used them to implement the New Deal and carry out the war effort. They had the great benefit of being able to hire all their personnel and of being free of the established bureaucratic rituals that inhibit quick action. I was fortunate enough to be part of one when I became an early member of the Peace Corps' staff. The most recent example is the Consumer Financial Protection Bureau. The idea behind it came from Elizabeth Warren, who also helped set it up. It is doing work that was badly needed, and doing it well enough to inspire Republicans in Congress to plot its emasculation. KIPP Public Charter Schools is another example. Its creators, Mike Feinberg and Dave Levin, thought of a more effective way to deliver public education and then demonstrated how it could be done so that it can be replicated elsewhere.

One of the great needs through all levels of government is in the area of information technology. As the launch of the Affordable Care Act demonstrated, the necessary expertise is often lacking. An organization called Code America has taken a first step in meeting the problem by enlisting volunteers to do coding for local governments.

To Obama's credit, when it became clear that he had screwed up the launch of Obamacare, he quickly recruited a crew of Silicon Valley hotshots who were able to get the system running smoothly within a couple of months. Among them was Mikey Dickerson, who took leave from his job at Google in order to lend a hand. Afterward Dickerson said, "I went back to my old job and tried to care about it. I was not successful." He explained that his brief tenure in government had been "more important and meaningful than anything I could have accomplished in a lifetime working at my old job." Dickerson returned to Washington to set up for the White House a new organization called the U.S. Digital Service to provide people with IT skills, not only for the healthcare program but for more than a score of other federal agencies. The recruits are not asked to commit to careers in government but to serve a year or two. Dickerson recruits them with this message: "The most sobering thing about my tenure in government was to really understand at an emotional level that this country belongs to you and me. Grown-ups are not going to fix it for us, and billionaires are not going to fix it for us. We either do it ourselves or nobody does."

The fact that the Digital Service has been set up by the White House demonstrates that Obama belatedly learned from his experience. He became personally involved in helping Dickerson. At a White House gathering of potential recruits in the Roosevelt Room of the West Wing, Obama told them that they needed to come to work for him. He said he doesn't care what it takes—he will personally call their bosses, their spouses, their kids to convince them. When the crowd laughed, Obama replied, "I am completely serious," explaining that he really needed them to overhaul the government's digital infrastructure.

My hope is that Barack Obama, as a former president, instead of making a lot of money and hanging out with Anna Wintour, decides to devote himself to teaching how government works using the inside story of his remarkable achievements and his embarrassing failures to help those who follow him in public service do a better job. I must say that I consider Obama's choice of his next career as having immense symbolic importance for this country. We cannot continue to have our role models continue to cash in.

And as long as I am dreaming, it would be great to see wise young men and women aspire to be the next Will Rogers, a comedian who appealed to practically everyone instead of a narrow slice of the educated elite, as has unfortunately been the case with liberal comedians Jon Stewart, John Oliver, Bill Maher, and Stephen Colbert. I have laughed with each of them, still miss *The Colbert Report,* and especially admire Oliver's use of comedy to examine public issues in depth. I do not think, however, that a comedian with broad appeal can afford to be as condescending as Maher, for example, has been about religion. Recently, as he was interviewing a believer he obviously respected, he said, "I can understand why a soldier in a foxhole would pray, but you are an intelligent man. Why you?" On the other hand, I would love to see the fun a new Will Rogers could have with today's 1,000 percent smarter CEOs— or with a Marylander's response to the Supreme Court's ruling that a corporation is a person with the right to donate to political candidates. The Marylander proceeded to file his corporation as a candidate for Congress.

I believe in appealing to religious values rather than condescending to them. Franklin Roosevelt and Martin Luther King, Jr., used Christianity to appeal to our better angels. There are fewer Christians today—roughly 70 percent of the country as compared to 90 percent back then—but it is interesting to recall that both Roosevelt and King, by appealing to those values, reached something in the hearts of people who were not Christians. American Jews were among the New Deal's most ardent supporters and were also prominent in King's civil rights movement. Many of them risked their lives in those early Freedom Rides and two, Michael Schwerner and Andrew Goodman, were among the three young men murdered by a Mississippi mob as they tried to register black voters in 1964. Just recently Christian forgiveness brought down the Confederate flag in South Carolina. And even many nonbelievers were moved when Barack Obama sang "Amazing Grace."

If you go into politics, you don't have to have a lot of money to start out. It takes nothing but volunteering to work in campaigns. That is where you will meet like-minded people who support change and will help you if you decide to run. If you run for a city council, where you can, for example, prevent the local police from beating up African Americans, and if you run for the state legislature, where you can repeal voter suppression laws and reform the state laws governing incarceration, you will find that in most parts of this country the most important factor in your success will not be money but door-to-door person-to-person campaigning. And once you demonstrate that you are a vote getter, it is amazing how you will attract money to finance a campaign for Congress. How that money affects your behavior in office is up to you. But if you are elected to Congress you can vote for all the reforms in federal policy that you want to see made, including laws that will bring about a fair distribution of income for all Americans.

Maybe you just can't stand the idea of running for office. You can still volunteer to help good candidates get elected. Volunteering, I can assure you, is not hard to do. I did it years ago, and my then thirteen-year-old grandson Jeffrey did it in the 2014 congressional election.

If you choose to participate in politics it is obvious by now that I want you to do so as a Democrat. It is not because I believe that Democrats have a monopoly on virtue. Exemplary private lives are lived by members of both parties. But mostly since 1994 and entirely since 2009, the GOP has been the party of no, rejecting any idea of liberal reform. Grover Norquist has persuaded practically every Republican member of Congress to sign a no-new-taxes pledge, making it impossible to finance desperately needed programs. In 2012, two highly respected political scientists, Thomas Mann and Norman Ornstein, published a book called *It's Even Worse Than It Looks,* concluding that Republicans are responsible for the gridlock in Congress. The threat of the alt-right should not obscure the fact that today's Republican Party as a whole is the main obstacle to liberal reform.

But being a Democrat does not require you to automatically assume that the party is always right. Far too many of its elected officials, for instance, are unconditional supporters of the teachers' unions and thus reluctant to take on the task of public school reform. Although we have to be wary of Republicans who would privatize public education, we also have to respect Michael Bloomberg of New York, a former Republican and now an independent, who has been a leader in the cause of public school reform. In general we have to beware of Twitter clusters, where political discussion is held in an echo chamber and no one listens to the other side.

Politics is an art of persuasion. It is least effective when we self-righteously call the other guy a racist and most effective when we bring out his pride in being generous and open-minded.

The New Deal provided the laws and regulations, but for "We Do Our Part" to take hold, something else had to change as well, and that was values. During World War II, what economists called "the great compression" of wages and executive salaries occurred. It happened because profiteering from the war effort was widely scorned. Franklin Roosevelt even proposed limiting after-tax income to $25,000 a year. Once those values took hold, they endured throughout the Roosevelt era with neither executives nor investors displaying the kind of greed to which we have become accustomed in the Reagan era. I believe we are still in the Reagan era because that greed persists today. Recall that Reagan slashed taxes from a top rate of 70 percent to 36 percent. Neither Clinton nor Obama dared raise it above 39 percent, while Trump proposes even more cuts.

Reagan's large tax cut reflected the haves' desire to contribute less to the common causes of the nation and keep more of their income for themselves. This, in turn, reflected the growing desire in the 1980s and thereafter to have more money—a lot more. It seemed to reach its most absurd heights with the 1980s television series *Lifestyles of the Rich and Famous*. But it even has since been topped by CNBC's *Secret Lives of the Super Rich*.

The need for wealth was fueled by high-end consumerism, which, as we have seen, has had its handmaiden in the snobbery that developed around the conviction that taste makes class. This snobbery spread not only to the identity of one's educational institution but to other areas of life, including politics.

Recall the Styles section's dismissal of local politics as the realm of mustard-stained polyester suits. Just as I was finishing this book I was dismayed to find a writer I otherwise admire, Sarah Lyall of *The New York Times*, praising a book for providing "a fascinating inside look at the mysterious forces—vanity, tribalism, self-righteousness, self-delusion—that fueled local government."

But snobbery has had its most baleful effect on the many members of the working class who feel they are being looked down upon, and who have been convinced by Rush Limbaugh, Fox News, and Donald Trump that the snobs are all liberal Democrats. Unfortunately, a good many of the snobbish meritocratic elite *are* liberal Democrats. But quite a few are libertarians.

Libertarians are anti-government and anti-regulation but liberal on social issues. They are ideological descendants of Ayn Rand, but not many of them would as openly exalt selfishness as she did, nor would they display as callous a disregard of income inequality. It is just that I fear that when it comes to really doing something about it, they will drag their feet. After all, many of them have become part of the 1 percent from their killings in Silicon Valley or on Wall Street or in one of its outposts among the hedge funds and private equity firms. If they are not part of the 1 percent they are almost certain to be among the 8 percent who make more than $200,000 a year, or one of the more than ten million households with a net worth of more than $1 million. In other words, they have reason to be wary of reform that might threaten what they have. But they will reassure themselves as to their virtue by their steadfast stands against racism and in favor of women's and gay rights. It should also be noted that quite a few of the liberals of the media elite, including several featured on MSNBC, seem more passionate about these issues than they are about economic injustice, and thus were slow to appreciate the appeal of Bernie Sanders. You can see why an unemployed coal miner in West Virginia or a factory worker in Ohio would want to see his plight given equal time with that of a transsexual seeking his choice of bathroom.

Still I find reason to hope. The liberal elite does seem to have finally awakened to the harm done by its snobbish disdain for the white working class. The few who winced when Barack Obama said, "They cling to guns and religion," as well as the good many more who cringed at Hillary Clinton's "basket of deplorables," were joined by practically every thoughtful liberal as they contemplated the results from Pennsylvania, Michigan, and Wisconsin on election night. We're beginning to see understanding books and articles about working-class and rural whites that see them as decent human beings with some deplorable views. Some are hooked on opioids that are being aggressively peddled by greedy drug companies and prescribed by equally greedy physicians. But I grew up with these people. I know they can be better than they seem today.

I also find hope in the fact that people are beginning to question the rampant consumerism that has characterized the Reagan era. My son, who teaches in a high school where most of the students are from working-class Hispanic families, tells me of the terrible pressure on their parents to buy them the athletic equipment they need to participate in the various sports that now are organized from childhood up and to purchase the electronic devices that all of us seem to feel we have to have in the latest model. Andrew Keene, in a recent book, asked whether Amazon is really the blessing that many thought it would be.

Another hopeful sign is the radical increase in awareness of income inequality that has taken place in the last decade. Countless articles have been written about it as well as at least four books—by Timothy Noah, Joseph Stiglitz, Jeff Madrick, and, of course, the best known, by Thomas Piketty. And Bernie Sanders made sure that millions of voters knew that the top 1 percent enjoy an excessive share of the nation's income and wealth.

Even some Wall Streeters seem convinced. Steve Rattner, whose decision to pursue wealth on Wall Street in the 1980s is noted at the beginning of this book, was three decades later leading the bailout of the auto industry that saved the jobs of thousands of workers and writing in *The New York Times* that the rich should be paying higher taxes. So there is reason to hope that at least some of the elite are ready to take the next step and to find a way to serve.

I think the moment might be right for people who want to do their part for the country, as John Kennedy asked, not for themselves as Richard Nixon asked. There are signs, including countless editorial cartoons, that the country is getting sick of selfies and the self-absorption they signify. More people are becoming aware of the merits of real conversation with real people to replace Internet messaging between phony Facebook identities. There are also indications that people are beginning to question their relentless pursuit of money, or at least some of the reasons why they think they have to make a lot of money. Do they really need to spend so much on junior's tutors, private schools, extracurricular activities, and college and graduate school? Are they worn out by helicopter parenting and beginning to wonder if it is the best way to raise kids? Frank Bruni of *The New York Times* recently wrote, "Childhood has been transformed—at least among an ambitious privileged subset of Americans—into an insanely programmed, status obsessed and sometimes spirit sapping race."

If it is a hopeful sign to see the liberal elite overcoming its snobbery to make a serious effort to understand the Trump voter, it is even more hopeful that some of them are asking the toughest question of all: When are we going to stop letting those hillbillies go get shot? For fifty years meritocrats have assumed that they had no duty to serve. Too many of the boomers, the founding generation of the meritocracy, assumed that whatever civic obligation they might have had was more than satisfied by their participation in antiwar demonstrations and their attendance at Woodstock. But, in recent years, as the pious hypocrisy of "Salutes to Our Servicemen" has become blatant, I have heard more people comment about the unfairness of leaving service to the less privileged. So there is reason to hope that the meritocrats are ready to take the next step and decide to find some way to serve.

There is also reason for optimism, at least over the long term, that demographics should deprive white voters of the electoral power they now hold and end the reign of Reaganism and of the nastier edge given to it by Limbaugh, Fox News, Donald Trump, and their more explicitly white supremacist allies. This is not to say that all white voters are lost souls. Far too many of them, however, are either too devoted to the defense of their wealth—not just Wall Streeters and real estate tycoons but surprisingly affluent tea partiers—or hopelessly rigid in their adherence to right-wing dogma and their opposition not just to the smug and silly side of political correctness but to its valid concern that ugly speech can lead to ugly action. Today, power is theirs.

But things can change. Consider California, where in 1978 voters passed Proposition 13, which limited revenues available for education and led to the decline of what had been the nation's most outstanding system of public primary, secondary, and higher education. It was a signal that the Reagan revolution was coming and that the country was turning from a politics of generosity to a politics of selfishness. In 2012, California voters passed Proposition 30, restoring funding for education. In 1996, California passed one of the nation's most anti-immigrant laws. Today the state ranks among the nation's most inclusive in its treatment of immigrants. In other words, a state that had been governed by the politics of selfishness now embraces the politics of generosity.

Even at my most pessimistic, as I have tended to be since the November election, I still see a compelling argument for a rebirth of "We Do Our Part." After all, what is the alternative? How else is change we need going to happen?

Now is the time to start. Recall that the great Democratic comeback that launched the New Deal began with the 1930 midterms. In the 2018 elections, Democrats may not be able to win back the House and Senate, but they can begin to chip away at Republican margins. In state elections they can do a lot more. Control of one house or both in thirty-eight state legislatures will be decided. The more of them Democrats can win, the closer they will come to controlling the redistricting that will take place in 2021, control they can cement with a strong nationwide victory in 2020. None of this is going to happen, however, unless liberals get busy now, as Barack Obama challenged them to do in his farewell address, becoming candidates themselves or helping good candidates win, not just for president and Congress but for state and local offices, from governor to the legislature to county sheriff and city mayor and council member. In the short term, victory will depend on turning out the voters in the present Democratic coalition. If other liberals are as haunted as I am by the image of Tony Bennett alone at that Stewart-Colbert rally in 2010, they will get out and vote in every election so that they can build a solid party organization that can prevail again and again. If they campaign for justice and fair play for all, they will prevail.

And if liberals listen to the legitimate concerns of rural and white working-class voters instead of dismissing them as boobs and bigots, they will gradually win back their natural allies in the "We Do Our Part" coalition.

It may be a close call, as it so often is as our better angels struggle for ascendancy, but finally I am optimistic. Having witnessed the wonders of the Roosevelt era, I know what the American people are capable of.

# ACKNOWLEDGMENTS

The indispensable man has been Kenneth Ikenberry. Ken, a former reporter and editor at the Washington *Evening Star* and a member of the editorial page staff at *The Washington Post*, not only performed much of the research but in countless other ways made this book happen. He understood my purpose from the moment we first discussed it. Whenever I was in doubt, I relied on his good judgment.

The indispensable woman was my wife, Beth, who has cheerfully dealt with the infirmities inevitable with my advancing age and managed to pull me together each day to do my part in the book's creation, to which she has made an invaluable contribution with both her editorial suggestions and her ability to impose order on my disorder.

Beth is responsible for my finding Ken. She had worked with Ken's wife, Sue, at Georgetown Day School. Sue taught social studies and used my book *How Washington Really Works* in her classes. When she pointed out that the last edition was a couple of decades old and urged me to do a revision, I found the idea depressing. Washington had become worse in so many ways, as indeed had the country as a whole. But in thinking about what to do about Washington and the country, I realized that my life had taught me some of the answers to today's problems.

At the same time I began thinking about this book, my friend and former colleague Timothy Noah began talking to me about *The Great Divergence,* a book he was working on about the growing inequality of income since the late 1970s. I had lived through a time of the greatest equality of income in our history and had some idea of how it had come about and how it was coming apart.

There was one part of the coming-apart story that I had been exploring for forty years with my colleagues at *The Washington Monthly.* It was the class division that began during the antiwar movement in the late 1960s, separating the educated elite from the working class. I am especially grateful to Suzannah Lessard for "Let Those Hillbillies Go Get Shot," to James Fallows for "What Did You Do in the Class War, Daddy?," and to Nicholas Lemann for christening the new elite as the meritocrats and identifying their characteristics, including their obsession with SATs.

As to why I was offended by that snobbery, I am indebted to my fellow seventh- and eighth-grade pupils in the sheet metal and woodworking classes at Thomas Jefferson Junior High School. I was smarter than they were in history and English, but they excelled in working with their hands and in commonsense decision making. Why should anyone look down on them?

I had seen the results of a government that worked during the New Deal and World War II, but I had not had an inside look at how to make one work until I joined the staff of the Peace Corps, where I learned how good a government agency can be if it is staffed by talented people and led by an inspiring leader who is willing to face his mistakes and learn from them. The leader was Sargent Shriver. If you haven't heard of him, read an amazingly good biography, *Sarge,* by Scott Stossel.

If FDR and Sarge taught me to respect what government can do, I owe my respect for politics and politicians to my parents. They were lifelong Democrats, both of them active in party affairs. One incident explains the family feeling. On the second night of the 1940 Democratic national convention in Chicago, Senator Alben Barkley delivered a passionate speech on behalf of Franklin Roosevelt that left the three of us so fired up that we decided to go to Chicago. At dawn the next day we piled in the family car to drive across Ohio and Indiana on mostly two-lane roads, long before the era of interstates, arriving just before midnight. The following day we were in the convention hall in time to see Eleanor Roosevelt practice politics at its best by skillfully defusing a rebellion by party conservatives and bringing the convention that nominated FDR for a third term to a close.

I owe special gratitude to four authors: Hedrick Smith for his account of the Powell memorandum and much else in *Who Stole the American Dream?*, David McKean for his splendid biographies of Clark Clifford and Tommy Corcoran, Zev Chafets for his sympathetic biographies of Rush Limbaugh and Roger Ailes, and Lou Cannon for his sympathetic understanding of Ronald Reagan in both his books about the Gipper and his coverage of him for *The Washington Post*. I am less admiring of their subjects than are Chafets and Cannon, but they helped me understand what made the three men so persuasive to so many Americans.

As I was writing, I asked several friends to review drafts of what I had written and tell me what they thought. They included my son Christian and my former colleagues James Bennet, Haley Sweetland Edwards, Robert Worth, and Jason DeParle. Jason went well beyond the call of duty to read two drafts. I am grateful to them for the pitfalls they helped me avoid and for making this a better book, but they should not be blamed for the shortcomings that remain.

I am grateful to the Random House leadership—Gina Centrello, Susan Kamil, and Tom Perry—and to its editorial team for *We Do Our Part*, including Jon Meacham, who commissioned it, and his colleagues Will Murphy and Mika Kasuga. Jon's keen sense of history and beguiling sense of humor made working with him a special pleasure. I suspect that his sense of humor also helped him endure the experience of dealing with an author not noted for being easy to work with. I was heartened by Will Murphy's sensitive understanding of what I was trying to say and his courageous support for my contrarianism. Mika Kasuga has been thoughtful, efficient, and a delight to work with, and I want to thank Steve Messina for the crucial role he played as production editor. I felt I was in good hands all the way.

# NOTES

---★---

## Chapter 1: The Age of Roosevelt

17   "I want to get out of"   William E. Leuchtenburg, *The FDR Years: On Roosevelt and His Legacy* (New York: Columbia University Press, 1995), p. 63.

17   "It begins to get to you"   Philip Weiss, "Hello Sweetheart, Get Me Mergers and Acquisitions," *Washington Monthly,* May 1986.

18   In the 1930s   Walter Shapiro, "The Case of the Missing Middle Class: Money Madness in Manhattan," *Washington Monthly,* December 1984.

18   "about having a lot of money"   Stuart Candy, "The Futures of Everyday Life: Politics and the Design of Experiential Scenarios" (dissertation, University of Hawai'i at Mānoa), https://www.scribd.com/doc/68901075/Candy-2010-The-Futures-of-Everyday-Life.

21   "We owned them"   Interview with Lesley Stahl on *60 Minutes,* Nov. 6, 2011.

21   "equivalent of war"   Walter E. Volkomer, *The Passionate Liberal: The Political and Legal Ideas of Jerome Frank* (The Hague: Martinus Nijhoff, 1970).

21   more important than any individual   Arthur M. Schlesinger, Jr., *The Age of Roosevelt*. Vol. 2, *The Coming of the New Deal, 1933–1935* (Boston: Houghton Mifflin, 1958), p. 19.

21   Walter Lippmann, an influential columnist   Robert Dallek, *Franklin D. Roosevelt and American Foreign Policy, 1932–1945* (Oxford, UK: Oxford University Press, 1995), p. 35.

23   "he has the guts to try"   Leuchtenburg, *The FDR Years,* p. 7.

26   "good food and a good place to sleep"   Errol Lincoln Uys, *Riding the Rails: Teenagers on the Move During the Great Depression* (New York: Routledge, 2003), p. 260.

27  **"we need to involve the macaroni growers"**   Arthur M. Schlesinger, Jr. paraphrased in Jim Couch, "The New Deal: Reputation and Reality," Hillsdale College Archives, 2006.

27  **"a trend toward fascist agriculture"**   James L. Roark et al., *The American Promise*. Vol. II (Boston: Bedford/St. Martin's, 2012), p. 800.

29  **In Hollywood, Busby Berkeley**   Robert S. McElvaine, *The Great Depression: America, 1929–1941* (New York: Crown, 1984), p. 214.

30  **Those who had little**   Uys, *Riding the Rails*, p. 177.

31  **"When did you boys last eat?"**   Ibid., p. 170.

33  **"a new moral framework"**   Martin Marty quoted in Ron Smith and Mary O. Boyle, *Prohibition in Atlanta: Temperance, Tiger Kings and White Lightning* (Charleston, SC: American Palate, 2015), p. 135.

33  **"so many speeches that were essentially sermons"**   James MacGregor Burns, *Roosevelt: The Lion and the Fox,* Vol. 1. (New York: Harcourt, Brace, 1956), p. 476.

34  **New Deal as applied Christianity**   Gastón Espinosa, ed., *Religion and the American Presidency: George Washington to George W. Bush* (New York: Columbia University Press, 2009), p. 189.

36  **"the best newspaperman"**   Bahman Dehgan, ed., *America in Quotations* (Jefferson, NC: McFarland & Company, 2003), p. 181.

36  **"stimulating and enjoyable interludes"**   Graham J. White, *FDR and the Press* (Chicago: University of Chicago Press, 1979), p. 11.

37  **"fair and accurate"**   Richard D. White, *Will Rogers: A Political Life* (Lubbock: Texas Tech University Press, 2011), p. 116.

38  **"'Soak the Successful'"**   Ben Procter, *William Randolph Hearst: The Later Years, 1911–1951* (Oxford, UK: Oxford University Press, 2007).

39  **"of the same mind"**   White, *Will Rogers*.

42  **Frances Perkins's first day**   Kirsten Downey, *The Woman Behind the New Deal: The Life and Legacy of Frances Perkins—Social Security, Unemployment Insurance, and the Minimum Wage* (New York: Anchor, 2010), pp. 140, 141.

43  **"toughs and hoodlums from Howard University"**   Samuel Krislov, *The Negro in Federal Employment: The Quest for Equal Opportunity* (New Orleans: Quid Pro Quo, 2012), p. 22.

44  **"the mob shouted, 'Lynch him'"**   *New York Times*, Oct. 19, 1933.

45  **"If there is objection"**   *The Crisis*, April 1943, p. 117.

46  **"*Everybody* loved *Amos and Andy*"**   Henry Louis Gates, Jr., *Colored People: A Memoir* (New York: Knopf, 1994), p. 22.

### Chapter 2: From Doing Good to Doing Well: The Pioneers

49  **Their careers ended**   Alan Brinkley, *The End of Reform: New Deal Liberalism in Recession and War* (New York: Vintage, 1996).

49   Corcoran had joined  David McKean, *Peddling Influence: Thomas "Tommy the Cork" Corcoran and the Birth of Modern Lobbying* (Hanover, NH: Steerforth Press, 2005).

51   "have more influence at the White House"  Brinkley, *The End of Reform.*

51   Frankfurter chose Cohen and Corcoran  William Lasser, *Benjamin V. Cohen: Architect of the New Deal* (New Haven, CT: Yale University Press, 2002), p. 106.

51   "the most brilliant man I ever saw"  Noah Feldman, *Scorpions: The Battles and Triumphs of FDR's Great Supreme Court Justices* (New York: Twelve, 2010), p. 80.

52   By getting Brandeis's guidance  Feldman, *Scorpions.*

52   "Corcoran gallery of lawyers"  Jordan A. Schwarz, *The New Dealers: Power Politics in the Age of Roosevelt* (New York: Knopf, 1993).

55   Playing the accordion  Feldman, *Scorpions,* chap. 9.

57   His government salary at the time was $9,000  McKean, *Peddling Influence.*

58   "and ask for the big defense contracts"  Stephen B. Adams, *Mr. Kaiser Goes to Washington: The Rise of a Government Entrepreneur* (Chapel Hill: University of North Carolina Press, 2009).

59   "This is Tommy Corcoran at the White House"  Robert A. Caro, *The Path to Power: The Years of Lyndon Johnson* (New York: Knopf, 1982), p. 679.

60   "Attorney Corcoran Faces Ethics Probe"  *The Washington Post,* Dec. 21, 1979.

64   "What can we do for you?"  Spencer Weber Waller, *Thurman Arnold: A Biography* (New York: NYU Press, 2005), p. 248.

65   "the wisest man"  Robert Dallek, *Flawed Giant: Lyndon Johnson and His Times, 1961–1973* (New York: Oxford University Press, 1998), p. 233.

68   an innate gift for hypocrisy  Douglas Frantz and David McKean, *Friends in High Places: The Rise and Fall of Clark Clifford* (Boston: Little, Brown, 1995), p. 108.

69   "dollars on the table"  Charles Peters, *Lyndon B. Johnson* (New York: Times Books, 2010).

### Chapter 3: The Snob Factor

76   "what he could see in O'Brien"  Kenneth P. O'Donnell and David F. Powers, *Johnny, We Hardly Knew Ye: Memories of John Fitzgerald Kennedy* (New York: Open Road Integrated Media, 1993).

82   making the highbrow list  Russell Lynes, "Highbrow, Lowbrow, Middlebrow," *Harper's Magazine,* February 1949.

93   Using taste as a demonstration of class  Suzannah Lessard, "Taste, Class and Mary Tyler Moore," *Washington Monthly,* March 1975.

## Chapter 4: The Rise of the Right

98    **"Mr. Norm is my alias"**    Alan Brinkley and Davis Dyer, eds., *The American Presidency* (New York: Houghton Mifflin, 2004), p. 458.

100    **" 'forced busing,' 'states' rights' "**    Lee Atwater interview with political scientist Alexander P. Lamis, author of *The Two-Party South* (New York: Oxford University Press, 1984).

101    **the Atwater strategy**    Lou Cannon, *President Reagan: The Role of a Lifetime* (New York: Simon & Schuster, 1991), p. 458.

103    **Limbaugh has preached a doctrine**    Zev Chafets, *Rush Limbaugh: An Army of One* (New York: Sentinel, 2010).

104    **"I don't want them to succeed"**    *Rush Limbaugh Show,* Jan. 16, 2009.

104    **Mary Matalin observed**    Chafets, *An Army of One.*

105    **"Reagan rejected the notion"**    Zev Chafets, "Late-Period Limbaugh," *New York Times Magazine,* July 6, 2008.

105    **it can be downright mean**    *Rush Limbaugh Show,* Oct. 11, 2010.

111    **"Let's face it"**    *Politico,* Nov. 1, 2010.

111    **"Your own mother"**    Gabriel Sherman, *The Loudest Voice in the Room: How the Brilliant, Bombastic Roger Ailes Built Fox News—and Divided a Country* (New York: Random House, 2014), p. 113.

112    **Ailes biographer Zev Chafets**    Zev Chafets, *Roger Ailes: Off Camera* (New York: Sentinel, 2013).

116    **lucrative jobs in the private sector**    Mark Leibovich, *This Town: Two Parties and a Funeral—Plus Plenty of Valet Parking!—in America's Gilded Capital* (New York: Blue Rider, 2013).

118    **cesspool of the country**    Andrew Ross Sorkin, "On Wall Street, a Culture of Greed Won't Let Go," *New York Times,* July 15, 2013, and "Many on Wall Street Say It Remains Untamed,"*New York Times,* May 18, 2015.

118    **one of the world's largest law firms, DLA Piper**    Peter Lattman, "Suit Offers a Peek at the Practice of Inflating a Legal Bill," *New York Times,* Mar. 25, 2013.

## Chapter 5: The Price of Glamour

120    **early fantasy of his**    Clay Felker (as told to Gail Sheehy) "My New York," *New York,* July 8, 2008.

122    **"*The New Yorker*"**    Tom Wolfe, "Tiny Mummies! The True Story of the Ruler of 43rd Street's Land of the Walking Dead!" *New York,* Apr. 11, 1965.

123    **Wolfe's "Radical Chic"**    Tom Wolfe, *Radical Chic & Mau-Mauing the Flak Catchers* (New York: Farrar, Straus and Giroux, 1970).

124    **"known in the business as 'Siberia' "**    Steve Fishman, John Homans, and

Adam Moss, eds., *New York Stories: Landmark Writing from Four Decades of New York Magazine* (New York: Random House, 2008), p. 97.

125 **"Redpants and Sugarman"**   Gail Sheehy, "Wide Open City, Part II: Redpants and Sugarman," *New York,* July 26, 1971.

127 **performed by Graydon Carter**   Jay Cocks, "Spy Magazine Draws Blood from the Stony Big Apple," *Time,* Nov. 2, 1987.

130 **Felker's self-invention**   Tom Wolfe, "A City Built of Clay," *New York,* July 6, 2008.

130 **There is something of the same flavor**   Gaby Wood, "Get Carter: Graydon Carter Edits the Most Influential Glossy Magazine in the World. And Now He's Produced the Perfect Movie About Hollywood Excess . . . ," *The Guardian* (U.S. edition), Nov. 9, 2002.

131 **putting together the seating plans**   Allen Salkin, "Many Called, but Few Were Seated," *New York Times,* July 1, 2009.

132 **Toby Young, a young**   Toby Young, *How to Lose Friends and Alienate People* (Philadelphia: Da Capo, 2002), prologue.

## Chapter 6: Main Street Goes Wall Street

134 ***Wall Street Week***   James Brant, "Louis Rukeyser, Television Host, Dies at 73," *New York Times,* May 3, 2006.

134 **Ralph Nader, on the other hand**   "The Lonely Hero: Never Kowtow," *Time,* Dec. 12, 1969.

136 **what's good for Wall Street**   N. R. Kleinfeld, "Enduring, Not Always Endearing 'Wall Street Week,'" *New York Times,* Nov. 11, 1990.

137 **Harry McPherson, a Texan**   Jacob Weisbert, "Liberal Tobacco Whores: Why Are Ann Richards, George Mitchell, and Others Working for the Cigarette Companies?" *Slate,* Aug. 10, 1997.

139 **Fred Dutton was the next**   Steven Emerson, *The American House of Saud: The Secret Petrodollar Connection* (New York: Franklin Watts, 1985), p. 88.

## Chapter 7: The Issues That Divide Us

153 **Irving Kristol, editor of *The Public Interest***   Douglas Murray, "'A Liberal Mugged by Reality,'" *The Spectator,* Sept. 23, 2009.

153 **Norman Podhoretz, the editor of *Commentary***   Norman Podhoretz, "In Defense of Sarah Palin," *Wall Street Journal,* March 29, 2010.

157 ***Rise of the Warrior Cop***   Radley Balko, *Rise of the Warrior Cop: The Militarization of America's Police Forces* (New York: PublicAffairs, 2013), p. 30.

157 **I saw an article**   Travis Crum, "W.Va. State Police Shooting Unjustified, Kohler Family Says," *Charleston Gazette-Mail,* July 21, 2013.

## Chapter 8: The Education Wars

167  **"Yes, but Where Are Your Credits"**  Susan Ohanian, "Yes, but Where Are Your Credits in Recess Management 101?," *Washington Monthly,* April 1984.

172  **In 1994, two alumni**  Jay Mathews, *Work Hard. Be Nice. How Two Inspired Teachers Created the Most Promising Schools in America* (Chapel Hill, NC: Algonquin, 2009).

173  **the school reform movement**  Diane Ravitch, "How, and How Not, to Improve the Schools," *New York Review of Books,* Mar. 22, 2012, and "The Lost Purpose of School Reform," *New York Review of Books,* Apr. 2, 2015.

173  **an admiring profile of Ravitch**  David Denby, "Public Defender: Diane Ravitch Takes On a Movement," *New Yorker,* Nov. 19, 2012.

174  **"will have a wide-ranging"**  Annie Lowrey, "Big Study Links Good Teachers to Lasting Gain," *New York Times,* Jan. 6, 2012.

## Chapter 9: A Cynical Age

176  **release of the Pentagon Papers**  Michael Cooper and Sam Roberts, "After 40 Years, the Complete Pentagon Papers," *New York Times,* June 7, 2011.

179  **to fire bad civil servants**  Leonard Reed, "Firing a Federal Employee: The Impossible Dream," in Charles Peters and Nicholas Lemann (eds.), *Inside the System* (New York: Holt, Rinehart and Winston, 1979), pp. 214–26.

181  **the Waco case**  Malcolm Gladwell, "Sacred and Profane: How Not to Negotiate with Believers," *New Yorker,* Mar. 31, 2014.

184  **"It violates the basic principle"**  President Lyndon B. Johnson's Remarks at the Signing of the Immigration Bill at Liberty Island, New York, Oct. 3, 1965, in *Public Papers of the Presidents of the United States: Lyndon B. Johnson, 1965,* vol. II (Washington, DC: Government Printing Office, 1966), entry 546, pp. 1037–40.

185  **an article entitled "Illegal Aliens"**  Leonard F. Chapman, "Illegal Aliens: Time to Call a Halt!" *Reader's Digest,* October 1976, p. 189. See also Chapman's statements to *The New York Times,* Oct. 22, 1974.

185  **Pat Buchanan was declaring**  Jeff Chu, "10 Questions for Pat Buchanan," *Time,* Aug. 20, 2006.

## Chapter 10: Fashionable Trouble

188  **"Two first ladies"**  John Koblin, "At Met Gala, Fashionistas Dress Up in Tribute," *New York Times,* May 5, 2014.

188  **"Obama was wearing play shorts"**  Robin Givhan, "Robin Givhan on Fashion: In Her Choice of Shorts, Michelle Obama Goes to Unusual Lengths," *Washington Post,* Aug. 23, 2009.

188 **"When Abedin posed"** Robin Givhan, "Anthony Weiner's Wife Huma Abedin Is Dressed for Distress," *Newsweek*, June 19, 2011.

189 **"What I Wore"** Bee-Shyuan Chang, "Outfits That Walk Between 2 Worlds," *T: The New York Times Style Magazine,* Nov. 17, 2011.

189 **Audrey Gelman lured chic New Yorkers** Alex Williams, "Audrey Gelman, the Girl Most Likely," *New York Times,* Oct. 4, 2013.

191 **the price of a basket of luxury goods** Suzanne Kapner and Christina Passariello, "Soaring Luxury-Goods Prices Test Wealthy's Will to Pay," *Wall Street Journal,* Mar. 2, 2014.

193 **An article on the decorator Stephen Sills** David Netto, "Pale Beauty" *T: The New York Times Style Magazine,* Sept. 24, 2014.

194 **Neil Irwin of the *Times*** Neil Irwin, "Special Sauce for Measuring Food Trends: The Fried Calamari Index," *New York Times,* Aug. 12, 2014.

## Chapter 11: Clinton and Beyond

201 **the Whitewater land development project** Jeff Gerth and Stephen Labaton, "Whitewater Papers Cast Doubt on Clinton Account of a Tax Underpayment," *New York Times,* Aug. 6, 1995.

205 **One state senator, Vada Sheid** David Maraniss, *First in His Class: The Biography of Bill Clinton* (New York: Simon & Schuster, 1995), p. 414.

208 **a black political activist named Sister Souljah** Sheila Rule, "The 1992 Campaign: Racial Issues; Rapper, Chided by Clinton, Calls Him a Hypocrite," *New York Times,* June 17, 1992.

210 **members of Congress who have served** "Most Members of Congress Have Little Direct Military Experience," Pew Research Center, September 4, 2013, www.pewresearch.org/fact-tank/2013/09/04/members-of-congress -have-little-direct-military-experience.

214 **90 percent are poorer** Matt O'Brian, "The Bottom 90 Percent Are Poorer Today Than They Were in 1987," Wonkblog, *Washington Post,* Oct. 22, 2014.

215 **Professional Air Traffic Controllers Organization** Jessica Desvarieux, "The Consequences of Reagan Breaking the 1981 Air Traffic Controllers Strike," Real News Network, Aug. 5, 2014, www.truth-out.org/news/item/25393 -the-consequences-of-reagan-breaking-the-1981-air-traffic-controllers-strike.

# BIBLIOGRAPHY

Adams, Stephen B. *Mr. Kaiser Goes to Washington: The Rise of a Government Entrepreneur.* Chapel Hill: University of North Carolina Press, 2009.

Balko, Radley. *Rise of the Warrior Cop: The Militarization of America's Police Forces.* New York: PublicAffairs, 2014.

Brinkley, Alan. *The End of Reform: New Deal Liberalism in Recession and War.* New York: Random House, 1996.

Brinkley, Alan, and Davis Dyer, eds. *The American Presidency.* New York: Houghton Mifflin, 2004.

Buchanan, Patrick J. *State of Emergency: The Third World Invasion and Conquest of America.* New York: St. Martin's, 2007.

Burns, James MacGregor. *Roosevelt: The Lion and the Fox, 1882–1940.* New York: Harcourt Brace Jovanovich, 1958.

Cannon, Lou. *President Reagan: The Role of a Lifetime.* New York: PublicAffairs, 2000.

Caro, Robert A. *The Years of Lyndon Johnson.* Vol. 1, *The Path to Power.* New York: Random House, 1981.

Chafets, Zev. *Rush Limbaugh: An Army of One.* New York: Penguin, 2010.

Clinton, Bill. *My Life.* New York: Vintage, 2004.

Couch, Jim. *The New Deal: Reputation and Reality.* Unpublished ms. Hillsdale, MI: Hillsdale College Archives, 2006.

Dallek, Robert. *Flawed Giant: Lyndon Johnson and His Times, 1961–1973.* New York: Oxford University Press, 1993.

———. *Franklin D. Roosevelt and American Foreign Policy, 1932–1945.* New York: Oxford University Press, 1995.

Dehgan, Bahman, ed. *America in Quotations.* Jefferson, NC: McFarland, 2003.

Downey, Kirsten. *The Woman Behind the New Deal: The Life and Legacy of Frances Perkins.* New York: Random House, 2009.

Emerson, Steven. *The American House of Saud: The Secret Petrodollar Connection*. New York: Franklin Watts, 1985.

Espinosa, Gastón, ed. *Religion and the American Presidency*. Lanham, MD: Rowman & Littlefield, 2008.

Feldman, Noah. *Scorpions: The Battles and Triumphs of FDR's Great Supreme Court Justices*. New York: Hachette, 2010.

Frantz, Douglas, and David McKean. *Friends in High Places: The Rise and Fall of Clark Clifford*. New York: St. Martin's, 1995.

Galbraith, James K. *End of Normal: The Great Crisis and the Future of Growth*. New York: Simon & Schuster, 2014.

Gates, Henry Louis, Jr. *Colored People: A Memoir*. New York: Alfred A. Knopf, 1994.

Kennedy, David M. *Freedom from Fear: The American People in Depression and War, 1929–1945*. New York: Oxford University Press, 2001.

Krislov, Samuel. *The Negro in Federal Employment: The Quest for Equal Opportunity*. 1967; reprinted New Orleans: Quid Pro Books, 2012.

Lamis, Alexander P. *The Two Party South*. New York: Oxford University Press, 1984.

Lasser, William. *Benjamin V. Cohen: Architect of the New Deal*. New Haven, CT: Yale University Press, 2002.

Leibovich, Mark. *This Town: Two Parties and a Funeral—Plus, Plenty of Valet Parking!—in America's Gilded Capital*. New York: Random House, 2013.

Leuchtenberg, William E. *The FDR Years: On Roosevelt and His Legacy*. New York: Columbia University Press, 1995.

Madrick, Jeff. *Age of Greed: The Triumph of Finance and the Decline of America, 1970 to the Present*. New York: Vintage, 2012.

Manchester, William. *The Glory and the Dream: A Narrative History of America, 1932–1972*. Boston: Little, Brown, 1974.

Maraniss, David. *First in His Class: The Biography of Bill Clinton*. New York: Simon & Schuster, 1996.

Mathews, Jay. *Work Hard. Be Nice.: How Two Inspired Teachers Created the Most Promising Schools in America*. Chapel Hill, NC: Algonquin, 2009.

McElvaine, Robert S. *The Great Depression: America, 1929–1941*. New York: Times Books, 1984.

McKean, Dave. *Peddling Influence: Thomas "Tommy the Cork" Corcoran and the Birth of Modern Lobbying*. Hanover, NH: Steerforth Press, 2005.

Noah, Timothy. *The Great Divergence: America's Growing Inequality Crisis and What We Can Do About It*. New York: Bloomsbury, 2012.

O'Donnell, Kenneth P., and David F. Powers. *"Johnny, We Hardly Knew Ye": Memories of John Fitzgerald Kennedy*. Boston: Little, Brown, 1972.

Packer, George. *The Unwinding: An Inner History of the New America*. New York: Farrar, Straus and Giroux, 2013.

Patterson, James T. *Grand Expectations: The United States, 1945–1974*. New York: Oxford University Press, 1997.

———. *Restless Giant: The United States from Watergate to Bush v. Gore*. New York: Oxford University Press, 2005.

Peters, Charles. *Five Days in Philadelphia*. New York: PublicAffairs, 2005.

———. *How Washington Really Works*. New York: Basic Books, 1992.

———. *Lyndon B. Johnson: The American Presidents Series: The 36th President, 1963–1969*. New York: Times Books, 2010.

———. *Tilting at Windmills: An Autobiography*. Boston: Addison-Wesley, 1988.

Procter, Ben. *William Randolph Hearst*. Vol. 2, *The Later Years, 1911–1951*. New York: Oxford University Press, 2007.

Reeves, Richard. *President Reagan: The Triumph of Imagination*. New York: Simon & Schuster, 2005.

Reich, Robert. *The Resurgent Liberal: And Other Unfashionable Prophecies*. New York: Random House, 1989.

Roark, James L., et al. *The American Promise: A History of the United States*. Vol. 2, *From 1865*. New York: Macmillan, 2012.

Schlesinger, Arthur M., Jr., *The Age of Roosevelt*. Vol. 2, *The Coming of the New Deal: 1933–1935*. New York: Houghton Mifflin, 2003.

Schwartz, Jordan A. *The New Dealers: Power Politics in the Age of Roosevelt*. New York: Random House, 1993.

Sherman, Gabriel. *The Loudest Voice in the Room: How the Brilliant, Bombastic Roger Ailes Built Fox News—and Divided a Country*. New York: Random House, 2014.

Smith, Hedrick. *Who Stole the American Dream?* New York: Random House, 2012.

Smith, Ron, and Mary O. Boyle. *Prohibition in Atlanta: Temperance, Tiger Kings, & White Lightning*. Charleston, SC: History Press, 2015.

Stiglitz, Joseph E. *The Great Divide: Unequal Societies and What We Can Do About Them*. New York: Norton, 2015.

Uys, Errol Lincoln. *Riding the Rails: Teenagers on the Move During the Great Depression*. New York: Routledge, 2003; Boston: T. E. Winter & Sons, 2014.

Volkomer, Walter E. *The Passionate Liberal: The Political and Legal Ideas of Jerome Frank*. The Hague: Martinus Nijhoff, 1970.

Waller, Spencer Weber. *Thurman Arnold: A Biography*. New York: NYU Press, 2005.

White, Graham J. *F.D.R. and the Press*. Chicago: University of Chicago Press, 1979.

White, Richard D., Jr. *Will Rogers: A Political Life*. Lubbock: Texas Tech University Press, 2011.

Wolfe, Tom. *Radical Chic and Mau-Mauing the Flak Catchers*. New York: Farrar, Straus and Giroux, 1970.

Young, Toby. *How to Lose Friends and Alienate People*. Boston: Da Capo Press, 2002.

# INDEX

## ABOUT THE AUTHOR

CHARLES PETERS was born in Charleston, West Virginia, and educated in local public schools. He earned a BA and an MA at Columbia University and a law degree from the University of Virginia. Peters served in the U.S. Army and the West Virginia legislature, practiced law, and managed John Kennedy's 1960 presidential campaign in Kanawha County. Peters also helped found the Peace Corps and served as its director of evaluation. The founder and longtime editor of *The Washington Monthly*, Peters is the author of several books, including an examination of the political system, *How Washington Really Works*; a history, *Five Days in Philadelphia*; and a biography, *Lyndon B. Johnson*, for the American Presidents series.